A Semblance
of Justice

A Semblance of Justice

St. Louis School Desegregation and Order in Urban America

Daniel J. Monti

University of Missouri Press
Columbia, 1985

Library of Congress Cataloging in Publication Data
Monti, Daniel J.
  A semblance of justice.
  Bibliography: p.
  Includes index.
  1. School integration—United States—Case studies.
2. Educational equalization—United States—Case studies.
3. Afro-Americans—Civil rights—Case studies. I. Title.
LC214.2.M66 1985   370.19'342   85-1008
ISBN 0–8262–0476–7

⊗^{TM} This paper meets the minimum requirements of the American National Standard for Permanence of Paper for Printed Library Materials, Z39.48, 1984.

For Nip, Danny, Chris, and several generations of Montis, DiSalvos, and Smits, who as recent immigrants pursued a uniquely American dream, and for countless generations of Buckleys and Nuckolls, who have been here forever and who did not blink when their daughter brought home an Italian with a beard.

Foreword

"Be not deceived," St. Paul assured the early Christians. "God is not mocked!" No such boast can be made by contemporary crusaders for racial justice, condemned as we are to ritual annual observances of the Supreme Court's *Brown vs. Board of Education* decision. Each year the once-powerful precedent gains in honors, as each year it becomes increasingly irrelevant to the educational needs of the black children who were its intended beneficiaries.

Even the most committed advocates of integration must now concede that what was an all-out court campaign to desegregate the public schools has degenerated into a scatter-gun of still-litigated cases, none of which is likely to alter the status of most black children who continue to receive inferior and inadequate schooling in facilities generally as separate in fact as they were once segregated in law.

How could this happen? Where and how did those of us who worked so hard to eliminate racially segregated school systems lose our way? Professor Daniel J. Monti, significantly a social scientist rather than a lawyer, seeks an answer using as his vehicle a painstaking examination of the decades-long St. Louis school desegregation experience.

In *A Semblance of Justice,* Professor Monti reveals a continuing commitment to the ideal of the racially integrated school far greater than my own and, I would add, far greater than that of most black parents. Neither they nor I any longer see educational benefits worthy of the horrendous struggle required to merge dozens of urban and suburban school districts and to bus thousands of children in order to make real a vision once shared by many but now still held by only a faithful few.

During the early 1960s, I supervised as many as three hundred school desegregation cases across the South as an NAACP Legal Defense Fund lawyer. I confess that in those days I, too, equated a racially balanced school with the *Brown* decision's promise of equal educational opportunity. But for a long period now, I have urged that whatever leverage remains in the *Brown* precedent be used to gain for black children an effective education even if, as is likely for most, the school where it is obtained serves black children predominately or totally.

There is no shame in this admission. Those genuinely concerned about the welfare of black people in America cannot afford the luxury of a consistency of approach rigidly held in the face of constantly changing events. Today, I am as committed to efforts to bring effective schooling to black children in black schools as earlier I was willing to close all black schools if such was the price of providing them with an education in racially balanced facilities. Tomorrow, I may reverse directions again as did black parents who since the 1790s have sought educations for their children alternately in racially separate and integrated schools.

I write this foreword because *A Semblance of Justice* explains why flexible strategies are necessary. It should make clear to civil-rights advocates and lawyers why the racial reform possible under *Brown* was destined to be limited whether the goal was racially balanced schools or effective schooling for black children.

Though little acknowledged, it is hardly a secret that the struggle by blacks first for freedom and then for equal rights has served well many interests of the nations as a whole. Indeed, it is not extravagant to suggest the individual rights that are the source of so much American pride would mean far less than they do but for the constant and too often futile struggle by blacks to gain for themselves that legal protection most whites take for granted.

Abraham Lincoln may be remembered as the "Great Emancipator," but his Emancipation Proclamation, by its terms, actually freed no slaves while providing much political benefit to the Union cause. Similarly, the Fourteenth Amendment, initially enacted to provide and to protect citizenship rights for the former slaves, became first a bulwark for corporate enterprise against government regulation and later by far the most important guarantee of individual liberty in the U.S. Constitution. Only in relatively recent years have its provisions been used to correct the most blatant forms of racial discrimination.

Harvard Law School Professor Paul Freund, in commenting on the general social reform made possible by blacks' quest for racial justice, observed that the "frontiers of the law have been pushed back by the civil rights movement in many sectors that are far broader than the interests of the movement itself." Professor Freund cited as examples the ruling gained at the urging of civil-rights lawyers prohibiting state courts from enforcing discriminatory property covenants, and the potential of that decision to transform the line between private and public sectors of choice and responsibility. He also cited the expansion of First Amendment rights to cover the group representation practices of NAACP lawyers charged in southern states with violation of barratry and other canons of professional ethics. Subsequently, the civil-rights precedents were used to broaden group representation plans operated by unions and other associations, and ethical canons were revised accordingly.

For decades, federal courts refused to enter the "political thicket" to interfere with gerrymandered legislative districts, even though the result was disproportionate political power to sparsely populated areas at the expense of heavily populated urban districts. When blacks challenged successfully the shocking districting of Tuskegee, Alabama, under which virtually all black voters were placed outside the city's boundaries, the Supreme Court acted to remedy the situation. The civil-rights precedent opened the way for successful challenge of nonracial gerrymanders leading to the Supreme Court's adoption of the "one person, one vote" standard.

Even the *Brown* decision, while the fruit of a decade of difficult litigation by civil-rights lawyers, was of as much help in improving the nation's image in the post–World War II challenge to compete with Communism as it was in lifting the burden of racially segregated schooling from black children. The decision did not mention the fact, but it must have been obvious to the Supreme Court that the country could no longer afford to maintain the nineteenth-century racial compromise of constitutionally supported segregation that had become an international embarrassment.

In any event, having struck down the now obsolete "separate but equal" principle, the Supreme Court, after another year's delay, dictated that the remedy for blacks could be implemented "with all deliberate speed." This initial venture in judicial prudence set a standard for racial remediation that has enabled perpetuation of the old game of subordination of black rights to white needs under new colorblind rules.

Professor Monti's book adds significantly to our ability to identify the real winners in school desegregation battles, an identification that explains why so much of *Brown*'s promise to blacks has gone unfulfilled. In St. Louis, we learn that school officials staunchly resisted any liability for segregation in their schools, then under court orders these same individuals utilized school desegregation mandates to achieve educational reforms, including magnet schools, increased funding for training, teacher salaries, research and development, and new school construction, all without giving more than secondary priority to redressing the grievances of blacks. The only sensible way to deliver educational resources to the metropolitan area of St. Louis, according to school officials, is a metropolitan school system, and they candidly told Professor Monti that desegregation was a tool to accomplish that end.

As importantly, *A Semblance of Justice* explains how school officials utilized the school desegregation controversy to increase their legitimacy as the proper policy-making location for public education. Indeed, as Professor Monti makes clear, neither side in the school desegregation struggle in St. Louis called for abandonment of the school board, even though it and its predecessors in office were responsible for the discriminatory policies attacked in the courts.

In explanation, *A Semblance of Justice* makes a fascinating and likely controversial analogy between school desegregation and the ritualized rebellions of primitive peoples in which relatively powerless groups formally act out their resentment and frustration by challenging the established social structure without actually threatening that structure with destruction and its accompanying chaos. These periodic rituals, far from endangering the social status quo, tend to legitimate it. Certain policies are shown to be unfair and arbitrary, but the protests do not reach a level requiring revolutionary change.

In this light, Professor Monti argues that school desegregation has performed a special service in our political culture. This is a surprising statement, but consider that America is a society in which racism is a systemic and essential support of the economic system. The historic exploitation and subordination of blacks is reflected in every statistic as otherwise unexplainable disparities of income, political representation, social class status, unemployment, educational level, quality of health, and even mortality. Given the broad landscape of black oppression, the racial segregation of all public facilities in the South and, in particular, the segregation of black children in public schools was hardly more than a dramatic instance of our manifest inequality.

Civil-rights lawyers and their supporting organizations, determined to expose the "separate but equal" interpretation that gave constitutional validity to segregation policies, had to start somewhere. Public schools seemed, and were, the most vulnerable links in a system of legalized apartheid that one school board lawyer argued to the Supreme Court should be maintained because "somewhere, sometime to every principle comes a moment of repose when it has been so often announced, so confidently relied upon, so long continued, that it passes the limits of judicial discretion and disturbance."

In the end, the longevity of the segregation principle bowed to the pressure of contemporary national necessity. Happily, for the proponents of school desegregation, their advocacy of racial justice for black children harmonized nicely with the nation's need to improve its racial image as it competed with Russia for the hearts and minds of third-world peoples just emerging after decades of subordination under European colonialism.

True, the *Brown* decision and the Warren Court that decided it have been roundly condemned for favoring black rights over the vested interests of whites. But legal commentators as prestigious as Professor Arthur S. Miller view the Warren Court's precedent-making decisions in civil rights and civil liberties as protective of the political and economic status quo. The decisions, coming at a time of relative prosperity, served to mitigate the most serious injustices borne by minorities and the poor at minimum social cost to the established order.

Professor Miller explains that while "the Supreme Court before Warren was mainly concerned with the protection of established property interests, under Warren, the High Bench, by moving to protect many of the poor and disadvantaged, also helped those highest in the social pecking order." Consciously or not, it was the unmentioned but perceived need to strengthen the status quo as much as the voiced concern for the inequities visited on blacks under the "separate but equal" doctrine that led the Court to *Brown* in 1954.

Given this motivation, we should not have been surprised at the glacial pace of judicial implementation or the meager results of what we hoped would be mammoth social change. The systemic racism that we saw as segregation was not a monster with a single head. Thus, the struggle that finally disestablished the dual school system simply cleared from the scene a racial policy grown obsolete, clumsy, and embarrassing. Already waiting in the wings was a new equal opportunity model, fashioned in the main with the approval of those who would find it provided for some student and teacher desegregation, that would maintain blacks in a subordinate status in regard to educational outcomes and policy making.

A Semblance of Justice provides in painful detail how this process worked in St. Louis. But the book also presents the obvious question. Assuming the accuracy of the assessment that school desegregation was a ritualized rebellion, how may blacks break free of societally self-serving struggles that, even when won, provide white "losers" with more gain than black "winners?" If meaningful racial reform in the schools and elsewhere requires change in the economic and political life of a community, how does a still relatively powerless minority marshal resources and support for such a challenge?

We may not be able to dissolve school boards and deal directly with school administrators as Professor Monti suggests, but at least future efforts must serve ends beyond enhancing the power of school officials and furthering the urbanization of a large, metropolitan area. Black children, particularly those whose parents are poor, need effective schooling now more than when the Court in *Brown* observed that its denial rendered it doubtful "that any child may reasonably be expected to succeed in life." It is that knowledge and that need which move us toward new battles for racial equality in which, at the least, we hope to avoid the old mistakes.

Derrick A. Bell
Professor, Oregon Law School

Acknowledgments

This book contains most of what I learned about school desegregation. In writing it, I hoped to make others better understand what this reform has meant not only to St. Louis residents but to all Americans. I know that some in St. Louis will be greatly distressed by what they read in this book. That, I am sorry to say, cannot be helped. My responsibility as a teacher and author is to help others look at what they might otherwise choose to ignore. On some occasions, there can be great joy in sharing that knowledge. On other occasions, it can be less fun. This, I believe, is one of those other occasions.

I did not know much about school desegregation when I began the research that eventually led me to write this book. And, I suspect, there is likely to be some consensus that I have not learned much in the ensuing ten years. If this is true, then the credit for such a sorry state cannot be shared with the hundreds of school officials, teachers, students, and parents who have tried to teach me all they could about this reform. The credit is mine alone.

I promised these persons that I would protect their anonymity. They trusted and confided in me, and I have not violated my pledge in this book. I would say only this: many of you have worked tirelessly, often making substantial personal and financial sacrifices, in order to obtain a better education for your own and others' children. I regret that I cannot offer you more than this book in return for that service.

The National Institute of Education funded most of the fieldwork included in chapters 6, 7, and 8. Generous support also was provided by the Center for Metropolitan Studies of the University of Missouri–St. Louis. I am grateful for the cooperation of the center and the project's staff. I wrote the book while a member of the Department of Sociology and a Fellow in the Center for International Studies at UMSL. Celeste Brown, Tib Lanham, Mary Hines, and Donna Eckerle flattered my scrawl with their competent typing skills and proofreading. Peggy Magee, who by tending bar has demonstrated rare insight into the most effective use of an undergraduate degree in sociology, proofread the final version of the book.

I have sought and received, at one time or other, assistance from several of my colleagues while writing this book. Among them have been Harry Bash, George McCall, John Hepburn, and Ron Denowitz from the sociology department at UMSL. Special thanks also is extended to Professors Ed Fedder, Don Phares, Norton Long, and Gene Meehan, whose feet seemed to have that special gift for inspiring the young scholar in just the right way to get him over the next hurdle. Finally, Professor Leila Sussmann of Tufts, Professors Mark Chesler and Louis Ferman of the University of Michigan, and Dr. Jennifer Hochschild formerly of the first floor of Barrows Hall and now at Princeton are to be thanked for their careful reviews of earlier drafts.

I have dedicated this book to both my families. They may not always have understood everything I was doing or everything I wanted to be, but they were always there when I needed them. I am especially grateful to my wife and sons, who helped to make all the nonsense I have endured in the past ten years worthwhile. They have shared their love with me and taught me much. I could always turn to them for support; but mostly, I did it just because it made me feel good.

I alone, of course, am responsible for the book's content and conclusions. In writing each page of this book I moved one page closer to fulfilling a promise made to a self-assured high school student in 1967. His edges are considerably smoother today, due in no small part to the efforts of friends in Oberlin, Chapel Hill, and St. Louis. Traces of that scrappiness still managed to slip through on occasion, despite their best efforts and those of the well-meaning editors of the University of Missouri Press.

D.J.M.
April, 1985

Contents

1. Introduction

More than twenty years after a black preacher stepped before the Lincoln Memorial and challenged his countrymen to build a more just and tolerant society, we are still a divided people. It is as true today as it was in 1963 that certain types of people have more of the things everyone wants while others have much less than they probably need. Inequality remains an important and uncomfortable fact of life in our country. The United States is not unique in this regard. Every "advanced" society has certain classes of people that control a disproportionate share of that society's wealth; and each society experiences problems because of these discrepancies.

The existence of inequality and poverty should not surprise us. On the other hand, how we sometimes address the problems they create might. Hints to the character of a people are discovered in their efforts to address such issues and the conditions that spawned them. More importantly perhaps, the persistence and forthrightness of these efforts can provide us with clues about how a society like our own manages to strike some balance between its need for order and the compelling desire for justice among its citizens.

Our own country has a history of treating many minority populations rather shabbily, at least until they manage to "prove" their worthiness or are discovered to be less objectionable than the newest immigrant group. Black people have occupied a peculiar niche in American history. They were among the first despised ethnic or racial groups "invited" to help build this nation. Yet most blacks have been hindered from proving themselves worthy of its bounty because of their status as descendants of slaves and, more recently, because changes in the economy have made it difficult for them to build a broad and stable middle-class base.

The anniversary of Martin Luther King, Jr.'s speech has prompted us to consider how far we have come in realizing his dream of equality and fair play. Some progress has been made, especially with regard to blacks' political power and the growing tolerance of whites for the legal and social rights of black persons. However, great concern is again being voiced over the plight of the black family. Poor economic gains evidenced by the majority of blacks since 1960 have been disappointing. The gap between the average income of blacks and whites has closed little during the past two decades. Many persons fear that someday blacks may constitute disproportionately a permanent "underclass" in our society. Occupational advances made by better educated black persons are threatened by decreasing employment opportunities in the public sector. Moreover, discrimination remains a factor in limiting the progress that can be made in the career of even a well-trained black person.

1

The failure of the civil rights movement to secure a "revolution" in the status of black Americans says more about the rhetorical excesses of some black activists and nervous whites than it does about the goals expressed by minority citizens.[1] It is clear today that "the movement" was designed to open the doors and windows of the house and let in some fresh air, not to tear the house down. That, in retrospect, was its primary accomplishment. The same might also be said of the reforms enacted during this period. Yet there are many persons who would disagree with this idea. They object to the "intrusion" of the federal government or courts into public schools and other institutions. That such efforts have been taken in behalf of minority citizens does not help. These angry persons have waited a long time to see these policies reversed. And now, at least in the schools, they may see their patience rewarded. Not only has the U.S. Department of Justice stopped initiating cases against allegedly segregated districts but it has moved to dismantle the fourteen-year-old busing plan of the Norfolk school district as well. To the extent that districts have done all that the courts have required, the argument goes, perhaps they should be allowed to reintroduce neighborhood schools. As long as officials did not intentionally redraw the new boundary lines to increase segregation, it really ought not to concern us if children go to predominantly one-race schools. Unintentional segregation is not unconstitutional.

To be sure, no democratic society can maintain indefinitely a large disenfranchised population within its own borders. Legally enforced segregation had to be ended, and the civil-rights movement helped to achieve that goal. The noisy and often violent repudiation of segregation witnessed during the last two decades marked an important passage in our history as a nation. Today we are on the verge of yet another period of self-discovery. We are moving beyond the legally enforced absurdity of segregated schools. We have begun to recognize the social and economic costs of having a great number of poor workers and consumers in our country, people who can neither produce nor buy things, but whose voices dare not be ignored too long. How the American public is likely to discover solutions to this dilemma is in a sense the real issue raised here. The particular subject matter of the book—school desegregation—may be of less immediate concern today. However, it provides us with a fascinating glimpse into how we have managed in the past to temper our desire for justice with the need for order and predictable change.

We are a conservative people, although we sometimes lose sight of what that means and how much of our strength is derived from that simple trait. The stubborn reluctance to move sharply in any direction is built into our government and routinely expressed in our public habits. This can be frustrating, but it is every bit as much a part of our culture as are the lingering effects of inequality and our willful pursuit of new economic challenges. School desegregation has always been viewed as a device to impel social change, to root out old injustices, and to help apprehend a new and more just society. The conflicts that erupt over this issue have been part of a bitter pill swallowed by an unwilling patient, as far as desegregation advocates are concerned. Conflict between the races, it was expected, would be resolved or at least greatly reduced as a result of things like desegregation.[2] Opponents of "forced busing," on the other hand, have consistently portrayed desegregation reforms as an ineffective and disruptive force in local educational affairs. Few proponents or detractors of desegregation, however, have been willing to step back from their partisan positions and view the controversies over segregated schools in the context of our broader political culture. Had they done this, a much different and decidedly conservative picture of desegregation might have emerged. Surely, there is much evidence to suggest that old antagonists have not been united into a new or particularly innovative concord as a result of desegregation controversies. Perhaps, then, such fights merely purchased the illusion of change, while providing a medium through which the legitimacy of old boundaries and institutions could be reaffirmed by virtue of having been tested so severely.

This is no small heresy. This idea contradicts everything we have been taught to believe about desegregation and like reforms. Yet it also provides a way of making sense of contradictory findings about the reform and its effects that we have failed to resolve. Foremost among these is the fact that desegregation has never obtained for minority youngsters the dramatic gains that were hoped for, either before or after they graduated from high school. Granted, desegregation never was the unmitigated failure most of its opponents have dismissed it as being.[3] Nevertheless, we expected far more definitive and positive results.

The same conclusion can be reached when we shift our attention from the students to the districts or schools they attend. Successful desegregation, according to those who have compared many districts at the same time, usually requires the movement of many students and staff, the introduction of new academic and training programs, and more community involvement, among other things.[4] On the other hand, detailed studies of how desegregation and related reforms prevail in a single district reveal a different picture. The very reforms most often cited as indicators of successful desegregation emerge as tools used by district leaders to ensure the continuing independence of their system and their authority over it.

Advocates of desegregation might find such observations disturbing; but extensive research into the problem of securing change in corporations or manufacturing plants corroborates the results of the desegregation case studies.[5] The most popular and frequently adopted strategies to induce change inside complex organizations involve changes at the individual level (through counseling, selection, or placement) or group level (through training and surveys). These are the levels at which school segregation is usually attacked. Such tactics, unfortunately, also tend to produce much less change in the organization's or members' conduct in the long run unless nested in changes at the organizational level (changes in the authority and reward structure or the division of labor). Yet neither school systems nor larger businesses display much interest in pushing such fundamental reforms.

Why should we tax ourselves over a reform that the U.S. Department of Justice has sought to abandon and that no longer seems very interesting to most people? There are several compelling reasons. First, school desegregation is not the educational dodo its critics would have us believe. While it is true that the federal government and courts seem to have retreated from advocating new or aggressive desegregation orders, there are many metropolitan areas that have segregated suburban and inner-city schools. The problem will not go away simply because some would prefer that it did. Moreover, if the recent decrees dealing with metropolitan desegregation in the St. Louis area are as pathbreaking as many persons think, then before too long we could see a new burst of litigation and reforms involving "voluntary" city/county desegregation orders.[6] We need to know what contribution such plans might make to the identification and resolution of nationwide problems like inequality.

The second reason for paying more attention to desegregation as a social reform is historical and philosophical. Education has always been an important part of our cultural baggage. Our faith in its redemptive powers is unshakable, even if a bit overblown at times. Generations of Americans have come to see our educational institutions as the single biggest factor in their advancement and as a source of community pride. Education is, as historian Diane Ravitch declares, our "noble flaw." It allows us "to believe in the future, to believe in what may be accomplished through the disciplined use of intelligence, allied with cooperation and good will." Education has been the answer to those hoping to better their station in life and to communities anxious to "improve the status quo" while avoiding the turmoil that can come with social change.[7]

How school desegregation fits into a much longer process of social change and community development, then, greatly concerns us today. We have entered a period in which basic and far-reaching changes are occurring in the ways people can expect to make a living. Whether a person, regardless of color, can expect to work at all may be more closely tied than ever before to the services provided by our schools. Yet we live in a time when our faith in that institution has been abused and its performance weakened by forces seemingly outside our control. That public education is in a state of crisis today is not disputed. Many believe that desegregation helped to create this crisis. They think that something needs to be done quickly. The kind of reforms needed most is open to debate, however. How school desegregation may have contributed to this current crisis in educational equality, therefore, is a topic worthy of our attention. My goal in this book is to show that while desegregation may have prompted a crisis in educational affairs, it also has contributed to the creation of a more workable social order that keeps the crisis within manageable bounds.

There are a number of ways in which one could demonstrate this. Diane Ravitch recently completed an excellent survey of educational controversies in the United States since the end of World War II. In it desegregation appears as only one of several elements in what she calls "the troubled crusade" to order and improve our lives through education. Several of the themes introduced in her work—the social discomfort prompted by industrialization and city building, our efforts to cope with these changes, and the tension between justice and order evidenced in those meager efforts—are described in greater detail here. I have the luxury of doing this in part because I have focused on only one of the educational crusades described by Professor Ravitch. At the same time, it probably has been the most important of these crusades. As Ravitch notes, "While some issues in American education waxed and waned . . . the problem of racial inequality in education grew in significance with each passing year."[8]

It is difficult to determine just how significant the impact of desegregation controversies is in the absence of fairly detailed information about specific places and plans. By focusing on one metropolitan area and the impact of desegregation plans on several districts in it, we will be able to get a finer grasp of how this educational crusade was interpreted on a local level. Although St. Louis is not like every other place in the country, we will see that there are parallels between its experiences and those of other communities. Moreover, we shall see that the manner in which communities dealt with this most recent reform crusade bears a striking resemblance to the way in which earlier efforts to improve Americans were initiated in urban areas.

Questions Prompted by St. Louis's Desegregation Efforts

St. Louis is a nice place, a bit too muggy in the summer perhaps, but a nice place nevertheless. Native St. Louisans are fond of saying that it is a good place to raise a family. I tend to agree. It also is an interesting place. St. Louis is northern enough to have suffered more than its share of industrial disinvestment and urban blighting. It is southern enough to have cultivated a modest image of itself as a conservative and cultured community, yet one that yearns to assume its rightful position among other "sunbelt" cities filled with commercial vigor and a renewed sense of purpose. And it is just midwestern enough to be satisfied most of the time with adopting someone else's innovations. If St. Louis is not a boring place—conventioneers have been known to complain that they really do attend workshops and speeches during their visits—it certainly lacks the good-natured rowdiness and corrupt charm of Chicago, its former stepchild to the north. For all these reasons, St. Louis would seem an odd place to stage a minor revolution in American race relations. Yet to hear and read reports of its plans to initiate the nation's first "voluntary" desegregation plan involving city and suburban school districts is to believe that St. Louis will show other areas how to solve their segregation problem. At least that is how this plan has been portrayed in the media across the country.

Until 1975, most children attending school in St. Louis City or St. Louis County went to school with youngsters a lot like themselves. White children sat next to other whites, and blacks were enrolled at schools attended by other minority children. Youngsters from more well-to-do families went to the same schools, and children whose parents had less money also tended to live in the same district and to go to school together. Today, more white and black children are going to school together than ever before. Many white students from St. Louis County are enrolled in city schools that have specialized programs. Many black city students take a daily bus ride to predominantly white suburban schools. No one really knows or cares how much "social class mixing" is going on with this "race mixing" in the schools. All they seem to care about is how much money it is costing and that desegregation has proceeded peacefully.

One of my concerns in this book will be to describe how St. Louis residents managed their race-relations crisis so well. In this sense, the book serves as a case study and can be read profitably on that level alone. The two cases considered in detail are interesting on a variety of grounds. The first involved three districts in suburban St. Louis County that were merged by a court order into the Ferguson-Florissant Reorganized School District. This kind of judicial activism is rare and it held many possibilities for mischief and disruptions in school affairs. But there was no obvious breakdown in the district because of desegregation. The second case involved St. Louis City. Required at first only to initiate a voluntary magnet school program, the St. Louis Public Schools' system was eventually ordered to undertake a more extensive and mandatory desegregation program. Since then, the district has become a champion for metropolitan desegregation.

The reasons for the city school system's conversion and the county district's successful campaign for home rule are not difficult to understand. Nor are the consequences all that surprising. The mandates for desegregation came to be renegotiated as each district continued its efforts to avoid formal condemnation for its practices and/or reasserted its domination in the formulation and implementation of educational policies over other concerned parties. Tentative efforts of citizens from both districts to form effective coalitions and influence desegregation policies failed in the absence of aggressive federal support for reforms. Something called desegregation was introduced into both districts. Institutional reform was not. The impact of these early efforts on the proposed metropolitan desegregation order is discussed in detail later. So, too, is the attempt by many citizens to help transform St. Louis into a modern metropolitan area.

Here, then, is the second level on which the book was written and can be read. Too often, I think, those who have studied and written about desegregation have treated this reform as an end in itself. Justice was to be served, and it was required that desegregation be introduced to satisfy that simple moral claim. I was driven by a different concern and question. Namely, how are we to make sense of school desegregation? What contribution can it make to our way of life when it is so bitterly contested? These are matters that have troubled me in my different roles as scientist, concerned citizen, and parent since I began a serious study of the reform nearly ten years ago. I found a good deal of research on the topic. Indeed, there were so many studies on the subject that it was difficult to figure out what desegregation was and how it fit into American society. The arguments I heard on these subjects, while fine examples of rhetoric thumping, did nothing to ease my nagging suspicion that we really had not tried to make much sense of desegregation. As someone with pretensions about being a scientist, this fascinated me. I wanted to know how desegregation could be connected with the big and not-so-big changes occurring in this country since World War II. What follows is some of what I think I learned.

Some Preliminary Answers

No issue before the American people since the end of World War II has stuck in the public craw so stubbornly as school desegregation. We have fought over it, prayed for it, cursed it, legislated for and against it, studied it beyond the point of reason, and it has refused to go away. People who are otherwise capable of making balanced assessments about difficult matters lose their tempers at the very mention of the reform. Politicians avoid the issue, long since convinced that it would bring them only trouble. Even the courts seem to have lost their taste for enacting desegregation plans. School desegregation is no longer a popular topic for polite conversation or a legitimate enterprise for public servants. Still it persists, lingering in the public's imagination. It is the issue we love to hate.

Although never as obviously flawed as its detractors stated, desegregation has not accomplished what many people hoped it would. Many white and minority persons, perhaps most of them, still do not care much for each other or concede much beyond a grudging recognition of the other's right to exist and earn a living. Whether they would prefer to live, work, and socialize with one another is questionable. That their children are manifestly better—intellectually and emotionally—for having attended school together is disputed.[9] It is for these reasons, among others, that school segregation is no longer a national concern, merely a national annoyance.

If this alone were true about segregation and desegregation, then much of what is written in this book could be dismissed as self-indulgent twaddle. However, I think there is much more to desegregation than we have been willing to see. Rough talk about busing may be good fun, but it obscures an important fact: the significance of desegregation lies not in what it forces us to learn about ourselves but in what it helps us to avoid doing to ourselves and learning about the fragile nature of social order.

This is a big statement and it deserves a fuller explanation. The better part of this book will be dedicated to that end. My argument is based on two related ideas. First, desegregation occasions a crisis in the conduct of public education that no one—black or white, civil rights activist or racist—really wants. All the participants in a desegregation process work to soften the effects of this crisis by implementing rather limited reforms that do not undermine the legitimacy of public school systems. Indeed, as we shall see, their behavior actually reinforces the legitimacy of that institution. Second, the conflict over school desegregation enriches and protects our civic culture during periods of change. It accomplishes this neat trick by providing an opportunity to talk about some of our problems in a relatively predictable manner without having to resolve them. We live in a world that is in equal measure often unfair and unjust. We are reminded daily that some people always seem to get more than others. Tension and conflict are to be expected under such conditions. Of greater interest is the fact that more of this tension is not expressed in nastier conflicts between the groups that have less of nearly everything and those that have more.

Historically, this is where desegregation and other reform efforts have made their greatest contribution to our social order. Desegregation, however raucous and violent it becomes, allows us to draw attention to such tensions without doing too much to overcome them. The conflicts surrounding desegregation, if not exactly staged, are ritualistically prescribed and ended to the apparent satisfaction of almost everyone. We have been made aware of our differences, expressed our displeasure with them, but failed to take decisive steps to correct the injustice or inequality we all can see. Modest and hard-fought changes may be achieved, but the security and prosperity of a known social order have been preserved—for those on the bottom as well as the top.

Cultural anthropologists use the term "ritualized rebellions" to describe such disruptions to the established order of "primitive" societies. Ritualized rebellions have been described as "an institutionalized means whereby those in relatively powerless and inferior positions can formally rid themselves of accumulated frustration and resentment."[10] An established social order is challenged and the appearance of turning a social world upside down is created. What is both regular and obnoxious to some persons can be treated as something exceptional and bizarre, at least for a while. Certain practices that keep some members of the society at the bottom of the heap are challenged, but not so strongly as to disrupt the society too long or too hard. Women might assume male roles for a time and enjoy the privileges known to men in their culture. The men, for their part, occupy themselves with distinctly female-types of activities during such periods. The world that they all know, including its built-in stresses and strains, is inverted, but the disruption to their normal routine and customs does not last forever. Indeed, the rightness and utility of their normal way of life, including the part that has some persons on the bottom of the heap, is in a sense legitimated by having been put through this periodic test. The members of the society have found a way to acknowledge that some of the customs practiced in their society are arbitrary and unfair while avoiding the chaos that would ensue if those practices were repudiated entirely.

I thought that there might be some important parallels between the so-called ritualized rebellions of tribal societies and the crisis and reforms provoked by school segregation in our own. Desegregation and its attendant conflicts, it seems to me, have provided us with an opportunity to talk through some of the arbitrary and unfair customs practiced in our society. School segregation and desegregation also have made us think about some of the consequences of changes that occurred in our economy and politics as a result of building bigger, more modern metropolitan areas. I was interested in determining how the arguments over desegregation might have helped us make sense of those changes. It became obvious that these arguments occurred in a relatively predictable fashion. The nature and pace of discussions about racial problems were controlled.

It was agreed among the contesting parties that something called desegregation would take place in their school districts. They were not sure what that would mean, but they were familiar with the established procedures for introducing school policies. These procedures were modified slightly but not permanently to accommodate desegregation. Attempts to introduce new actors to the process or additional issues to the disputes were strictly controlled. Plans were developed under the guiding hand of school officials and presented to the public as "court-ordered busing." People got upset by the intrusion of the courts into local school affairs. Parents feared for their children's safety. There were some scuffles, some suspensions, and some uneasy socializing. Knowledge of a sort was passed on to the children. Minor adjustments were made to the desegregation order. The court was pleased with reports it received, reprimanded officials for their minor indiscretions, and declared the districts' program a success. People complimented one another on a difficult, but rewarding, job well done. Life went on, if not exactly like it used to be, with few major changes.

If there is a winner in this scenario, it must surely be the school system that has helped to create the illusion that big changes were occurring while maintaining most of its control over educational affairs. There are other winners, however. There is the court that has cleared its docket of a troublesome case. There are the civil rights attorneys who have created a little more law, added the scalp of another district to their belts and résumés, and then left town. There is the media that has gotten some splashy coverage of the first day of court-ordered busing. There are the activist parents appointed to prestigious committees and pleased by the news that their children were discovered to be gifted. And there are the desegregation experts who sometimes earn a good deal of money working for one group or another and otherwise try to feather their nests by writing scholarly articles and steamy desegregation exposés. Winners all, they share a common interest in making desegregation work, if only for themselves.

Through this posturing and service for or against racial equality, the desegregation crisis is transformed into a complex but well-understood ritual. The ultimate contribution of this culturally inspired crisis and our contrived responses to it is order. We have bumped up against the limits imposed on us by a segregated world and found them inefficient and highly annoying. Not wishing to disrupt our lives more than is necessary, however, we negotiate new limits within which most persons can operate comfortably as citizens and workers. Modest changes are secured and order is preserved. School desegregation has served as an important medium through which these negotiations could proceed, while keeping the disruption to more critical economic and political institutions to a minimum.

The prospect of accomplishing little when faced with a troubling problem is distasteful to many, myself included. We fancy ourselves people of action and resolve. There are times, however, when we may be better served by noisy and principled ineffectiveness. I think that school desegregation provides such a service.

Organization of the Book

When I looked at St. Louis's experience with school desegregation, I tried to understand how something thought to precipitate a "crisis" could have such a meager effect on most people's lives. Virtually everyone with whom I spoke and everything I read told me that the answer had something to do with justice and racial equality. Desegregation was needed to right a wrong. If people were not actively resisting its introduction, it must be because they had come to accept that fact. Appealing as such an argument was, it left me unsatisfied. It just did not fit the events that I had seen or had recollected to me. An alternate explanation—one that focused on efforts to create a workable civil order—seemed to make more sense. Perhaps the crisis passed so quickly and quietly because people found a way of softening its impact. Maybe the real achievement of desegregation is that it allowed us to talk about some sticky problems we all face without drastically changing the way we lead our lives. Order rather than justice was the real accomplishment of desegregation. People came to tolerate desegregation because they believed not in what it changed but in what it left alone. One thing became apparent. Regardless of who was right, the question of whether justice or order was the primary achievement of desegregation had to be addressed. This I attempt to do in the second chapter.

That desegregation is more important in facilitating the process of urbanization than the cause of justice may not be a popular idea. Nevertheless, I think a general review of what has (and has not) been considered as part of St. Louis's desegregation efforts will help to make the argument clearer, if no more convincing. Desegregation, especially insofar as it involves a metropolitan plan, ought to contribute to efforts to transform St. Louis into a modern metropolitan area. The ways in which this might be accomplished are described in the third chapter.

How far one can push an argument based on a few cases, like desegregation activities in the St. Louis area, is a problem for scientists who do fieldwork. It would be nice to be able to say that every other community dealt with these issues as did St. Louis, but that is not so. There have been some excellent case studies of desegregation in other places; and these provide some clues to how general a pattern has been identified in the St. Louis case. Another way to achieve the same end would be to look backward, not just to the early 1970s but to the early 1800s, and see how urban residents have altered the ways they tried to cope with rapid changes brought on by urbanization. These arguments are summarized in the fourth and fifth chapters. The lessons that our own urban history could have taught us about desegregation and other reform efforts are there too, as is a defense of desegregation as an article of our civic faith.

A more detailed account of how desegregation progressed in two St. Louis area districts will allow me to show how their plans contributed to the larger process of urban expansion alluded to in the earlier chapters. Chronicled in the sixth, seventh, and eighth chapters also is how St. Louis residents worked to moderate the effects of a racial crisis on a local level. Not always a pretty picture, it nevertheless provides an interesting counterpoint to the official propaganda laid out by the districts and some outside experts they brought in to justify their activities.

That persons like myself or jurists interested in desegregation have accomplished little of substance with all our energetic pronouncements may upset some people. They should remain patient, however, because in the last chapter I will try to describe what it was we were doing wrong. I also will try to describe what we can do better in the future. I will use this discussion to show how desegregation experts shaded their work so as to help achieve a civil, if not much more just, social order for minorities in the United States.

It is not that any of us intended to hide the "truth" about desegregation from the public, though that may have been the practical effect of our work. It is rather that we chose to overlook certain aspects or consequences of the great desegregation crisis just like everyone else caught up in it. After all, both those opposed to and in favor of desegregation agreed that the purpose of this reform was to bring about big changes. They simply ignored the possibility, well known to any student of social theory, that conflicts are just as likely to conserve old divisions as they are to melt them away. I will try to show how this happened in desegregation controversies and the service these disputes rendered to our public life in the chapters that follow.

2. Is the Major Achievement of Desegregation Justice or Order?

The Case for Justice

To the Supreme Court and its petitioners in 1954, segregation was much more than an offensive token of the black man's subordination to an outdated custom. It was a moral outrage. The separation of minority from white children in the public schools was an affront not only to the minority students and their parents but also to a democratic way of life. It was a crime of immense proportions whose solution could lie only in the affirmative actions of governments at all levels on behalf of minority citizens' civil rights. The promise of *Brown* vs. *the Board of Education,* however, went beyond the simple denial of the states' power to create segregated schools.

> What *Brown* had begot was a union of the mightiest and lowliest in America, a mystical, passionate union bound by the pained depths of the black man's cry for justice and the moral authority, unique to the Court, to see that justice realized.
>
> The black, at last, was to be Americanized: the cultural and psychic isolation . . . would be dispelled. The Court and the nation . . . believed that with *Brown,* education would break . . . the old, oppressive cycle of ignorance and poverty. Education's promise was the thrilling one of upward mobility. Integration improved one's chances for college, which, in turn, improved one's shot at a job. If, as *Brown* observed, success was doubtful without an education, it was achievable with one. Education was . . . truly "the great equalizer of the conditions of men."[1]

Brown was the promise to recast American society, an urban and industrial society, with blacks sharing in the wealth and knowledge that would be gained from a better education. It was a grand dream and an admirable goal.

The spiritual and intellectual reclamation of minority students was the primary concern, but white students would also benefit from the experience. Yet desegregation was an untested walk through legal terrain few had the training or inclination to initiate. For the most part, higher courts and legislative bodies passed the responsibility for enacting the law to lower courts and legislative bodies. Ultimately, the responsibility for articulating the promise of *Brown* was delivered to school officials who had only their experience as caretakers of segregated institutions to guide them. On a few occasions the courts flirted with ambitious plans for restructuring public education; but cooler heads prevailed, and desegregation quickly reverted to a question of how many youngsters to bus before minority rights could be validated.

The bright promise of school desegregation that once touched the conscience of this nation and fired the imagination of its citizens seems more subdued today. It has been clouded by time but also tempered by a realization that both the conditions that originally inspired it and the nation itself have changed. Although its passion may be muted by the shadowy rhetoric of statistical analyses and probabilities, the belief still shared today by supporters of desegregation is that this reform can be an effective tool for achieving social change. Desegregated schools can assist children in preparing for society as it ought to be, it is argued. To accomplish this, educational institutions must offer fresh notions about citizenship and alter the conception of who is qualified to receive and dispense these new ideas. Contemporary critics do not deny the merit of desegregation as an important strategy for exposing children of different races to each other's way of life. Nor do they necessarily doubt the constitutional validity of efforts to dismantle segregated schools. However, they do have reservations about the apparent recklessness of federal officials who in the past seemed intent on stretching the constitutional fabric beyond recognition. They believe that advocates of desegregation ignore the substantial damage that aggressive court orders impose upon communities without any promise that children of either race will benefit greatly from the experiment.[2] The question asked by contemporary critics is not whether we will continue to tolerate the stain of segregation in our public schools but whether we can long endure the trauma associated with its removal and its replacement with something of dubious educational value.

What is noteworthy to me is the apparent polarity of these positions, that public schools must or cannot be used effectively to achieve racial justice. Laymen and experts may have fought among themselves regarding the necessity of racial equality or the best means to apprehend it. Nevertheless, for the last thirty years, there has been no doubt about the issue at hand. It should be no surprise that the public has been taught to see these matters so clearly. That teachers, jurists, and scientists should also share this singular vision of school desegregation cannot be so easily dismissed. One expects that such involved persons should have been more sensitive to the subtle accommodations that pass for radical change.

People who write about desegregation can be placed into one of three categories. There are the supporters, who have dedicated a good part of their adult lives to studying this reform and fighting in its behalf. Their steadfastness to the principles implied—but never quite realized—in desegregation has not diminished with time or changing political tastes. Another group are the opponents. They, too, are honorable people no less committed or thorough in their work than their liberal peers. A third and much smaller collection distinguishes itself by its members' willingness to defend and to criticize desegregation at the same time. This might not seem terribly noteworthy, but in matters related to desegregation, this is a fairly rare combination. A discussion of ideas central to this approach will be reserved for the last section of this chapter.

Most people can be labeled easily as being either for desegregation or against forced busing. Curiously, however, their respective positions on how to construct and implement a desegregation plan have grown more similar the longer this issue has lingered before the public. These adversaries could probably get downright chummy when talking about the prerogatives of school officials and the regrettable harm done by an overzealous court. They differ only in the degree to which a particular intervention strategy should be used. Their remarkable consensus as to what constitutes an appropriate range of desegregation-related activities belies the image projected by their constant squabbling.[3]

Advocates will howl at the idea that they share anything in common with opponents. They will argue—not without some justification—that both sides are confined by what the law permits and the courts are willing to order. I point out only that social scientists have had a good deal of opportunity to shape what the courts have looked at.[4] Social scientists generally chose to ignore problems related to the administration and politics of educational reform. Jurists considered these questions but avoided them whenever possible. Critics maintained that the courts had no right or ability to "run" school systems. There were better ways to create more workable desegregation orders. The best desegregation plans, as they and almost everyone else came to think, are those composed and administered by local officials and citizens.[5]

For people who worry about tallying such matters, this represents a complete victory for opponents. The most likely beneficiaries of this approach are school officials and their defenders, because no one proposing such a strategy could seriously believe that school critics would be permitted to acquire more power.[6] Observers taking a more detached view of citizen participation know that school systems are filled with enough blind alleys and sinkholes to lose the average brontosaurus. A group of grass-roots activists would hardly be missed. Moreover, a distinct social class bias enters into any effort to affect policy. People with a higher class standing tend to participate more, and more effectively. Differences in power between those who have it and those who hope to acquire it may even grow during a conflict. For those people or groups accustomed to getting their way, it seems that "participation communicates and reproduces power." For those unaccustomed to wielding influence, "participation has been a symbolic substitute for power, a means of reproducing the absence of power."[7] Such matters will be addressed in detail later.

Of greater and more immediate interest is the reason for this growing intellectual affinity between supporters and opponents of desegregation. In truth, they have never been that far apart. However else they may have bickered and sniped at each other's work, both camps have always viewed desegregation as a tool to promote social change. As such, their work fits squarely and comfortably into a tradition of scholarly thinking about racial and ethnic conflict and accommodation. Central to this line of thought is the notion that the differences between racial or ethnic populations eventually will be resolved, or at least greatly reduced. These populations may continue to compete with each other; but the harshness of subsequent disputes will be lessened by the fact that both parties have "institutionalized" their conflicts. They will have developed new rules for processing claims, defining their common interests, and even preventing outbreaks of civil unrest.[8]

The scientific importance of desegregation—as compared to its moral correctness or political advisability—is that it so nicely captures the process of institutionalizing conflict, the moment in the supposed cycle of race relations when two people earnestly begin to teach themselves the difficult habits of self-constraint and mutual accommodation.[9] Social scientists were quick to seize the opportunity to evaluate how the American public had adjusted to desegregation. There are literally thousands of studies in which the good, bad, or indifferent effects of desegregation on people have been discussed. Though not always brimming with optimism, a number of these studies provide readers with some hope that desegregation can work. They often contain hints on how to achieve that end. Attention most often focuses on the decisiveness and scope of desegregation orders. More ambitious plans, it is reasoned, may yield better results for minority children in the long run.[10] Tensions and overt conflict may be greater for a time; but the purgative properties of conflict help to reconcile whites to the inevitability of change and accustom blacks to their improved status. Desegregation conflicts are thought to be "self-dampening" for this reason; that is, they would not polarize the community and create a basis for new conflicts.[11]

To the extent this is true, it would make desegregation-related controversies unique among the events typically thought of as intergroup conflicts. This, of course, is precisely what students of desegregation have long maintained. At least one recognized expert in the field, for instance, has argued, "There are virtually no theories of social change that are applicable to this type of 'forced' community social change."[12] One might take exception to such a bold declaration. The fact remains, however, that most explanations of why desegregation does or does not work in particular communities are based more on psychological reasoning and faith than on political compromise. Why people adjust better in some instances than in others depends on their willingness to change their beliefs and attitudes about themselves or members of another race. The institutionalization of interracial conflict through school desegregation supposedly makes this possible.

Desegregation was called for by jurists and scientists with only a vague notion about educational equity to guide their work.[13] Given this fuzzy mandate, debates over the reform tended to be confined to topics that dealt with changing the people who attended or worked with the schools. These topics included the legal barriers to educational equality, student achievement and emotional well-being, busing and white flight, race relations in schools, and post-graduation opportunities at college or in the work force. The results of this work have satisfied no one. Desegregation is still seen as either a painful intrusion or a necessary experiment in democracy and racial temperance. Research can be cited to defend both positions. Individual students, teachers, and citizens—white as well as minority—have had their lives altered by school desegregation.[14] Sometimes these changes have been beneficial; on other occasions the impact has not been so positive. Under no circumstances, though, have the results been sufficiently dramatic to warrant the idea that an entire race was being success-fully overhauled or ruined by desegregation.

I do not wish to make this appear a trivial conclusion. If our traditional notions about the beneficial effects of institutionalizing racial conflicts had been correct, we should have expected far more definitive and positive results from these scientific studies. This reasoning clearly underlies arguments for the aban-donment of school desegregation. It would not be unreasonable to wonder how far the process of racial accommodation could progress in light of such scientific findings. Ignoring for the moment the significance attributed to changes in individuals thought to be brought on by desegregation, perhaps we should have been looking at the whole school system or community for signs that racial justice was being secured. Maybe it was too much to expect that individual people, even great numbers of people, should show the effects of such a big change so soon.

When we shift our attention from the individual to the institutions, we tend to find the positive signs that we have been seeking.[15] This is a more sociological approach to the problem. Sociological treatments of desegregation are often subsumed under general discussions of institutional change and the civil-rights movement. While seemingly reasonable, this assemblage ties desegregation to a larger body of literature concerned with all types of social movements. Observ-ers tend to share the notion that such collective actions are designed to effect substantial changes in society.[16] Like his psychological cousin, therefore, the scientist looking at desegregation as an organizational phenomenon would be disposed to seeing it as something that would encourage social change.

This view is most evident in studies that contain comparisons of desegregation programs or their impact in numerous communities. Success or failure is gener-ally gauged by how many students were reassigned to integrated schools or the variety of educational programs introduced as part of a desegregation effort. Other factors often considered include changes in voting behavior or signs of resistance like student suspensions, fighting, and more rigid attitudes toward members of the opposite race. A composite picture of the desegregation process based on a review of such items has led a number of scientists to conclude that desegregation can work well. Overt resistance to desegregation does taper off after a year or two. There are signs that attitudes toward members of the opposite race soften, white flight declines, and voters start to turn away from antibusing candidates in school-board elections. These and similar expressions of inter-group and interpersonal conflict seem to give way to an accommodation between the races just as theories predict.[17] Insofar as such things can be taken as signs of progress, one might say that these communities had fashioned a more just society.

It is not altogether clear, though, that one acquires a fair or complete picture of desegregation and its impact on school districts when so many communities are studied simultaneously.[18] When only a few schools or towns are studied at once, school districts appear far less like self-conscious purveyors of rationality and justice or passive vehicles for mandated changes.[19] District caretakers seem more intent on ensuring the continuing independence of their system. The dis-trict may have to adapt to changes in the outside world; some negotiating can occur over the treatment of its personnel and clients. More important things seem immune to negotiation, however. The legitimacy and authority of the public schools to make and to carry out educational policy, for instance, have not been seriously threatened. Contrary to speculation, courts and federal agen-cies rarely and reluctantly intervene directly into the daily operation of school bureaucracies. Moreover, even among the most vocal advocates of desegregation, one finds little support for the idea that this situation should be changed. Thus, the administrative routines and political customs through which discriminatory school practices were implemented seem equally immune to criticism and change. The underlying tensions and inequities built into the way this institution operates have not been removed, even if some say they feel better about their situation.[20] The possibility exists, therefore, that aggrieved parties will again find reasons to doubt the institution's ability or its caretakers' willingness to adapt to a changing world.

These suspicions, it turns out, can apply equally well to the community in which the desegregating school district is found. Some scientists, as I noted above, claimed to have reconstructed and measured the impact of desegregation on community politics. They were optimistic because many people, at least in terms of their expressed attitudes or personal behavior, seemed less resistant and maybe even a bit more supportive of desegregation as time passed. They had adjusted to this "big change" in their lives. Yet a community's collective reaction to social change is far more than the simple summing up of its individual members' ballots on election day. What they do or fail to do as a group may reveal a different, and, in this instance, a less optimistic picture. This seems to characterize community reactions to racial controversies like desegregation. Communities, it appears, are far more adept at resisting than embracing change.

American urban ethnographers have just begun to examine how local communities seek to identify and defend their common interests.[21] The available evidence, though somewhat sketchy, complements and extends what we know from studies about the response of particular school systems to touchy reforms. In such a case, reform may provide an opportunity for the institution's guardians to continue their customary behavior while enjoying the protection of the courts and the status accorded to all harried innovators.[22] Local communities faced with similar challenges often mount collective actions that reinforce existing class divisions and frustrate efforts to change local politics. Parochialism is not an attribute peculiar to school systems and white ethnic enclaves, however. Minority groups and communities can also share this trait. Their ascension to the ranks of the politically active is no guarantee of progress either for themselves or for the larger community. Their acquisition of power, boisterous and violent as it often is, may be more cantankerous than threatening, more conventional than revolutionary. Conflicts and reforms ordinarily taken as signs of scornful ridicule for established and time-honored customs may be nothing more than expressions of an uncomfortable stalemate, a way of controlling the introduction of disorder more to keep the community together than to provide a medium for changing it.[23]

The Case for Order

This is not what most people think desegregation is intended to achieve. They believe that the purpose of this reform is to relieve the members of a despised minority population of their stigma, to make them more equal, and our society more just. Yet inequality seems to be a by-product of the way more advanced societies are organized. Most of the time these inequities are tolerated, even accepted. But for this, revolutions might be a lot more common than they are. Broad changes in society, like those prompted by industrialization and city-building, make differences in the life chances of one or another group more obvious and annoying. Changes need not result in violent upheavals or in realignment of social classes, and yet there are many indications that this has been the case in the United States.

Sometime during the early nineteenth century, parts of the country—most notably the Northeast and Northcentral sections—began to witness a dramatic growth in the number and size of cities. Although the South and West had a number of large cities, their period of rapid urbanization did not begin until the 1930s. In both cases, the rudiments of an urban way of life also were observed cropping up in smaller burghs.[24] The process of urbanization, however unevenly it might have been initiated and absorbed, had a profound impact on the communities it touched. Well before citizens resolved the sticky matter of the states' subordination to a central government, a distinctly "urban" way of doing things or looking at the world had already begun to exercise its disquieting affect on the nation.

City-building has long been considered a seditious process. Social and political theorists, pulp writers, and street-corner prophets warned about the evils of urban society and the attendant threat to civil peace. Implicit in their critiques was the idea that cities erode the basis for meaningful social contacts among people.

The quick and varied pace of city-living as well as the superficial character of human interaction seemed to make it difficult to achieve a sustained and stable community inside urban areas.[25] The organization and size of cities were thought to frustrate the efforts of well-intentioned people to reinforce social order and to involve others in more worthwhile enterprises. In the absence of firm moral standards for good behavior or more effective secular props for a crumbling sacred world, it was feared that chaos would ensue. "Scientific" confirmation of these impressions about urban life—surveys of the poor, studies of cephalic indexes, and the like—reinforced these fears.[26] Intermittent outbreaks of disease, labor or political unrest, and the annoying presence of personal differences substantiated them.

In retrospect, the bad effects of urbanization were greatly exaggerated. Urban dwellers are no worse off than anyone else. They are capable of carrying on satisfying social lives. They are not abandoned by their families, and they can enjoy close friendships. They are not emotional cripples.[27] If they are alienated from themselves, each other, or the products of their labor—as Marx expected victims of industrialization would be—they appear not much more vulnerable than persons who live in rural settings.

Evidence to contradict the view that urbanization has detrimental effects on persons' social and emotional well-being accumulated gradually from the United States and abroad. Left somewhat unsettled, though, were questions about the effects of urbanization on civil order. Urban life in itself had not been shown to disrupt the development of customary forms of group life. One might have expected such evidence to be used to counter arguments that urban life predisposed people to engage in less institutionalized forms of collective action. It was not. Many analysts could not abandon the idea that cities were the most likely sites for civil decay because of the kinds of people who lived there or the tensions they experienced. However, there appears to be nothing peculiar about people who live in urban areas, the mere fact that so many do, or how quickly they assembled in cities that would dispose them to commit acts of civil disorder. The conditions under which people violently disrupted the civil order of urban areas are no doubt more complex than had been believed; such conditions probably had a good deal more to do with local political customs and community organization than typically was supposed.[28]

Academic types like myself who are interested in how group life is sustained during periods of great change have been unable to get much beyond this point. In fact, we have been stuck with two very different, even contradictory, guesses as to how forms of civic restlessness fit into our political culture. Some of us have talked about how groups retreat into their neighborhoods and wage quiet and not-so-quiet wars of resistance against the outside world.[29] The idea that neighborhoods can become island fortresses is appealing, even though we know their walls are always in danger of being breached. Moreover, this idea suggests no way in which the reconstituted moral and social order of these small places could be extended to a whole metropolitan area. Other academics have noticed that forms of social protest have changed, becoming bigger, more organized, and politicized, along with the rest of society. This is crucial, if people are to use such devices in order to identify and overcome inequities built into their way of life.[30] These academics see civic restlessness making an important contribution to efforts to forge a new, and more egalitarian, social order. In this way, they manage to avoid the problem of how disorder could help spread new ways of conducting public and private affairs. Unfortunately, they have been unable to account for the failure of such efforts to achieve some final solution to inequality or, barring that, at least to blossom into bigger, nastier battles in which these matters would be confronted more openly.

Class warfare may be neither inevitable nor possess the redemptive qualities ascribed to it by doctrinaire Marxists. Students of U.S. conflicts have noted how little of our civil unrest has been directed toward the state and how racial or ethnic disputes have retarded the growth of conflicts between social classes.[31] If our culture possesses inherent stresses and strains that make class tensions inevitable, perhaps it also has developed customary ways of moderating their effects. The process by which class conflicts are "submerged" has not escaped the attention of social scientists, particularly those who study the American educational system.[32] It is contended here that school desegregation is a good example of such a process.

Reforms like desegregation perform a very special service in our political culture. They soften the effects of annoying problems in our social order without undermining the authority and legitimacy of important institutions. In the case of desegregation, segregative practices whose lingering presence seems quite out of place in a modern urban and industrial society are exposed. Yet, as was noted earlier, the public schools condemned as repositories of obsolete and officially repudiated customs rarely lose their ability to carry out their traditional mandate. School desegregation, in terms of its modest accomplishments and provocative nature, is reminiscent of "ritualized rebellions" in primitive societies. These stylized displays of community conflict appear to turn the "natural order of things" upside down, if only temporarily. For instance, women may be allowed to assume more dominant male habits for a time, and these occasions may be marked with considerable animosity or violence. After a while, however, things return to their normal state. Members of the community have expressed their recognition of inequality while ensuring that customary economic and political routines are allowed to continue.[33]

This pattern, of course, is modified in societies like our own in which change does occur, where the progress of industrialization and city building was never checked. In the struggle to compose a workable civil order, ways had to be discovered to preserve the economic vitality of cities without seriously altering the basic relations among their several social classes, ethnic groups, and religious communities. Conflicts were unavoidable, but the nature and occasion of confrontations could be influenced and, in a manner of speaking, institutionalized, just as race relations experts predicted. However, such staged rebellions do not guarantee that things will change much. Ritualistic conflicts and reforms enable people to adapt to changes brought on by urbanization and industrialization at a manageable pace and in a piecemeal fashion. They offer people an opportunity to transform familiar tensions with poorly defined causes into something explicable and at least temporarily remediable. The ritualized conflict affirms the inconsistencies of our social order. The ritualistic reform softens their impact without jeopardizing the legitimacy of that order.

As part of a ritualized rebellion, desegregation conflicts and reforms serve the social order as "rituals of reaffirmation" through which the "true" meaning of norms and values we all ostensibly share is better realized.[34] Some writers have argued that educational reforms were designed to preserve the American class structure; they essentially were a "capitalistic trick" to create a docile work force and electorate. I think, however, that desegregation crises and reforms have enabled us to avoid more punishing displays of class conflict while growing accustomed to new ways of urban life. There may be advantages to hiding class conflicts, and they are not confined to a "ruling" class.[35] The whole community benefits.

*   *   *

Primitive and advanced cultures exhibit similar responses to the problem of maintaining order across generations or in the face of large-scale economic and social changes. Intermittent displays of civil disorder provide opportunities to reaffirm the importance of this problem and its permanent challenge to community members. While all such displays are governed by cultural traditions to some extent, one class of civil disorder—the ritualized rebellion—seems particularly important in ensuring continuity and order within the community. In primitive cultures the outbursts are occasions for people to acknowledge inequities built into their way of life without having to reduce those disparities in any permanent fashion. In advanced cultures it is more difficult to avoid the influence of social and economic changes and the possibility that some reduction in inequality will be required. Under these circumstances, the ritualized rebellion serves to soften the community's introduction to new changes by drawing attention away from the basic divisions among its several economic classes. The threat to the community's established order is reduced in this manner, if not eliminated entirely.

School desegregation illustrates how this process works in an advanced urban and industrial society. Its arrival is anticipated and greeted with a good deal of apprehension, tumult, and, in some cases, violence. People are compelled to reconsider how their society has acted to deny certain members a proportionate share of wealth. The reforms introduced to achieve this end, however, do not alter the basic arrangement of social classes within the community. Indeed, the reforms may unintentionally reinforce the existence of such divisions by avoiding any definitive or direct fight over them. A case in point is the agreement among districts in the St. Louis area to initiate a voluntary "metropolitan" desegregation plan. The agreement presumed that there would be no resolution to the problems posed by the area's political fragmentation across two states and into hundreds of separate municipalities, and legislative, service, and school districts. Nor did the proposed plan require area residents to consider, much less do anything about, the underlying economic conditions that keep more well-to-do citizens separated from their less prosperous neighbors.

Of course, these matters were never intended to be considered in a final desegregation order. The controversies surrounding a decision to desegregate do incorporate such questions. It is an important element in ritualistic reforms, though, that such issues be ignored so that the legitimacy of the social order is not questioned too long or severely.

The achievement of ritualized rebellions is cultural compromise. All cultures must find a way to draw their members' attention to the problem of inequality. Ritualistic conflicts and reforms negotiate a path between two culturally unpromising solutions to this dilemma. They avoid, on the one hand, the need to adopt unscheduled collective actions that call the legitimacy of existing institutions into question. No society could long tolerate such challenges, no matter how valid the claimants' grievances. Perhaps that is why successful challengers to established leaders learn to modify their demands and tactics.[36] On the other hand, ritualized rebellions enable groups to do more than retreat to the safety of their isolated neighborhoods and engage in satisfying, if ultimately unsuccessful, attempts to resist unwanted changes. The incrementalism that passes for meaningful social change as a result of ritualized rebellions would not satisfy many activists or theoreticians.[37] Yet as a compromise between chaos and ossification in our social worlds, ritualized rebellions seem to have served us very well.

*   *   *

Ritualized rebellions in more developed countries do not prohibit change. They can, as school desegregation and the history of other educational reform efforts will illustrate, help manage the pace of change and ensure that some fundamental barriers between one or another class or race are left intact. Again, the desegregation case in St. Louis serves as an example of how this works. The original case against the city district was initiated in 1972. It yielded a voluntary magnet school program in 1976 and a compulsory intradistrict plan four years later. While neither effort spawned violence of the sort seen in other cities, there was and continues to be a good deal of bitterness and muffled resistance to desegregation within St. Louis City. The city school system and the NAACP pressed to expand the city's desegregation order so that it covered the twenty-three separate districts in contiguous St. Louis County. Several were already cooperating in a voluntary plan, and all but one of these districts agreed in principle to the provisions of a voluntary exchange and magnet school program on the eve of the trial for a mandatory plan. The voluntary agreement was hailed as an unprecedented achievement that would serve as an example for other metropolitan areas. Because the contribution of ritualized rebellions is what is overlooked about our social order, however, it is important to see what sources of inequality and problems were papered over in this artful compromise.

A review of the St. Louis County Board of Education's deliberations between the 1950s and 1970s reveals three overriding concerns among professional educators and the lay leadership: the merger of all county districts with the city district, the equalization of school tax rates in the area, and the consolidation of districts within St. Louis County. All would have led to a substantial reorganization of public education *and* would have removed an important barrier to the reconsolidation of St. Louis City with the county. Desegregation became a concern only as blacks began to make a dramatic and contested move into the county in the 1960s; but such a reform would not have required massive changes in school organization and educational financing. The current plan does not draw more attention to the disparities in wealth across districts. It does not threaten to disrupt the structured inequality evidenced in the schools that is derived from the wealth of persons living in one or another community. Indeed, the decision ratified that inequality by supplementing existing revenues through student transfers. Districts sending students to more integrated settings lose only a portion of the state funds they would have gotten for each student. Districts receiving these students receive additional state funds. Such funds are welcomed in districts that have been losing students and revenues, particularly in a state that does not support public education very well in the first place.

Thus, some progress has been made in helping people recognize that they are part of a larger metropolitan area. A few steps have been taken to make the area's public institutions and civil rituals a bit more consistent with the realities of a metropolitan economy. Neither of these signs of progress, however, has been fixed in the area's political culture through the creation of a permanent institution. Nor has progress or change been purchased at the risk of disrupting the basic social class divisions either separating the city and county or among blacks.

Even a cursory review of the demographic profiles of St. Louis County communities shows that recently arrived blacks often have income and educational levels comparable to their white neighbors, and sometimes higher. City blacks fare less well relative to city whites or departed blacks. Educational observers acknowledge that black students with better academic preparation—and by extension a higher social-class background—have been more likely to apply for inclusion in city/county transfers and are more often placed in county districts.[38] This pattern has been demonstrated since 1976 by magnet school enrollments in the city. Desegregation in metropolitan St. Louis may effectively reinforce existing social-class differences even as it appears to be heralding a new age of race relations. Such is the nature of ritualistic conflicts and reforms in urban-industrial states.

Conclusions: A Semblance of Justice

The fragile nature of social order is never more obvious than when a society is confronted with large-scale changes, like industrialization and urbanization, over which no person or group can hope to exert complete or predictable control. Under such circumstances, stylized forms of disorder may help to legitimate and dramatize the passing of a way of life already rendered obsolete by basic changes in the social and economic order. The emergence of desegregation as an issue, for example, did not occur until well after blacks had established themselves as an urban population and more potent economic force. Collective actions or controversies like those associated with desegregation are not effective devices for working out contradictions within the political and economic order.[39] The contribution, instead, might be simultaneously more modest and persistent. Displays of emendatory zeal or collective outrage in themselves may not substantially hasten the introduction of new ways of behaving and believing in the communities they touch. Were such efforts routinely successful, social change would be a constant and disruptive feature of community life.

The significance of intermittent attempts to make over the world or at least one's small corner of it may be that such acts are accepted by the public as a customary way of ratifying big changes or acknowledging the inability to halt them. Otherwise, it becomes difficult to account for the persistence of relatively primitive forms of corporate action in our distinctly unprimitive bureaucratic world, except as atavistic expressions of pent-up rage. The historic vitality of the "mob" as a form of collective behavior, for instance, has been chronicled in Western Europe and to a much smaller extent in the United States. The character of this behavior may have changed with the times, yet it remains as normal a ritual in our political culture as the modern recall and referendum that also register displeasure without toppling public institutions.

Ordinarily, in this context, the term *ritual* is used to describe practices that enable members of "primitive" societies to find an indirect and stylized way to resolve disputes without having to address the underlying problems that inspired the conflicts. It is not thought to be applicable to the ways that "advanced" peoples solve their problems.[40] Nevertheless, if we forgo the luxury of this kind of cultural absolution, we find that the term *ritual* can apply in our society to community conflicts and not just the quaint customs of someone else's religion. This certainly makes it easier to understand how both the supporters and opponents of desegregation can reasonably claim that the issue has been settled in their favor. Advocates point with pride to the introduction of a much despised reform. Adversaries show how effectively they resisted and continue to resist the plan, that racial problems still exist in the schools, and that many have abandoned the public schools.[41] Both are correct. We have achieved a semblance of justice while ensuring the continuation of our social order.

This is a strange argument indeed. For three decades we have believed that the purpose of desegregation and other race-related reforms is to help minority citizens acquire more of what this society has to offer and to teach others that this is good and proper. There was never a question that justice was the issue at risk. Raised now is the possibility that we were fooling ourselves, that wrapped up in desegregation is a much stronger impulse than anyone might have suspected to protect our communities from time and growth. Implied further is that the modest progress evidenced by minorities as a result of desegregation—and its concomitant failure to break down the economic and social order of communities in any fundamental way—was the reform's primary achievement.

3. In Pursuit of Metropolitan St. Louis

Conditions that change and conditions that cannot change provide a stage on which efforts to control and redirect our lives must be played out. They define some of the boundaries within which those attempts to control the process of social change or temper its effects must fall, if reforms are to have any chance of succeeding. Not all things can or will be considered open to modification. There are limits beyond which no negotiations dare be pressed, lest the foundations or guiding assumptions of our social order be questioned and possibly repudiated. If the school-desegregation movement has served the public by approaching sensitive matters indirectly or by avoiding more serious issues altogether, then one should describe what those more critical problems might have been. This is not as difficult as it may seem. We will begin with a discussion of things that have changed in the St. Louis area and then consider several factors frustrating St. Louis's efforts to rebuild itself.

Building Metropolitan St. Louis

The St. Louis metropolitan area has undergone major changes since the end of World War II. At that time, both jobs and people began to leave the city in large numbers. A substantial number of whites began moving away around 1950. Blacks did not start their own outward trek until the mid-1960s, but had by then established themselves as an integral part of the city's population. The movement out of the city was exaggerated by a general increase in the population of surrounding counties.

The cumulative effect of these changes has been staggering. By 1970, the physical boundaries of the metropolitan area had expanded to include five counties (three from Missouri and two from Illinois) that are not contiguous to St. Louis City. No longer is the city the region's dominant population center, having lost half of its 1950 population of eight hundred and sixty thousand. St. Louis County now enjoys that honor. Its population has grown to approximately nine hundred and seventy-three thousand; this represents an increase of 140 percent over its 1950 population of four hundred thousand. Nearly a million additional persons are spread throughout the eight other counties in the metropolitan area. This, too, represents a marked change from the way things were in 1950.

What has happened in St. Louis, then, is almost a textbook case of central city abandonment and suburban expansion. Blacks, once largely segregated in inner-city neighborhoods, have participated in this process, but not in such large

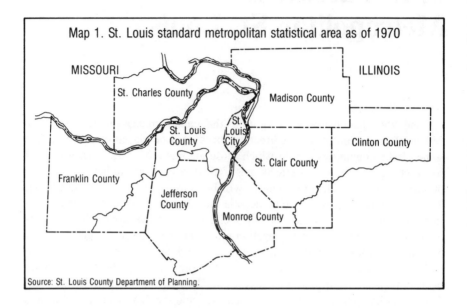

Map 1. St. Louis standard metropolitan statistical area as of 1970

Source: St. Louis County Department of Planning.

numbers as whites. Their presence in St. Louis County has grown since 1960 both in absolute numbers (from twenty thousand to one hundred and ten thousand) and relative to whites (from 3 percent to 11 percent). Still, almost 60 percent of all blacks in the metropolitan area live in the city of St. Louis. More of these people, when compared to black county residents, are likely to hold skilled and unskilled blue-collar jobs. The income profile for black city residents also is lower than that for blacks from St. Louis County. This is not to say that middle-class blacks have abandoned the city. (The numbers of blacks employed in the professions or as managers, for example, were comparable in St. Louis County and City as late as 1979.) It means only that they constitute a smaller class in the city's black population.[1]

The city of St. Louis has experienced losses in its population and business capacity that rival anything seen in other older central cities of the Midwest and East. While the fortunes of St. Louis have declined, however, not all parts of the city have suffered in equal measure. In general, the areas noted on Map 2 as the Northside and Near Northside have undergone the most painful transition since 1950. The population of these areas has become overwhelmingly black. The Southside and Near Southside have suffered losses, but far less so than other parts of St. Louis. These areas were populated primarily by whites in 1950, and that is no less true today. An area known as the Central Corridor separates the north and south sections of the city. Containing most of the city's major businesses, civic institutions, recreation centers, and railroad lines, the Central Cor-

ridor was once the population and slum center for the city. It was and remains
the most racially heterogeneous area in St. Louis.

Pictures of downtown St. Louis after World War II—along the eastern edge
of the Central Corridor—reveal an uninspiring landscape pocked by old ware-
houses and tenements against a rather modest array of government buildings,
office complexes, hotels, and department stores. The city's central business
district was crowded in a few square blocks adjoining a riverfront that held
neither the charm nor the energy of St. Louis when dozens of paddle wheelers
queued along its levee. Several miles west of the riverfront lay a second area of
substantial business and entertainment activities, including a symphony hall and
large movie theater. Farther west one found Forest Park, a large and lovely green
space that marks the city's western boundary and stands as a permanent monu-
ment to St. Louis's triumphant 1904 world exposition.

Much has changed in this area since the close of World War II. The original
central business district now stretches some fifteen blocks west of the riverfront
and is filled with new and renovated office buildings, a new sports stadium, the
world headquarters for several large corporations, and a new convention center.
The crown jewel in St. Louis's redevelopment effort, of course, is the Jefferson
National Expansion Memorial or, as it is more commonly known, the Arch. It
stands between the Mississippi River and the downtown area and has quieted
early critics by spurring on redevelopment efforts and becoming the most visited
of all national parks.

The impact of population changes and the loss of manufacturing jobs and
smaller retail stores has been telling. Residential segregation, especially in the
city, has not decreased substantially and probably is worse in many places today
than it was in 1960.[2] The migration of poor blacks left the downtown area
available for redevelopment, and the slums from which they were ejected were
torn down. At the same time, however, this forced march left a trail of abandoned
residences that neither the people nor any business or government leaders were
equipped to deal with competently. It also created a legacy of bitterness that
people in the metropolitan area have yet to address forthrightly.

The transformation process has not been easy. The idea that one's job and
private life may be tied to some transcendant metropolitan reality is less satisfying—and more difficult to personalize—than a comparable belief in one's
god. It is also easier to ignore. That is why, I suspect, we have been more willing
to build churches than public institutions that affirm the claim of the community
on our lives. Our urban history, as we shall see in the next chapter, is replete
with examples of city leaders and concerned citizens first denying the need for
public action and then jerry-building some institution to address a pressing
social problem. Contemporary St. Louis has struggled with the problem of
transforming itself from an old industrial and manufacturing city into the hub

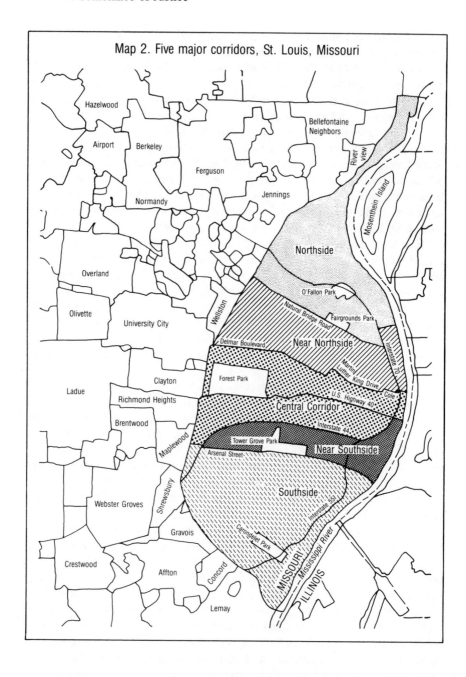

Map 2. Five major corridors, St. Louis, Missouri

of a modern service and commercial center. Many of the population and economic changes are consistent with such a process. When attention turns to the matter of public accountability for untidy consequences of this process, however, denial is the most frequent response one observes. Thus far, the public arena has been the most reluctant to acknowledge the importance of metropolitan development. Among the more critical obstructions to the kind of progress implied in metropolitan expansion have been the division of the region across two states and the exceptional political fragmentation between St. Louis County and City and within St. Louis County itself. If the St. Louis area has not been able to realize its potential as a modern metropolitan region, it is in part because it has lacked an institutional base geared to addressing metropolitan-wide concerns.

The existing organizational base of the city and county has frustrated such efforts. Groups are not able to mobilize satisfactorily in order to overcome the barriers to more effective metropolitan governance. There are regional boards to discuss common commercial and political concerns, and occasionally one hears talk of giving these bodies more authority and funds to conduct the region's business more efficiently. Unfortunately, the fact that this metropolitan area includes parts of two states frustrates any serious effort to combine resources and to address common problems.

Discussions on matters such as subsidies for the region's bus system or the possible relocation of the region's major airport to Illinois are rancorous and by no means fights between equals. Barely one-quarter of the region's 2.5 million people live in Illinois; Missourians control much of the region's wealth as well. For these reasons, perhaps, attention to the area's problems and proposed solutions to those problems usually focuses on Missouri. This is especially true when the subjects being considered are social issues like desegregation. Rarely does word of social problems cross the state line. The major exception is reference to East St. Louis, in Illinois, which is used in some quarters to illustrate how worse off things could be for Missourians.

That desegregation has been viewed as a problem peculiar to St. Louis and Missouri is notable because segregation is at once more obvious and manageable in Illinois. East St. Louis's impoverished and virtually all-black school system stands in marked comparison to surrounding districts. Yet no suit seeking to merge substantially whiter districts with East St. Louis has been filed. Such a suit would have two advantages for proponents of desegregation. First, it would be easier to win. Unlike a proposed merger between St. Louis City and St. Louis County districts, any case involving East St. Louis would probably be confined to St. Clair County, of which it is a part. It would be reminiscent of southern cases in which black and white schools were merged into a single countywide district. Still, it would serve as an example of metropolitan segregation insofar as one could show how suburban housing and school policies had locked blacks into a segregated central city. Proving a case of intentional segregation across county lines is much more difficult. Yet that was precisely what was being considered in the suit in Missouri, where St. Louis City also is an independent county, and its schools would have been merged with those of at least one other county. The second reason filing a suit in Illinois would be effective is that it would expand the debate over segregation to the whole metropolitan area. Even if a suit involving both states never were initiated, it would be impossible to ignore the regional scope of the problem and potential solutions to it.

Right at the outset, then, we see how important aspects of metropolitan segregation have been ignored by parties with an interest in the subject. People do place limits on the amount of school segregation they are willing to discuss. School segregation on the east side of the metropolitan area does not exist as far as anyone involved in negotiations over desegregation is concerned. It seems in this case that the negotiable limits of school segregation cannot cross the Mississippi River into Illinois, even though both parts of the metropolitan area might logically be involved in such a dialogue. There is no conspiracy involved here. Proving that districts across state lines behaved in a fashion to segregate students in East St. Louis and in the city of St. Louis would be even more difficult than proving a similar fact across county lines in the same state. Besides, I doubt that school officials and political leaders in both states ever worried about such a contingency, much less set up policies that would create it.

It is not possible to say whether the fragmented and local orientation of St. Louis County institutions helped the county's development when both its population and economic fortunes were expanding. There is little disagreement that this arrangement hurts the county now that the economy is sluggish, population movement has all but stopped, and more needy people must be served. The parochial quality of life in St. Louis County is reflected in its 92 municipalities, 20 townships, 47 state legislators, and 23 school districts. The 206 political subdivisions in the county are complemented by 70 additional taxing districts and 170 service districts for everything from the metropolitan zoo to local fire departments.[3] There is one county government, but in many instances it has direct authority over only the unincorporated areas of the county. Routine affairs in its municipalities are directed by local officials working in one of five types of administrative and political arrangements.

Difficulties created by a fragmented and parochial political structure are compounded by great discrepancies in the size and wealth of these units. The 92 municipalities in St. Louis County had in 1970 populations ranging from 19 to 66,000 and varied in size from .02 to 16.7 square miles. The median family income for one black community was only six thousand dollars in 1970. Another community had a median family income of thirty-two thousand dollars. These disparities are also evidenced in public education. The assessed valuation of one small district in 1976 approached only $18.5 million. In that same year it had

805 students. At the other end of the scale was the largest county district with over twenty-four thousand five hundred students and an assessed valuation of $475 million.[4] Under such conditions, it would not be easy for people to identify, much less resolve, sensitive and important problems they have in common.

St. Louis is not a unique case, of course. Many metropolitan areas have the same bewildering maze of public institutions through which their business is conducted. A coordinated response to areawide problems is unlikely, if only because metropolitan policy making lacks proper guidance. We live in something called a metropolitan area, but we lack the history of collaborative action that could give this meaning. As if this were not enough, problems thought to have been left behind in the cities—poverty, a declining tax base, crime, minority concerns—have not disappeared. They have stuck doggedly, and they may even have worsened because they were avoided and given more territory to fill.

There is nothing new in any of this. Earlier urban residents likewise despaired over the mindless confusion before them as they struggled to regain some control over their lives and their cities. They experimented with ways to recommit city residents to one another and to larger communities, but they did not wish to compound their problems by calling into doubt basic economic and social divisions. There were occasional attempts to talk about such things openly, but discussions did not succeed. The current generation of St. Louis leaders is well aware of this phenomenon. These leaders were embroiled in a bitterly divisive campaign during the late 1950s to create a metropolitan government without merging the city and county. Such a plan, if affirmed, would not have resolved all the inequities noted among county towns and between the county and the city. It would have made their identification and resolution more feasible, however. In two previous efforts in this century, city residents had supported similar proposals while county voters rejected them. This time, both city and county residents failed to approve a formal plan to draw them closer together politically.

Some opposed the plan because of its timidity: no merger was called for between the city and county. Others saw the plan as being too far-reaching.[5] Opponents in general decried the additional expense for taxpayers. Informal talks in 1976 between the St. Louis County executive and a former mayor of St. Louis about city/county consolidation foundered for the same reasons. Another problem involved the public schools. Both men apparently agreed to exclude the schools from any consolidation plan. This had been a sticky matter in 1959 and proved no less an impediment to joining the city and county in 1976. Had this plan been carried out, we know from what happened in Indianapolis and its surrounding county that the schools eventually would have been consolidated.

Other proposals to consolidate policy making under representative boards were stopped in the state legislatures. One plan to consolidate school districts that would have provided more equal educational expenditures across the state of Missouri died in the state legislature in the late 1960s (whatever its faults, elements of this plan eventually emerged in modified form in a proposal for desegregation submitted to the federal court by both its appointed experts and the city school system). The Illinois and Missouri legislatures in the mid-1970s both rejected a plan that would have given two regional planning agencies authority to coordinate development efforts in the region. Finally, some advocates of government reorganization in Missouri hoped that a proposal to amend the state's constitution might lead to the dissolution of the barrier between St. Louis County and City.

There is a demonstrable gap between the problems created by urbanization and the capacity of our civic institutions and rituals to cope with them. Somehow that gap must be bridged. In the present case that would probably involve vigorous efforts to reduce institutional fragmentation. Without such a reconciliation, it would remain difficult to explore metropolitan-wide problems and exploit the region's resources more effectively. Coping with city problems is not a trivial concern if one wishes to keep the area competitive in national and international markets and serving its people more efficiently than in the past.

If history serves as a guide for expectations, the effort to reduce fragmentation would probably fail as well. Such delicate matters are better handled less obviously and with more limited goals in mind. We shall see how moral-reform crusades served earlier populations in this fashion. It is my contention that school desegregation and other civil-rights efforts continued this tradition.

Parochialism is a luxury that a modern metropolitan area cannot afford. Of course, old habits are hard to break. This is why reform crusades like desegregation are so important to the process of social change. Changes in time-honored traditions are introduced slowly without jeopardizing the security and order underlying our customary ways of doing things. An introduction of this sort accords us the privilege of protesting an intrusion into our lives—without tearing apart our world.

In the case of a metropolitan area like St. Louis, desegregation has provided a sustained excuse to debate the proper form and responsibility of metropolitan governance and the uneven distribution of private and public wealth in the area. Routine politics have failed to provide an avenue through which such matters could be resolved directly. Nonroutine politics in the form of desegregation have provided a way for these issues to be discussed, if only in an indirect fashion. School desegregation has addressed tensions brought on by the transformation of St. Louis into a modern metropolitan area. Moreover, school desegregation has done this without either altering fundamentally the process of urbanization or resolving the problems made more obvious by it.

Routine Failures: Electoral Politics in St. Louis

The failure of routine politics to address and resolve obvious problems inspires people to adopt nonroutine ways to consider such matters. Already alluded to in this chapter was the failure of officials and citizens in St. Louis County and City to do anything substantial about the effects of economic inequality and political fragmentation in this area. Ten times between 1926 and 1971 efforts were made to consider some form of intracounty or city/county cooperation.[6] Only four succeeded. A plan for creating a Metropolitan St. Louis Sewer District was approved in 1954. A new charter was passed by county residents in 1968. In 1970 city and county voters both approved a County Home Rule Amendment to the state constitution. One year later they also supported the creation of a common tax to fund area museums and the St. Louis zoo. Area residents voted additional taxes on themselves for these services in 1983. More ambitious plans to join the city and county failed.

A review of the minutes from St. Louis County Board of Education meetings between 1955 and 1971 reveals that a good deal of energy was spent debating and inspiring public votes on proposed mergers among different combinations of districts. Dozens of proposals were brought before the board during this period. Only a small portion of these ever reached the voters for their review. An even smaller number of these was approved. There were twenty-seven local districts in 1952. Thirty years later that number was reduced by only five; two of those districts—Kinloch and Berkeley—were merged with a third only because of a court order. Thus, the fragmentation and political inertia apparent at other levels of government in the area infected the schools as well. More to the point, there were no efforts to pursue even modest reorganization proposals through regular political channels after 1971. It was after 1971 that court proceedings involving desegregation began in the city and county. Those discussions came to include consideration of a merger of at least the city district with most, if not all, of St. Louis County's local districts. The consideration might easily have been extended to districts in parts of St. Charles, Franklin, and Jefferson counties, but that seems unlikely today.

What emerges from the formal record of discussions about proposed mergers between 1955 and 1971 is a picture of calculated incompetence and lethargy in the face of change. There was substantial consensus among both St. Louis County board members and the many school officials who testified before the board that there were great discrepancies in the size and wealth of districts in the county. There was agreement that something needed to be done if all children were to receive a good education. Most of the attention focused on three alternatives: create a single city and county district, a unified county district, or a uniform taxing system that would equalize expenditures over all districts. Proposed mergers were discussed with the hope that these three things could be avoided. Elected officials and school personnel struggled for nearly twenty years to find some minimally sufficient arrangement among independent districts that might satisfy everyone. After 1971 they stopped trying to pretend that they could or had accomplished much of anything.

No one, it seemed, wanted to propose mergers unless the districts and their students were similar or could enhance one another's financial standing. At different times people spoke of the need to ensure "a high degree of homogeneity" in the populations of reorganized districts or, alternately, the need to ensure the preference stated by the people in one small, poor district "to be left alone."[7] Race was not necessarily a consideration in these proposals. Wealth always was. A student's color could be overlooked as long as he and his peers came from a well-endowed district. Such was the case with the Scudder School District that had many black youngsters but much industry to tax. The Berkeley School District, having expressed sympathy for Scudder's inability to mount an efficient high school program, annexed the district in August 1960. Two years later a recommendation by a team of analysts from the University of Chicago that Kinloch—a small but poor and all-black district—be merged with Berkeley was dismissed. The "attitudes and disposition" of the Berkeley people regarding the "financial and social" problem posed by a merger with Kinloch made such a proposal untenable.[8] Similar opinions were voiced in 1971 when a merger between Kinloch and the Ferguson R-2 School District was considered. The latter's superintendent hastened to point out that his, too, was a poor district and that nothing would be served by such a union.[9] A federal court later disagreed and imposed a merger that local officials had discussed but avoided.

Questions about race increased after 1960 when blacks finally began to move into the county in large numbers. By the 1970s blacks had substantial enrollments in several school districts, but discussions involving mergers ended by 1972. The presence of black students continued to grow throughout the 1970s, as can be seen in Map 3. There is no doubt that racial considerations helped to dampen whatever enthusiasm people might have expressed about interdistrict mergers. It would be inaccurate to say, however, that racial prejudice was the deciding factor in killing discussion over the need for some kind of relief for minority-dominated districts. Well before "the race issue" became critical for St. Louis County, people were reluctant to threaten the autonomy of local school districts or to propose mergers that would prove to be a financial burden. The movement of blacks into the county did not cause people to stop discussing the uneven distribution of wealth among county districts; but it did make avoiding the question somewhat more attractive. Phrases like *the social problem* or *students with different expectations* may have been used as part of a genteel code for avoiding baldly racist language, but no one had the stomach for an open debate on "the race issue." People preferred instead to acknowledge the existence of a problem and claim that it was the state's responsibility to watch over poorer districts.[10]

The county board chose to ignore a direct appeal by the U. S. Department of Justice that local authorities find some solution to the situation involving Kinloch, and a suit was initiated on behalf of Kinloch's students. Defendants in the case included state and county officials and school officials from Kinloch, Berke-

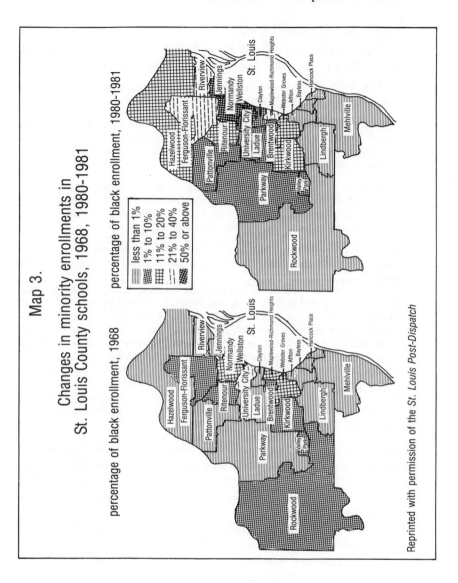

Map 3.

Changes in minority enrollments in
St. Louis County schools, 1968, 1980-1981

percentage of black enrollment, 1968

percentage of black enrollment, 1980-1981

less than 1%
1% to 10%
11% to 20%
21% to 40%
50% or above

Reprinted with permission of the *St. Louis Post-Dispatch*

ley, and Ferguson-Florissant. After evidence by all the concerned parties was presented, U.S. District Court Judge James Meredith ordered a merger of the three districts. Four points seemed especially salient to the court.[11]

1. Prior to 1937, Kinloch and most of Berkeley had been in one district, but schools were segregated in accordance with Missouri law.

2. The City of Berkeley was incorporated in 1937 and promptly formed its own school district. Kinloch was excluded from both. (Some persons maintain that a deal was cut with Kinloch residents. Kinloch would get its own school district if it did not fight for inclusion in the new City of Berkeley).

3. Despite one of the area's highest tax rates, Kinloch's financial resources did not permit the creation of programs comparable to those of nearby districts. At the time of the trial, Kinloch was found to have an inferior curriculum, physical plant, library, fund of equipment, and salary schedule.

4. State and county officials had failed to alleviate this situation. For example, Kinloch had not been included in most of the school district reorganization plans during the 1940s and 1950s. Ferguson-Florissant protested its inclusion in the case, contending that it had not been responsible for creating Kinloch. But the court noted that the Ferguson-Florissant School District had helped to maintain the all-black district. The rejection by area voters of a school reorganization plan that included Kinloch was a constitutional wrong. (Officials from the former Ferguson-Florissant School District would contend later to project staff that their inclusion was not well-founded on constitutional grounds, but it did make practical sense for the court. Their district and staff, they argued, was the largest and most sophisticated of the three. The court needed to put them "in charge" to ensure that a sound, long-term plan would be implemented. Officials from the other districts just "weren't up to running such a large district.")

The tone of Ferguson-Florissant officials' explanation for their plight was not overstated. Even the court seemed to share it, deeming the plan advanced by the state and county boards of education to be "the least disruptive alternative which is educationally sound, administratively feasible and which promises to achieve at least the minimum amount of desegregation that is constitutionally required." The Ferguson-Florissant School District was reorganized to include Kinloch and Berkeley; its board of education was restructured to provide the other districts with some representation. A new tax levy was imposed by the court "at a higher rate than previously voted by any of the three districts."[12] It was subsequently reduced to the rate paid by Ferguson-Florissant citizens, thereby increasing only the rate levied on Kinloch and Berkeley residents. A whole year was set aside for administrative reorganization and to complete plans for student desegregation for the 1975–1976 school year. The court monitored the implementation of its order with the assistance of a committee drawn from people across the newly constituted district.

A precedent was established for reorganizing school districts through something other than the routine political procedures available in Missouri. Race was the excuse for prompting this particular reorganization plan. It was not a plan, however, that was or could have been designed to address the more pervasive and serious signs of economic and fiscal inequality apparent in the St. Louis area. It was not even a plan that raised the specter of the three measures area school officials had hoped most to avoid. Former Ferguson-Florissant officials worked hard to gain acceptance for the "court order" in their community. They trivialized its impact in public while shrugging their shoulders over the unwarranted intrusion of the courts into local school affairs. At the same time, they privately congratulated themselves for orchestrating the acceptance of "their little desegregation plan" by the court.[13] If a desegregation crisis was not avoided in St. Louis County, at least for the time being it was contained.

Nonroutine Successes: Desegregation Politics in St. Louis City

The same could not be said of the crisis that occurred in St. Louis City. A suit was filed in 1972 by a small group of black parents, Concerned Parents for North St. Louis, against the board of education. The parents alleged that the school system had not done enough to desegregate the schools after the 1954 *Brown* decision. City schools were still segregated and, as the parents contended, "continuing racial isolation was not an accident but the direct result of unlawful official actions."[14] This position ultimately prevailed, but many argued that the legal victory was hollow. Eight years elapsed between the filing of the suit and start of mandatory student desegregation. The city's school population was barely half the size it had been in 1967 and already well more than 70 percent black. Several parties, including the former defendant school board, decided that relief could be secured only if a metropolitan plan were fashioned. The transubstantiation of the city board and school administration from reactionary racists into progressive visionaries may be unprecedented, but it was predictable. The secret to its strange transformation can be found in the politics of metropolitan governance and institutional greed.

The city's board of education was compelled to review its role in perpetuating a segregated school system and to take steps to reverse the effects of its previous policies toward minority children. Lawyers for the board of education acknowledged the existence of segregation, but they contended that the board had been unable to adjust attendance zones or build new schools quickly enough to compensate for massive changes in the city's school-age population. Under a consent decree worked out with the plaintiff parent group in December 1975, the board admitted no guilt but promised to take certain actions that might undo some of the damage to minority children. This decree would have desegregated faculty, weighed the impact of subsequent school closings on desegregation, studied the realignment of feeder school patterns to reduce segregation in the high schools, and introduced curricular improvements and voluntary desegregation.

Dissatisfaction with this agreement was extensive and strong. The most vocal critics were St. Louis City, the state and federal governments, the NAACP, and the Concerned Parents for Neighborhood Schools (a group of parents who supported the neighborhood school concept). Faced with a bewildering array of contestants and the prospect of a long trial, Judge Meredith conducted hearings in 1977 and 1978 that "dealt simultaneously with the . . . questions of liability and remedy."[15] He heard testimony from thirty-nine witnesses in five separate sessions that lasted a total of thirteen weeks.

The major plaintiffs (Concerned Parents for North St. Louis, the NAACP, and the U.S. Department of Justice) pointed out how attendance areas had not been "color blind" after 1954. The boundary lines changed as did residential patterns, and most children continued to attend segregated schools. Busing did take place, but most of it was done to relieve overcrowding in Northside schools, not to further desegregation. In fact, as one observer noted, when it was "necessary to transport black students to white schools, it was accomplished by 'intact busing,' i.e., whole classes of black students were bused to a white school where they maintained their own schedules, were taught intact and were not integrated into the procedures of the receiving schools."[16] Witnesses for the school system defended its record and argued that they had done the best they could under difficult circumstances. Judge Meredith agreed with the district's position in his dismissal of the board in April 1979. The Eighth Circuit Court of Appeals reversed that decision eleven months later in a stinging rebuttal.

The board of education was given the responsibility of developing a mandatory desegregation plan. It chose not to appeal the decision and with considerable dispatch submitted its proposal to the court. Under the plan, some twenty-six thousand of the district's sixty-three thousand students would have attended "integrated" schools; an integrated school was defined as one having an enrollment between 30 and 50 percent black. Easily two-thirds of the district's black students in the elementary grades would have been left in schools that by most reasonable standards were considered segregated. With the voluntary magnet school program expanded, the board would have continued its efforts to improve the quality of education in all schools. It was thought, however, that special attention ought to be paid to those schools in North St. Louis that would remain predominantly black. All of this the court accepted. In addition, the court ordered the state to underwrite one-half of the expenses of the plan—about $11,076,000—and, along with the United States government, to develop plans for an interdistrict plan that might relieve the burden of those black youngsters confined to segregated schools.

The mandatory desegregation plan for the city went into effect during the

1980–1981 school year. At the same time, the board of education and the NAACP initiated suits to draw several additional counties and more than forty districts into a metropolitan desegregation plan. Expanding the geographic and political focus of the controversy made sense because the city district and, more generally, the array of institutions located in the city's Central Corridor had an interest in bringing larger, more varied, and certainly wealthier areas under their influence.

Viewed in this way, metropolitan desegregation would have been much more than an opportunity to find a bigger group of white children with whom the city's black youngsters could be mixed. It would have imposed a degree of order over a fragmented system of public education involving dozens of separate districts and a hundred communities with gross disparities in wealth. Moreover, as some metropolitan leaders privately confess, it could have removed the most emotional barrier to consolidating St. Louis City with its more prosperous neighbor, St. Louis County. It would most certainly have placed the administrators of the city school system in the enviable position of assuming leadership in a metropolitan reorganization effort of those smaller districts that contested the suit and lost.

Conclusion: On Negotiating the Limits of Segregation

It is because most people are not inherently cynical that they struggle to change their communities for the better. Their efforts may seem fatuous to a critical observer, but they are pursued with a single-minded devotion and vision of human perfectibility. People may fail; more often than not they will fail. Our history has shown, however, that what is crucial is that people try to make a difference. This has been the precedent for people in modern metropolitan areas who were compelled to reconsider the meaning of segregation in their lives.

People could see that the process of metropolitan growth did not always have good consequences. Many older areas like St. Louis expanded their boundaries and population bases; but they also experienced severe changes in their economic fortunes and political responsibilities. The redistribution of differently colored people and wealth in such areas reintroduced some unpleasant realities about urban living. Something had to be done.

During the early period of industrialization, we will see, people tried to develop new or better institutions to cope with the ugliness around them. They usually discovered that established political routines were not well suited for addressing the problems they had identified. People found greater satisfaction, if no more success, through the use of nonroutine forms of political action. The most common expression for this amendatory zeal was the moral reform crusade.

The school desegregation movement is the most recent example of this kind of crusade. In St. Louis it emerged in earnest only after established political institutions had failed to take any affirmative action to address metropolitan problems. Yet not all types of inequality have been discussed at this point. Economic inequality has been mentioned but not seriously debated. The need for newer forms of metropolitan governance through which problems could be reviewed gets slightly more attention; but a straightforward assault seems all but impossible. Insofar as people use desegregation to talk about such matters at all, they discuss them in a highly indirect and limited fashion.

Desegregation may be used to achieve a certain degree of social equality among people living in a broad geographic area. That people appear willing to accept. Political equality, at least as much as may be secured through a reasonable system of metropolitan representation, is a more sensitive issue. Here, however, there may be room for compromise. Some types of metropolitan governance may be less threatening than others. The schools with their politically powerless constituents may be one of those less threatening arenas. Economic inequality is quite another matter. No one, it seems, seriously wishes to question or disrupt the basic sources and expressions of class segregation in our society. We know that educational experiments have generally had little discernible impact on the long-term economic fortunes of people exposed to them.[17] I suspect that such reforms were not really expected or intended to achieve economic equality for all or even most people.

Nevertheless, many different parties do become involved in these campaigns and express their interest in removing the painful signs of inequality in our lives. Some of these groups were discussed in the present chapter. We saw that there were substantial differences among them. All these various groups bring different histories, skills, and agendas to their crusade. What is remarkable is that despite their great differences and frequently bitter confrontations they seem intent on not pushing their disagreements too far or questioning the legitimacy of their social order too strongly. Even more surprising, perhaps, is that it seems to work. How it has come to work as well as it apparently does is the subject of the next chapter.

4. Civil Rites and Civil Wrongs

The broad outline of an argument regarding the significance of school desegregation in our civic culture has been laid out. Contrary to most informed thinking on the subject, desegregation is not an especially effective tool for securing great changes in either ourselves or our communities. Sometimes in some ways its effects are beneficial; on other occasions or in other ways its impact has been less positive. To make matters more frustrating, we are not really sure why this is the case or how to improve the chances for success in any reliable fashion. Yet it is this very quality of indecisiveness that makes desegregation such an important element in our civic culture. It allows us to promise ourselves more than can be delivered and more than we want to be delivered. If every society has inherent stresses and strains, then perhaps every society also has developed techniques to moderate their effects without either jeopardizing the benefits of a known social order or introducing too quickly a new and ill-defined world.

The most important service that desegregation has rendered, then, has been not to secure a greater share of this society's wealth for minority citizens and to drag white people to concede grudgingly that this is a good idea, but rather to permit us to talk about the distasteful consequences of racial intolerance in an increasingly more urban world without undermining the economic and political institutions we rely on for meaning. The failure of established routines and institutions to meet all of the demands or answer all of the questions generated from urbanization inspires a search for novel, but not too novel, devices with which to address our concerns. Though never entirely successful, attempts to institutionalize conflicts enable most people to capture a measure of the order they rely upon, and these attempts help to make sense of a passing order. It is in this fashion that people hope to apprehend a new urban community.

Hints of this can be seen in the general approach of St. Louis residents to the issue of school desegregation. As the city began to make the difficult transition from a population and industrial center to a less populated center for a post-industrial metropolitan area, it was confronted with a host of problems. Some were pretty mundane. Others raised basic questions about how the region's limited economic resources and tax dollars would be distributed among its people. Unable or unwilling to address these issues head-on, residents instead began to argue about the lingering effects of inequality by way of the public schools and their role in perpetuating a segregated social order that favored white people. No permanent, far-reaching solution to that problem was discovered. Yet most parties seemed relatively satisfied with the solution arrived at through the courts. At least they did not continue to press their concerns so forcefully as to undermine the credibility of institutions that bolstered the very inequalities troubling them.

The question is how St. Louis residents came to work out such an artful compromise among themselves. Why did they not press their concerns? Why did they settle for a less-than-final solution to the problem of racial separation and inequality? How did they come to convince themselves that their solution was fair and also held at least the promise of being effective? How does one build a single community in the face of great differences in wealth and culture or over great distances?

These questions could be answered in a number of ways. In this chapter, the first great period of urban growth, which occurred in the nineteenth century, is examined in order to understand how our ancestors coped with similar problems. If there is something in our civic culture that enables us to avoid more punishing fights over inequality, then it probably took root during that early period of city-building. In subsequent chapters the way that St. Louis residents put those historic lessons into practice will be examined in greater detail.

Desegregation and the Politics of Redemption

City life, it seemed to many nineteenth-century Americans, was not only different from life in small towns but also qualitatively worse. Traditional prescriptions, standards for human conduct that had been passed from generation to generation, seemed inappropriate for the conditions people had to cope with in cities. New modes of work and government were being developed in cities, and there appeared to be no limit to the number and diversity of persons that could be absorbed. Urban settlers were allegedly stripped of their agrarian past with little regard for its impact on them. Many argued that the communal rituals they had known were abandoned. People had few opportunities to overcome the differences among themselves and, hence, were more likely to engage in collective acts of fantasy and self-destruction. At least this is what many observers perceived. For all its ugliness, there was some comfort to be gained from this vision of cities and their effect on human sociability. It provided a ready explanation for the source of discomfort.

The power of these theories was based in faith rather than knowledge or understanding. Translating that faith into a workable program of action to improve city life was left in the United States to urban reformers. Regrettably, urban reformers shared the same attitudes about city life as the nineteenth- and twentieth-century critics of urbanization. Their saving grace was a profound belief in the mutability of human beings and their habits: if the city had brought people to the brink of social and spiritual disaster, residents could be redeemed with the help of new social conventions and stiff doses of Protestant civilization. The problems reformers faced in realizing their dream, however, were immense.

As late as 1800 the vast majority of Americans lived in rural areas and occupied their time growing crops or reaping the nation's other natural resources. A comparatively tiny urban and mercantile population was still concentrated in the coastal cities, although a solid foundation for city-building in the Midwest had already been laid by that time. Those living in cities had no experience with sprawling modern business districts or tenements to which contemporary urbanites are so accustomed. Theirs was a rather compact settlement, a "walking city," where residents of different means lived fairly close to each other and their respective places of business or employment. Yet that situation changed dramatically.

Beginning around 1820 and continuing throughout the nineteenth century, the United States experienced a remarkable increase in both the size and number of cities it possessed. Coastal cities, especially those in the Northeast, began to develop an industrial base that within sixty years rivaled anything in Europe. In the meantime, the commercial impulse that prompted this early success and the competition for western markets touched the newer midwestern cities, and places like St. Louis started their ascendancy into the ranks of America's bigger cities. The pressure for building cities was fed largely by waves of immigrants from Europe, people who needed cheap housing and the jobs being created in a burgeoning industrial economy. But there were many native-born Americans who found their way off the farm and into the cities as well. Together their contribution to the population growth of cities was staggering. So great were their numbers that, "from 1790 to 1840, every decade but one saw a rate of urban growth double that for the population as a whole," and places like New York showed population gains of 50 percent or more in a single ten-year period.[1]

The consequences of rapid urbanization were only hinted at in the works of social theorists and critics. For many people who lived in America's great cities, the effects were a daily challenge to their survival. Historian Paul Boyer has captured both their fears and responses to the urban crisis nicely, and I will draw heavily from his research as well as the works of others on reform crusades throughout this chapter. About the early reactions of frightened city residents Boyer notes,

> Sometimes the threat was described in terms of revolutionary violence—a possibility underscored by the riots, gang wars, and turbulent street brawls of the period. More often, observers dwelt on the equally disturbing possibility that the slum's miasmic evils would infect the larger society by more insidious means.[2]

Bringing People Together

To good people in early nineteenth-century cities, the nature and sources of urban decay were painfully obvious. Open displays of gambling, prostitution, and profanity were inflamed by an all-too-casual observance of church services by profligates and decent folks alike. Yet, as offensive as such acts were, they were but signs of a deeper calamity befalling all city residents. The true source of distress was the disintegration of the community's public life. Potential sources of "moral authority or social cohesion"—churches and local government—seemed either powerless or reluctant to take steps that concerned citizens thought were necessary to cure the city of social and moral disease.[3]

Religious revivals could draw hundreds of converts, perhaps even thousands, on a single day. Unfortunately, such intermittent celebrations left little in the way of a sustained institutional presence to cope with the convert's subsequent temptations and the need for strong public ceremonies. More organized Protestant churches appeared no better equipped to guide a growing number of working-class laborers than to meet the calls for help from their own parishoners.[4]

Civil authorities were even less likely to respond to the mounting crisis identified by the cities' leading citizens. Public services had already been stretched threadbare by the demands of a burgeoning urban population, and leaders showed few signs of breaking an established pattern of supplementing charitable works, improvements to property, and other services underwritten by the wealthy. More importantly, city governments eventually became symbols of the same moral and civil depravity that reformers attempted to remove. Urban growth led to the "emergence of political organizations that drew their strength from precisely those who . . . represented the greatest menace: the poor, the immigrants, the laboring masses."[5] Even worse, the political machines that relied upon the vote of such people to stay in power not only refused to attack existing sources of corruption but seemingly worked at a feverish pace to expand them. The public rituals extolled by supporters of those organizations were not the kind urban reformers thought should be the centerpiece of a civic renaissance.

Having found existing public and religious institutions wanting, early-nineteenth-century reformers in effect created a set of ceremonies and beliefs that filled the public vacuum left by churches and city governments. Strategies and ideologies were drawn in large measure from those institutions. Contemporary religious doctrine provided the basis for moral pronouncements and beliefs about saving the underprivileged from themselves. Also borrowed from the churches was the idea that reform crusades could reassert a sorely needed degree of social control over the public and private behavior of city residents. True to the missionary appeal of their efforts, urban reformers relied heavily upon various kinds of educational techniques to hold the interest of their potential converts.

Reaching them was another matter. The prospect of trying to proselytize tens of thousands of people in densely populated neighborhoods created special problems. Clearly, the evangelistic crusaders with their patented one-shot doses of spiritual restoration were not doing the job. Nor could the ward-heeler approach to mobilization practiced by the political machines be given serious consideration. But a hybrid of the two seemed to work. The basic strategy that came to be settled on ironically drew reformers closer to the very mass politics that helped to undercut their genteel control of municipal affairs. Through what might be loosely termed "Pentecostal ward heeling," urban reformers hoped to sustain the spiritual fervor of evangelistic crusades by practicing the kind of grass-roots organizing that was later accomplished so successfully by the despised political bosses.

The moral reform crusaders also shared the same ambivalence for the lower classes as their archenemy did. Despite the shinier finish on the reformers' beliefs, their goal was not dissimilar from that of the political boss. Confronted with problems attributable to a growing urban population, both sought to create a sense of fraternity with working- and lower-class people. They nourished this ideal with beliefs about democratic rule and personal salvation and reaffirmed it through prescribed rituals like voting and attending church services. In truth, the ceremonial reenactment of this fraternal bond was the key to understanding the promise of reform activities and machine politics. Both were designed to bring some degree of order back into the way public life was conducted in big cities, but the difference can be found in the direction each wished to see public life move. The political boss brought the first hints of professional administration to city government and attempted to provide services needed by a growing city and its people. In exchange, he frequently gave up any pretext of running an uncorrupt government and any wish to change the bad habits of his constituents. The moral reform crusader tried to reassert the prerogative of ceremonial caretakers such as ministers and lay teachers to oversee and correct such personal shortcomings in the hope that this would reenervate city life. Ultimately, this required reformers to issue a broader challenge to the authority of political leaders. On the part of both the moral reformer and the political boss, however, there was a desire to control the urban masses from a safe distance.

Bibles and Bible Schools

The first comprehensive movement to recapture the moral and civil idealism of village life in cities was built around the thinly veiled propaganda contained in hundreds of religious pamphlets and in the organizational efforts of the American Bible Society. Throughout the nineteenth century, members or affiliates of this group spread the gospel as if they were huckstering a political candidate. The work of New York City's American Tract Society (ATS) shows how this was done.

> By 1850 the ATS had built up a back-list of more than 500 titles and was annually producing more than 5 million tracts and other publications. Subsidized by . . .

contributions and endowment income, these publications were attractively printed, well illustrated, and made available either free or at a nominal cost.

Distribution was as efficient as production. A network of branches and auxiliaries served as outlet centers, supplying thousands of agents and volunteers. Bulk shipments went to Sunday schools, poorhouses, prisons, orphanages, and immigration depots. In city after city, local tract societies conducted systematic house-by-house distributions.[6]

The content of these tracts was as impressive as the marketing. Always phrased with an eye toward creating new friendships and melting away the anonymity of cities, the pamphlets implored, wheedled, and excoriated the reader to lead a clean and virtuous life. Some contained theology. Others merely condemned vices of one type or another. "More typically, however, the tracts [took] the form of brief, readable narratives whose moral [was] woven into the story itself."[7]

Impressive as the tract movement was, it offered readers little beyond slickly packaged slugs of morality. The movement clearly was a more enduring vehicle for the evangelical spirit that had inspired earlier revivals against prostitution and the like. Yet it never offered a sustained institutional presence for reform in the cities. Nor did it create the kind of invigorating ceremonies that would have given substance to the search for a new fraternal order. Instead, it relied on a relatively sure but modest strategy for making contact with the masses, a strategy whose impact probably was greater on those distributing the tracts than on the prospective convert.

The Sunday-school movement was an implicit response to these continuing problems in moral reform efforts. This movement tried to fill some of the institutional gaps left by the tract societies, if only on a part-time basis. Yet its adherents pursued their task with a remarkable single-mindedness. There were already hundreds of Sunday schools across the country in 1824 when the American Sunday School Union (ASSU) was established to serve as a parent body to dispersed groups. Within six years, however, the number of students enrolled in its various programs jumped from fifty thousand to three hundred and fifty thousand. Additional thousands of children attended Sunday schools sponsored by different religious denominations. Together, these organizations managed to reach every city in the antebellum United States and to provide what was thought to be the "best shield against immorality" for their members.[8]

Implicit in the work of the Sunday schools was the idea that parents were not up to the task of rearing their children properly. "At best," argued spokesmen for the movement, "slum parents were either guilty of 'indifference' toward their offspring or [were] the hapless victims of a disordered social environment where a child could go bad before his parents were even aware of the danger. At worst, they were an actively destructive agent in their children's lives."[9] In either case, urban family life as practiced by the lower classes was thought to be a contributing factor in the social and moral degeneracy of the next generation of city residents. Proponents and detractors of the Sunday-school movement understood its challenge to replace the family with a more effective socializing agent, one that might save children from their circumstances, families, and themselves.

Social order depended on the success of such programs. "The spread of indiscipline among the working people—their refusal to accept their place . . . their continued agitation at workplace and poll—[was] traced back to the households in which they had been [improperly] raised."[10] The object of the Sunday school was not to convert lost souls but to prevent them from being lost initially. The only hope, according to the ASSU handbook, was "to lay in the children's minds the foundation of obedience to their governors in church and state, to make them contented with the station which providence has appointed to them in the world."[11] In so doing, the fabric of society might be saved from any further unraveling and its better elements spared the expense of future prisons, poorhouses, and orphanages.

Achieving such an ambitious goal, however, proved to be quite beyond the grasp of the movement's supporters. Classes were taught by volunteers with little apparent training or experience. More interesting was the curriculum that emphasized not only Scripture and morality but also reading, writing, and mathematics. Such secular topics combined with the movement's pronounced advocation of distinctly social goals created problems for adherents among the organized Protestant churches. Resistance to its good works also emerged from the very segment of society that the Sunday schools targeted. At one point in the 1830s, for instance, the ASSU chapter in Boston noted "that its efforts were encountering 'indifference' and even 'reproaches' among the urban masses." Given the attitude of Sunday-school workers toward the parents of the children they taught, it is small wonder that they were not always warmly received. Beneath all these problems, though, lay a far more fundamental dilemma that Sunday-school activists could not resolve. The emphasis on punctuality, order, physical regimentation, and compulsive obedience that was central to the philosophy and operation of the schools had little relevance to students outside of class. Even the movement's most devout supporters seemed to recognize the Sunday school "as a contrivance for producing an artificial version of a social order whose natural roots were withering."[12] Pursuing a strategy to prevent children from following a life they knew by training them once a week for a society that no longer existed, and perhaps never did, became untenable. Something more permanent and applicable to the lives of these young people was quickly developed.

Charity and Common Schools

For all their popularity and sophisticated marketing, the tract societies were charmingly provincial in their approach to personal and communal redemption. The lessons and source book were timeless. A universal message was addressed to the city as if the audience was as uniform as its rural homilies. Subsequent reformers were more careful to take account of the city's varied population and to create more specialized marketing techniques to reach different parts of that audience. The Sunday school represented a good start.

Although the charity school suffered from some of the same limitations as the Sunday school and was developed around the same time, it held out new promise to those seeking a permanent and compulsory way to reach younger people. Charity schools were purely secular institutions and were not burdened by the problems involved with wrapping social themes in religious rhetoric as the Sunday schools were. In other important ways, Sunday schools and charity schools were virtually mirror images of one another. Both were founded by well-to-do persons and were supported by religious leaders. The primary goal of each was to drill obedience and respect for authority into the tiny brains of slum urchins, but they also endeavored to wean children from the corrupting influence of their parents. Ultimately, the poor tried to avoid the charity schools just as they had tried to avoid the Sunday schools.

The rejection of the schools by the very people they were designed to serve compelled supporters to change their professed mandate. Trustees of New York's Free School Society, for instance, were themselves weaned from the condescending philosophy of their own early efforts by 1830. In fact, they came to see schooling as "a right of free men," "to espouse common schooling for all children, rich and poor, and to demand full public support for their schools." The idea that a relationship existed between education and the social class structure of cities, Diane Ravitch tells us, was understood by the more radical Workingmen's party whose "leaders feared that industrialization would harden class lines unless workers had equal opportunity to advance through education." That this theme was echoed by the aristocrats of the Free School Society as well was quite a step forward. Indeed, it was the first step toward the creation of free public schools in New York. The subsequent consolidation of the Manumission Society's six schools and one thousand four hundred black students with the newly renamed Public School Society's schools in 1832 stood as additional evidence of the movement to a truly common school system. That same year, however, a controversial decision to permit the Catholic Orphan Asylum to draw from the common school fund foreshadowed the battles to come between the Irish Catholics and the "Protestant" School Society.[13]

The predicament in which the New York drive for public schools found itself was not unlike that faced by supporters of common schools in all big cities. Caught somewhere between its aristocratic heritage and a nascent populist ideology, the Public School Society was forced by a suspicious and belligerent Catholic population to review the beliefs on which the common schools were founded. The Catholics, or any predominantly lower-class population for that matter, thought there was cause to be suspicious. Notwithstanding the progressive noises made by the Public School Society, the philosophy of school reformers was laced with the same kind of Protestant work ethic espoused in the Sunday-school movement.[14] Unlike the students in the Sunday schools, however, rich and poor students were to have attended classes together in the common schools. That did not happen as often as reformers wanted.

The rationale for "class-mixing" has a strangely familiar ring to it. According to historian David Nasaw, "all would profit . . . in the common schools."

> The rich man's son would come away a better man by learning firsthand as a child "that it is by rough contest with the rougher members of society, that he is to work his way through life." The poor would profit even more. They would be "excited to emulate the cleanliness, decorum, and mental improvement of those in better circumstances." They would learn directly from the more prosperous, if not how to be prosperous themselves, at least how to act like it.[15]

The moral education received by the poor in the common schools, it was hoped, would surpass anything ever dreamed possible in the Sunday schools. Those weekly gatherings were intended to acquaint city children with an ideal way of life they had forgotten or never known. Sunday-school lessons were passed along with the help of the ubiquitous tracts distributed throughout cities. Notions about order, respect for one's superiors, and morality were communicated to children through stories about people they may not have recognized but seemed destined to become. In the common schools all that would change. Rather than emulating some barely believable image of rural life, one would instead sit next to the very model of Protestant civility for the new urban age. Those who wished to improve themselves could ask for no better opportunity to advance their social standing. It was also intended that others would learn to be more reliable citizens and workers.

Vocal support for the common schools among working-class organizations did exist for a time and might have served the cause by encouraging people to attend, but their ideas about the content and philosophy of public education tended to set them apart from, if not against, the reformers. Moreover, by the middle of the 1830s these groups were embroiled in issues of more immediate relevance to their vulnerable position in the economy such as child labor, debtor legislation, and the ten-hour workday.[16] Workingmen's groups did not object to the concept of common schools so much as they found it inapplicable to their situation.

Catholics suffered from no such ambivalence. They opposed the common schools as a matter of principle and used the issue of public taxation in support of such schools to mount their campaign against reformers. New York's Governor Seward began this feud in his state in 1840 by declaring that common schools ought to be established with teachers of the same faith as the students. Catholics applied for part of the common school fund in New York City, were refused, and took their fight to the state, where they fared somewhat better.

While still denied access to public funds as sectarian schools, the Catholic hierarchy helped to secure passage of a bill that decentralized control over public schools and ensured that curriculum would be "religiously neutral." It was a blow to the Public School Society, which had fought against separate administrations in each ward. The response by non-Catholics in New York as well as other cities where similar debates were occurring was swift and frequently violent.

Although the experiences in other cities and states differed from New York's, several common themes emerge from these early fights over the common schools. First, titular authority over the schools remained in the hands of the community's upper-class citizens. As in city politics, however, their actual control over the day-to-day operation of the institution quickly eroded. Having been remanded to the "blighting influence of party strife and sectarian animosity," a noble aristocratic experiment was awarded to the very persons it had been designed to redeem and rehabilitate.[17] The ascension of such people to power was on occasion challenged by the city's more prosperous and enlightened citizens, but with only passing and limited success. Protestant hegemony over vital public institutions faded with losses in the common-school movement. However, Protestant influence in the conduct of those institutions did not end with the common-school movement. In 1849, for instance, the Boston School Committee "proposed to make schooling compulsory for all children" and helped to secure passage of such a law in the state legislature three years later.[18]

Outmaneuvered and outvoted, the well-to-do did not lose, but merely displaced, their philanthropic zeal. For the next fifty years leading citizens had to be contented with serving as the school systems' fiscal watchdogs, mounting economy drives, and retaining as much power for central boards as they could. In New York these citizens also sought to redefine "the proper limits of public education" by leading the battle against City College and Normal College, places that provided "higher education to public school students at public expense."[19] They later defended during the 1890s more positive positions in the debates over reorganizing school systems and staff accreditation. On no occasion, however, did they view themselves as bitter, moralistic curmudgeons whose only concern was to dampen the democratic fervor of the less fortunate. Rather, they believed themselves to be the guardians of social order and progress in a new urban and industrial society that no one understood. If their energies could not be spent satisfactorily on matters related to the public schools, there were other groups of people to serve and other projects to undertake. If they were to lose control over the ceremonies of established institutions, they could easily afford to go out and create new ones. And that is precisely what they did.

The Voluntary Service Industry

Their grievances against machine politics notwithstanding, patronage of a sort came easy to the more prosperous and civic-minded residents of cities.

Indeed, support for the arts and private societies or social clubs had long been seen as their special responsibility. These activities not only enriched public life but also added a certain grace "in a society which provided no formal recognition of aristocratic standing."[20] To advance such causes, the private leaders of cities had invested since the early 1800s large sums of money and a good deal of energy to promote libraries, lecture series, art collections, concerts, gardens, and other such philanthropies. After 1850, the efforts of these people were directed increasingly toward redefining such projects as public rather than exclusively private affairs. City taxes, it was thought, should be used to support these kinds of services for the entire population. So successful were their campaigns that by the early twentieth century public libraries and many neighborhood branches were established in all the bigger and medium-sized cities. Many communities also acquired publicly supported museums, art galleries, and theater groups; a few even had public universities.[21]

These things, while not services in the same sense as welfare or public housing, are essential parts of city living in most places today. More importantly, the evolution of such institutions from aristocratic preserves to public concerns set a pattern for the subsequent public adoption of other services provided at first by private organizations. The well-to-do elements of urban society pioneered the kinds of social programs in housing, employment, and health that we consider commonplace today. The gradual acquisition of such responsibilities by city governments was a tribute to the influence of these people in urban affairs and was also an indication that they could no longer control the ultimate effects of their reform activities or mobilize sufficient resources to bring them before the entire public.

That frustrating reality had already begun to be recognized, if not yet accepted, by reformers as early as the mid-nineteenth century. Tract societies, Sunday schools, and missions were firmly part of the urban scene, but they failed to rouse the kind of moral rebirth in city residents or their customs that had been promised. "Symptomatic of the frustrations of urban moral reform in the 1840s and 1850s were the bursts of moral vigilantism that punctuated the urban scene" across the nation.[22] The destruction of brothels, burned in Boston, St. Louis, and Detroit during this period, was especially popular. Further west, San Francisco merchants organized up to five hundred people and created the Committee of Vigilance that took credit for the lynching of several criminals between 1851 and 1856.[23] The first period of moral-reform crusades drew to a close with few hints as to what lay ahead.

Earlier campaigns to halt the spiritual rotting of American cities failed, in part, because it was impossible to replicate a rural community and its alleged benefits in the big city. Aggressive marketing schemes for religious tracts and the tentative use of new forms of social control in the Sunday school could not carry their own weight and that of a dated rural ideology as well. The common-school movement stripped reformers of whatever illusions they might have had about dominating a large, public bureaucracy in this new age. It also began to teach nominal activists how their private organizations could or could not be used effectively to address public problems. These lessons were put into good use after 1850.

Three distinct but complementary organizations emerged in New York City around that time: the Association for Improving the Condition of the Poor (AICP), the Children's Aid Society (CAS), and the Young Men's Christian Association (YMCA). The reform movements spawned by these groups were quite different from previous ones. Although driven by a similar evangelical dream, these crusades were decidedly secular and urban in their focus, manned by paid staff instead of volunteers, and had very specific target populations in mind. They did not try to create a facsimile of rural villages in cities. Instead, these three organizations worked to develop alternative institutions to those lost as a result of urbanization.[24] The moral and social order their members hoped to create more closely resembled the realities of urban life.

Of the three organizations, the AICP had the closest ties with previous reform efforts, and the YMCA was the most removed. The ancestral roots of the AICP could be traced to the antipauperism societies of the early nineteenth century. Unmoved by any sense of guilt over the plight of the poor, AICP members feared the threat to social stability posed by the unemployed and sought to reduce it by helping the poor acquire spiritual salvation. To accomplish this, the organization used the services of volunteers who visited the homes of the poor and, while investigating the condition of their lives, tried to get them to help save themselves. This strategy was used by the tract societies and Sunday schools; many of the visitors, in fact, had been tract distributors at one time. Unlike earlier crusaders, however, AICP members moved from their strict moralistic explanation of poverty to a critique of the degrading physical conditions that helped reduce the spiritual capital of the poor. In this way, the AICP anticipated later movements to change the environment the poor lived in rather than the poor themselves.[25]

Saving the children of the underprivileged was always an interest of reformers. While strategies for dealing with these children varied, two basic approaches had developed over the past half-century. One could educate them to behave and think properly in the common schools, or one could confine them in reformatories and asylums for a period of time or in Sunday schools once a week. Either way, these children would be spared from the influence of their degenerate parents and receive a proper measure of discipline. Leaders of the CAS detested the practices of the asylums and Sunday schools and their "obsession with discipline, conformity, and hierarchical authority."[26] CAS members saw no advantage to turning children into machines. Rather, their goal was to harness the energy of these children and redirect it in socially useful ways.

Capturing the rugged individualism of such youngsters could be achieved in two ways.

The first was to establish dormitories, reading rooms, and 'industrial schools'
. . . to which youthful news vendors and other street boys could repair for brief
intervals while continuing their independent life.
> The second and . . . more 'permanent and useful' aspect of the CAS program
> was to transfer street urchins to towns and settlements in the West, placing them
> with local residents who would provide for them in return for work.[27]

Rather than encouraging these boys and girls to take up permanent residence
with each other as a group, it was hoped that such actions would keep them an
inchoate mass. They posed little danger as long as they remain disbursed. Col-
lectively, they might form street gangs or, "grown to maturity, . . . 'come to
know their power and *use it!*'—perhaps at the ballot box, perhaps in the
streets."[28] Approximately ninety thousand potential urban guerrillas were relo-
cated in the West by the mid-1890s, and the threat of revolutionary violence in
the industrial cities was lessened, at least in the eyes of CAS members.

Leaders of the AICP, CAS, and YMCA shared a common desire to reimpose
a cohesive moral order over an increasingly disordered urban landscape. They
thought they understood how the anonymity of city living ate away at the foundations of that order by limiting the opportunities for fellowship among people.
Only the YMCA, however, consciously set out to counteract such forces by
creating a voluntary but permanent fellowship among those in the largest detached group in the cities, unmarried young men. Not everyone in that category
proved to be a candidate for inclusion. Attempts to attract and hold working-
class men failed. The YMCA was an organization for native-born Protestants
with a real or declared membership in the middle class.[29] Membership was
voluntary and guaranteed no one of a job, but it was a good and secure place
from which to start one's search. YMCA leaders did not expect to transform
cities into the small towns where many members had been raised. In this regard,
the YMCA represented a great step forward from earlier and even contemporary
moral reform crusades. Its rapid growth after 1850 testifies to this fact. In 1860
there were nearly twenty-five thousand members in the two hundred YMCA
chapters from the east coast to the Mississippi. By 1900 the number of members
had grown to two hundred and fifty thousand, and there were about one thousand
five hundred chapters in cities across the country.[30]

Although the YMCA leadership seemed willing to negotiate a separate peace
with city life, there was never any question about the terms of the settlement. In
the battle against urban corruption there were to be no prisoners. The starch-
collared armies of the YMCA would march through cities and vanquish all
sources of wickedness and decay. Here, too, the organizational sophistication of
the YMCA made its purity campaigns stand out from previous ones. The tent
fever of evangelical crusades was redirected toward surveys of "moral destitu-
tion" in cities, conventions, and lobbying efforts in government offices. In New
York, for example, the YMCA got the state legislature to pass stricter regulations
on the sale of liquor and obscene literature. It also helped launch the New York

Society for the Suppression of Vice, which, in turn, sponsored similar efforts in Cincinnati, Chicago, Louisville, St. Louis, and San Francisco.[31] These anti-vice groups attacked what they thought were the actual purveyors of corruption such as prostitutes and proponents of birth control. Combined with the YMCA relief programs for the poor, these organizations took a major step toward insti-tutionalizing the fight against urban decay.

At the same time, however, they also moved reformers one step further away from achieving the mystical union of the upper and lower classes that some hoped would save the cities. This could not be helped. Upper- and middle-income people were already scurrying to the suburbs, while those who remained in the cities were rapidly abandoning the downtown areas to the foreign immi-grants.

Still, there were those who continued to think that the old evangelical tricks might yet work. "The tract societies issued an array of updated tracts aimed at a new generation of readers, and the Sunday-school movement, despite . . . the shift to a predominantly middle-class base, renewed its concern for the urban poor."[32] Revivals also enjoyed renewed popularity, but, as in the tract societies and Sunday schools, a substantial decline in attendance by the middle class occurred. Meanwhile, many from the middle class were becoming converts to the newest crusade, the charity-organization movement.

This reform effort was nurtured by the idea that a more comprehensive and less fragmented attack on the sources of urban decay was needed. Its organiza-tional approach was drawn from the common-school movement, but its philoso-phy concerning slum problems was derived entirely from the textbook written by the AICP. The basis of poverty "lay in the moral deficiencies and character flaws of the poor" and would only be overcome when the poor recognized and corrected these shortcomings. Charity organizations could help the poor in this process of self-discovery. This would be accomplished by coordinating the activ-ities of various groups, "compiling dossiers on everyone requesting relief," and by using middle-class visitors "to approach the uplift task on a family-by-family basis." Data on each applicant were collected, and, unsurprisingly, much of the information solicited was concerned with attitudes and character. Arranging these data into some logical pattern "offered deceptively tangible assurance that the . . . disturbing human reality documented had somehow been subdued and rendered manageable."[33] These data, in turn, were passed by the friendly home visitor to relief agencies, landlords, employers, banks, and even the police. If such tactics increased the tension between the self-appointed "friend" and the family, they also conveyed to the poor a sense of their proper place in society's pecking order. The goal here, as for some early proponents of the common school, was to show "them" how to adjust to their "preordained" slot in the world.

Leaders of the charity-organization movement eventually tried to amend their ideology to soften its outrageous paternalism, but they met with little success. The coercive elements of their philosophy and tactics no longer satisfied a public that had begun to understand that the poor may not be in control of their own fates, regardless of their faith. The redemptive works of charity organizations had never been received warmly by the poor. Nevertheless, this movement did accomplish three things between 1870 and the early 1890s. First, the charity organizations sustained the idea that it was still possible to fashion a strong moral order in cities based on sound Protestant principles and upper- and middle-class leadership. More importantly, the movement provided a focus for such beliefs even as the leaders were "fleeing to the suburbs, retreating into tight neighborhood enclaves, dismissing municipal politics, . . . and allowing the industrial capitalism that was shaping the city to proceed unchecked and uncontrolled."[34] Second, the movement inspired several states and dozens of cities to consolidate their relief efforts into a single coordinating board. Third, by broadening the array of programs formally defined as welfare-relief efforts and certifying their activities by some central board, the charity movement promoted the development of "new professional leadership."[35] The movement thereby helped to subvert the very evangelical volunteerism it had sought to promote and to lay the groundwork for even more comprehensive public relief programs in this century.

Civil Rites and Civil Wrongs

It would be unfair and inaccurate to attribute the growth in city governments to the withdrawal of more well-to-do people from public affairs. Nor was the expansion of public services simply the result of the rise of political machines intent on capturing the vote of illiterate immigrants with patronage jobs. Yet both sets of factors figure prominently in the gradual shift of moral-reform crusades from the private arena to the public stage. Indeed, various reform efforts of the late nineteenth century and early twentieth that are referred to by the term *Progressivism* were the last gasps of Protestant revivalism in our major cities. Subsequent attempts to recast the moral order of urban areas in terms that earlier reformers would have understood took the form of defensive or holding actions. À little "good government" here, some throwing out of the rascals there, and an occasional victory in behalf of the public control over vital services all contributed to the development of morality crusades from a public to a government phenomenon.

Traditionally, city governments had not been directly implicated in the identification or resolution of civil improprieties. Slowly, almost imperceptibly, this began to change. Violations of codes for right conduct came to be seen as a government concern, subject to government intervention, persisting because of government complicity. Civil rites became more closely identified with civil wrongs. The enthusiasm to reform public life and morality was translated into movements to change the central rituals and institutions of government itself.

The Push for Public Reform

Maintaining the cities' barest physical needs—roads, docks, and sewers—in the nineteenth century became too great a burden for even the most generous civic patrons to carry alone. Services such as relief for the poor, which customarily had been supported through philanthropic efforts, were redefined as public and ultimately government problems. Fire and police protection, parks, sewage, construction materials, epidemics, street lights, and even the provision of water joined the list of problems that private citizens could no longer resolve effectively for themselves. The better classes responded to these challenges with a mixture of fear and disdain. Even as they left the cities in large numbers, they took great comfort in knowing that the source of these problems could be traced to the character and spiritual flaws of the people who were taking their place. Up to this point in time, the moral-reform crusades were intended to fix those deficiencies and, in the process, reenervate important civil rituals that would help keep everything in order. The thousands who volunteered their time to these crusades apparently received great inspiration for their efforts. For the even greater number of underprivileged people at whom such crusades were directed there seemed to be far less gained. Their chances for a better life were not improved noticeably because of the reformers' good works.

The continuing failure of these crusades to bring about a spiritual and social renaissance in cities helped perpetuate the very institutional crisis reformers had envisioned engulfing urban America. There were other people for whom the institutional crisis was equally real, however, who did not share the reformers' desire to save the poor from themselves. They were interested in harnessing the spirit of the industrial city rather than purifying it. As good urban technicians, they understood the need to provide services to a growing population and knew how to convince businessmen that economic expansion could only be sustained by making such human capital investments possible. They were political bosses, and the institution they created in response to the challenges posed by urban development was called the *machine*. It is a term that captures nicely both the way it worked and a sympathy for the mechanics of running a government to which upper-class reformers later tried to claim exclusive rights.

The order inspired by the political rituals of the machine may not have been particularly moral or cheap—public indebtedness under the bosses grew substantially after the Civil War—but it was effective. Franchises to companies providing better street lighting, water services, and mass transit were expensive, but American cities got these things long before European communities did.[36] It was not an accident that support for public relief programs increased during this period.

Yet for all their corruption and carousing with scruffy immigrants, political machines were not the carriers of social and economic subversion that critics pictured them to be. In fact, they mounted no greater effort to undermine the existing social and economic order of cities than did the YMCA. The political machine was a rather conservative device, notwithstanding its support of many issues, such as voting rights and antiprohibition, dear to immigrants' hearts. Contrary to the impression left by some observers, the machine did not provide a channel for professional mobility for entire groups.[37] It did permit selected members of immigrant populations to acquire considerable wealth and power. Still, many secured only low-paying jobs. Others never worked at all. Poverty was a constant feature of their lives.

Political machines fought the nativist movements in behalf of their immigrant supporters and even displayed a measure of racial tolerance that was progressive for its day. Nevertheless, the bosses needed to keep these people in a dependent state in order to maintain their own position. What made the political machine unique among other efforts to control the pace and direction of urban growth was that it used the city's existing resources to drag it closer to the twentieth century rather than pushing it back into the eighteenth. It did not seek to save the city or the people in it. Yet it exhibited a paternalistic style that had much in common with earlier reform efforts, and its leaders shared the same cynical view of the lower classes as their more high-minded opponents. The bosses preferred to use the social and spiritual "flaws" in these people rather than attempting to change them. In this way, the crisis spread. Now, not only did the working class need reforming but the institutions and rituals of public life required purification as well.

Politicizing the moral reform effort in cities in the 1890s and early twentieth century had a big impact on urban politics. To be sure, crusades blossomed against the machines, but there were also renewed movements to change the schools and root out personal vices such as prostitution and the consumption of alcohol. Finally, there were attempts to alter the entire physical appearance of cities. Impressive as all of this undoubtedly was, it must be recalled that these various crusades were occurring even as their leaders were completing their abandonment of the larger cities or hiding themselves away in restricted neighborhoods. The subsequent dimming of reform movements had more to do with the ability of persons to seal themselves off from the painful realities of urban America than it did with any rebirth of optimism about city life. Cities had always enjoyed their boosters in the academies as well as in the press and among popular writers.[38] The brief hiatus in moral-reform movements is better explained by reference to the world wars and great depression that interrupted the attention of reformers and redirected it toward the nation as a whole. Even during this relatively quiet period, however, the city's stage was being readied for the greatest reform crusade since the Progressive era: the civil-rights movement.

Toward A Civil Religion

Campaigns to purify public life in the cities after 1890 moved along two distinct but frequently converging paths. According to historian Paul Boyer, some reformers "drifted toward . . . coercive measures to uproot vice and impose a higher standard of civic virtue, others were drawn to a subtler, less direct approach: that of remolding the city's physical environment as a means of elevating its moral tone." The repressive movements tended to attract middle- and lower-middle-class persons as followers. Environmentalist efforts appealed generally to members of the business and commercial elite and complemented their attempts to restructure governments so as to offer "a more efficient and patently superior alternative to misgovernment and waste."[39] Together, these two movements rekindled the dream of a united and moral city. In this way, at least, reformers remained true to the original morality crusades of the 1820s.

There were ways, however, in which the reform efforts of the Progressive era differed sharply from their predecessors. Foremost among these differences was the reduced attention paid to the Scriptures as the basis and defending rationale for movement activities. Religious beliefs still played an important part in the minds of many participants, but secularization in the movements' ideology and organizational base was pronounced. Even members of coercive movements now understood that the churches could not transform urban society.[40]

Gone also was the emphasis on attacking expressions of degeneracy at the level of the individual or his family. Accompanying this push for a new civic morality was the realization that only citywide agencies could possibly accomplish the task. Campaigns to cleanse local politics took on broader meaning than that implied in the Progressives' challenge to tame city governments and make them more "businesslike." The once tentative excursions of temperance and antiprostitution leaders into local politics in the 1880s developed after 1890 into aggressive campaigns to infuse government with Christian goodness. There were parallel developments in the private arena. Private organizations mimicked the consolidation they had been witnessing in the charity movement and built coalitions among groups interested in the same issue in order to multiply their power. Mass politics had come to the purity crusades of the 1890s. After nearly a century of struggling with the problems posed by urban and industrial growth, Americans finally had established a basis for a civil religion.[41]

Liquor and prostitution after 1890 again were turned to as the quintessential urban vices to be purged from public display, if not from private practice, by the coercive faction of reformers. The objectives of these reformers had not changed much over the course of a century. As they grew stronger, their demands grew increasingly more strident and less amenable to compromise. This movement was fed by the Protestant fundamentalism of its participants; barely middle class, if middle class at all, the native-born rural transplants who poured their energy into these crusades were lost in the tradition of earlier reformers. Like their predecessors, these people had every intention of turning cities into small villages. Yet at times their message was wrapped in some fairly progressive rhetoric. No longer was the cause of one's downfall attributed to personal shortcomings. Rather, an urban environment that presented insurmountable barriers to living a wholesome existence was blamed for these individual deviations. Also, gone from the reformers' speeches was the emotional appeal to the "common body of values and standards" that allegedly could unite people from otherwise disparate backgrounds and social classes. Instead, these reformers used a rational approach to the problems they attacked. Their "reliance on statistics, sociological investigation, and 'objective' social analysis" was unprecedented in moral-reform crusades and greatly contributed to the "secularization of the urban moral-control movement." Although such devices placed the morality crusaders more in the mainstream of Progressive-era reformers, the association with tent revivals and witch hunts that the contemporary upper class found unpleasant could not be dispelled. Sponsorship of the coercive movements by upper-class persons waned. The reforming impulse among the upper classes and businessmen found its outlet through more positive works.[42]

The "positive environmentalists" held views about the moral decay of city life that were not dissimilar from those made by their less esteemed working-class colleagues, but they differed markedly in the strategies they preferred to use. The key to achieving moral control and social order "was not repression but a more subtle and complex process of influencing behavior and molding character through a transformed, consciously planned urban environment."[43] Unleashing that philosophy on urban America, these patrons of genteel reform undertook an ambitious program for changing the face of the city. Included among their targets were parks, playgrounds, housing, public utilities, schools, and even the local government. It was an unparalleled outpouring of civic pride and faith in the regenerative powers of the city. Such an effort was needed, however, if the class divisions opened up by labor violence in the preceding two decades were to be healed.[44]

One of the first and most enduring monuments to this civic revivalism was the settlement house. Living where and what they preached, settlement workers took up residence in tenements on the same blocks as the people they wished to assist. Their approach was straightforward: "investigate to see what needs to be done, then do it." This pragmatic but ill-defined sense of their mission inspired a wide array of reform activities and social programs. They sponsored clinics, educational programs, cooperative coal yards, boarding clubs, athletic facilities, referral services, and campaigns in behalf of child-labor laws, factory safety, and work-and-hour legislation. Critical of the charity organizations' "friendly visitor" strategy, they chose to serve as living examples of what could be done for and by the slum dwellers. Antagonistic toward machine politicians, they worked to raise the consciousness of the poor and championed laws that would help them. Yet these noble experiments made little progress in the larger campaign to "unmake" the urban slum or to bring whites and blacks together.[45]

In spite of their sincere efforts and enormous energy, Progressive-era reformers accepted the same paternalistic responsibility as their predecessors for saving the poor from themselves. Settlement-house patrons and charity workers, for all their caterwauling, had more in common than they cared to admit. The settlement volunteers were "simply 'friendly visitors' who actually took up residence in the poor neighborhood, creating a model middle-class household: orderly, cultivated, temperate, and industrious."[46] Bound by their own class and, later, racial biases, these persons were unprepared for the changes that would overtake cities after 1900. Reaching white immigrants who had an idealistic but alien vision of rural American morality had been difficult enough. Tempting native-born blacks from the South with that same vision was quite a different matter. Even the followers of Chicago's indomitable Jane Adams were not equal to this task.[47]

The little islands of middle-class civility represented in these settlement houses failed to become institutions around which slum residents rallied and agitated for social reforms. Indeed, such nonconciliatory gestures were not really part of the settlement-house movement. Led by boards of trustees with upper-class pedigrees, settlement-house democracy extended no further than their public baths. Members of these organizations could not reverse the suppressed class divisions that were rapidly becoming institutionalized through residential segregation. Nor did they ever seriously try to close the gap between the races.

Still, all was not lost. Reformers slowly were getting a better indication of the most effective measures to secure a new moral order. Early attempts to redeem the community by proselytizing individuals or their families, though never completely abandoned, had revealed serious weaknesses by the time of the Civil War. Initial efforts to establish citywide institutions that could serve as a moral breeding ground faltered with the common-school movement in the 1840s and 1850s. However, reformers studied the organizational strategies of both the antislavery movement and machine politicians and learned some valuable lessons. Ideas about grass-roots organizing and coalition building at the local and even national level were put into practice in some of the charity crusades and most certainly in the settlement-house movement. But the lower classes proved far less susceptible to the appeals of well-meaning reformers than anyone expected, particularly when they were in their own communities. A new moral and social order could not be fashioned successfully by working at the neighborhood level either. The purity crusades, notwithstanding their blatant paternalism, had shown that only citywide efforts held any promise for success against the arrogant ward captain and his army of bushy immigrants. Their efforts foundered, among other reasons, for lack of a credible institutional base that could work on a sustained basis and compete with the likes of a political machine for control of the city. Thus, reformers worked hard to pass legislation or secure tax revenues to upgrade housing conditions and build neighborhood playgrounds and parks. Changing important parts of the environment allowed the rich some measure of control over the poor by giving the latter a place to heal the emotional damage wrought by impoverished surroundings.

Backers of the "city-beautiful" movement were playing for big stakes. They were striving to "promulgate a single civic ideal" that, "if pursued vigorously in the poorer wards, . . . would 'awaken ambition,' . . . and ultimately create 'purer souls.' " There was more. Not just specific groups would be caught up in this movement. It was hoped that the whole city would be invigorated by a new picture of itself as a living thing. A civil religion, after all, was possible only if one had a vision of the city as a spiritual entity with its very own soul.[48] Not only was the city finally accepted as a legitimate form of social life by the upper classes but its problems and moral order were being manipulated by people with good technical skills. City-planning as a profession eventually evolved from this movement as people looked for sound, long-term solutions to the city's physical and social problems.[49] Before that, however, the goal of achieving a new civic ideal guided the efforts of Progressive reformers to gain control over city governments.

Government Crusades

Who led the great crusades to reform city governments has been the subject of intense debate among historians.[50] It seems certain that the established elite and many businessmen were at the forefront of virtually all these efforts. At issue is how far down the social class ladder these movements had to reach before exhausting the population most receptive to their message. To refer to these "good government" campaigns as "middle-class" achievements is inaccurate, but such crusades did acquire considerable support from middle-class and white-collar workers. We also know that such people were not especially active in the coercive moral-control movements. It appears more likely that these people followed the lead of upper-class, professional, and business groups. These different groups, for reasons peculiar to their positions in urban society, sought to extend principles of rational management and of control over the metropolitan market into the operation of city governments, school systems, public health, and other areas. More importantly, perhaps, the absence of substantial pockets of upper-middle-class and elite residents in the older central cities is clearly associated with the failure of governmental reforms in those places. The adoption of reforms was far more likely in the smaller, newer, socially homogeneous cities where these classes fled after abandoning places like Chicago and Detroit.[51]

The history of "good government" campaigns, as the settlement-house movement already had shown, was marked by the growing spatial and social separation between urban elites and those whose behavior and morals they hoped to repair. Lines for the contest were drawn along natural or symbolic barriers that partitioned cities into segregated residential neighborhoods.

Sometimes these barriers broke down. Many "reform bosses" looked for corruption well beyond prostitution, gambling, and saloons. The political machines that protected such corruption and the companies that profited from alliances with the boss politicians also came under attack. Campaigns to secure public ownership of utility and transit companies emerged as important strategies in the battle against the old-style bosses and for "the larger moral reclamation of the city and its inhabitants."[52] Yet those with socialist proclivities who organized public boycotts of private transit companies were the exception among Progressive city reformers. Using the machinery and ceremonial clout of city governments to work in behalf of social justice was not what most reformers had in mind. Whatever justice or moral reclamation resulted from such projects might have been ideal, at least in the eyes of Progressive reformers, but the connection between them was indirect and undoubtedly obscure to the lower classes.[53]

The immediate goals of reformers were far more practical. Universal suffrage had greatly reduced their voting power, and the decentralized style of municipal governing practiced by the machines had further eroded their impact on public affairs. Progressive reformers responded by attacking the unrestrained manner in which local governments were run and the ward system of representation.

The self-serving motivation underlying the reformers' program for civic improvement was no clearer than in their campaigns to purge the public schools of the machine's influence. Overcrowded and yet still turning away students, orderly but condemned by a stultifying curriculum and poorly trained teachers, city school districts under the ward-trustee system perpetuated ignorance and poverty. The school, reformers maintained, "was the key to the battle with the slum. Other reforms would ameliorate poverty. School reform . . . would break its grip."[54] To be sure, reformers achieved a measure of success at the state level in securing property taxes and curricular guidelines. But they were not able to shake control of the schools at the local level away from ward leaders and other political hacks. Educational decisions, argued the reformers, ought to be left to professional educators, not to the machine's friends. Politics should be taken out of the schools. The only way to accomplish this was to centralize control over school affairs in the hands of boards of education, dominated, of course, by businessmen and upper-class reformers. By 1920 most city school districts had this kind of administrative organization.[55]

The dream of Sunday-school crusaders, "friendly visitors," the YMCA, and every reformer since 1800 who fretted over the moral probity of city children was finally realized. There would be an institution constantly reviewing the child's social and spiritual progress. All that was yet to be determined was what the reformers would do with it. Untethered, the school reformers initiated a series of innovative organizational and curricular changes that promised to alter not only the face of public education but its spirit as well. Reformers in New York, Diane Ravitch tells us, were anxious to remove the child as much and as long as possible from the influences of street and slum life. To this end, they "pressed the schools to lengthen the school day, week, and year." Teachers were expected to do "preventive social work," impart "the attitudes, the values, and the skills" not provided at home, and even inspect children for lice and chastise them about "cleanliness and sound nutrition."[56] All of these responsibilities were now added to the more traditional role of the public schoolteacher. Children had to be prepared to assume their appropriate places in an industrial economy.

Nineteenth-century advocates of the common school promoted the idea that all children, rich as well as poor, should be exposed to a good educational experience. More talented youngsters of humble origin, reformers thought, would raise themselves above positions achieved by others in their class. Children from well-to-do backgrounds would benefit from their contact with the rougher elements of society in a safe and controlled setting. The remaining children would assume a place among the masses. Twentieth-century reformers were far less reluctant to specify where each class of youngsters should end up and how they should get there. Though less democratic, it was decidedly more efficient than the common-school concept. The key to their program was the expansion of enrollment and curriculum in the high schools.

The simultaneous goals of reformers were to reduce the number of young people on the streets and direct them into "appropriate" career lines. Little concern existed over the ultimate fate of most children, especially those of immigrant stock. Eventually they would find jobs as unskilled or at least semi-skilled laborers in factories. Nor was there great apprehension over the future of "the abstract-minded and imaginative children . . . whose ancestors were in the professions and the higher occupations." For them, a "classical" education and attention to "intellectual skills . . . judgment, taste, fancy, imagination, and reason" was expected and appropriate. The question was what to do with the large number of children with some ambition and intellectual capacity, given the increasing need for persons to fill supervisory positions as "foremen, overseers, superintendents," and the like. The answer for Progressive-era reformers was vocational or industrial education, a system of tracking whereby students could be nudged into fields by pursuing curricular programs. This, according to Robert Nasaw, was to be "the new educational democracy."[57]

In truth, many youngsters managed to overcome the real and symbolic barriers to achieving a "classical" education and scrapped their way into the professions. The percentages of such youngsters from different ethnic groups who were able to overcome both the impediments of class and their teachers' biases have been quite remarkable. Twentieth-century Jews and Germans on the east coast, Japanese on the west, offer some of the most compelling evidence in this regard. The children of Italian and Irish immigrants, on the other hand, continued to lag behind in their occupational and educational achievement throughout this century. The same could be said of black and Spanish-speaking Americans today. Surely, the customs of these various groups and the importance they attributed to educational excellence had a good deal to do with the academic achievement of their children. Without ignoring these differences, however, one still must acknowledge the impact that standardized testing and the firm advice of school authorities have had on curbing the educational appetite of countless thousands of students since 1900.[58]

The campaign for vocational education, like that for staff and administrative professionalization, did have its opponents. As Progressive-era reformers grew bolder and tried to introduce fresh educational ideas, they began to bump heads with the same centralized, professional teaching staff they had been instrumental in creating. Jealous of their territory in the schools and allied at times with unions and some old-style politicians, school authorities resisted some of the more aggressive educational packages advanced by reformers.[59] In the case of the proposed shift to industrial schooling, educators had no intention of stepping aside for mere "job trainers." Emerging from this campaign was a compromise that most late-twentieth-century students have had to live with: the comprehensive high school.

That the reformers had to compromise at all indicates how much their once unassailable position as dictators of urban morality and civil conduct had eroded. By 1920 their energy had been spent, not only on school matters but in other areas of social reform as well. An era of Protestant evangelical crusades to transform the city had come to an end. A century of frustrated attempts to mold the character of the poor or those who were not native-born and white had met with little success. Cities could not be made over into small towns and residents could not be taught to behave, think, and feel like good rural folk. Upper- and middle-class people had been abandoning the older central cities for some time. Those who remained hid in segregated neighborhoods and expressed their demands through protective neighborhood associations. Reaching out to other areas of the city would be painful and long-awaited. In Baltimore, for instance, it was not until the 1950s and 1960s that the upper and middle classes began "to broaden their membership and address more comprehensive socioeconomic

problems that were destroying large sections of the inner city."[60] In the meantime, the traditional reforming classes continued their retreat and fought back
when they could. Their bitterness was expressed most forcefully in 1924 when
Congress set up immigration quotas to limit the influx of the most recent, and
objectionable, European settlers. If these people refused to be saved from themselves or could not be redeemed, they could damned well be kept out.

Conclusions: Morality Crusades and Civil Rights

They could not be kept out, of course. Jews, Italians, Slavs, and the like
merely were replaced by Puerto Ricans and blacks. Immigration by foreign
nationals might have been held in check; immigration by persons from one's
own country or its territories could not. The exodus out of the South by blacks
did not make itself felt until World War I. Spanish-speaking migration began
even later. Yet like the earlier European immigrants, these newer refugees did
not become the subject of intense and sustained reform efforts until after their
numbers had rendered them unavoidable and their problems undeniable. It was
not until after World War II, then, that these immigrants actually merited consideration of their situation on a grand scale. What they had inherited from
previous immigrant populations bears repeating: discrimination in employment,
housing, schools, health care, and a host of other public services and private
resources. However, they were cursed with several other problems with which
most previous immigrant groups had not been forced to contend. The most
obvious one was skin color, although we are now told by some persons that this
no longer is a serious impediment to their advancement.[61] Second, there were
no other ethnic groups waiting to take their poor housing and bad jobs or to
inherit the wrath of the dominant white population. Third, and perhaps most
important of all, in most instances they were received into cities that shortly
began flirting with bankruptcy and that were no longer centers for unskilled
industrial labor. All things considered, it was not a good situation.

Responses to these problems by minority and nonminority reformers varied
widely. Many sought to attack the root causes of segregation by increasing
minority representation in the work force and ending practices that limited
selection of housing to ghetto areas. Others concentrated on expanding minority
voting rights and opening up certain facilities once considered privileged areas
for whites. Each of these reform efforts contributed to the overall successes and
failures of the civil rights movement in its own way. None of them, however,
held as mystical an appeal or evoked such impassioned resistance as the quest
for desegregated schools. Why so much faith would be placed in a reform that
focused on such a limited and powerless segment of the population is beyond
reason. More vigorous assaults on job discrimination, argues Diane Ravitch,
"would have improved the economic status of Negroes faster than school inte-

gration; eliminating residential segregation would have at once ended school segregation."[62] To answer why school desegregation commanded our attention the way it did for as long as it did requires us to look further than the grooved answers of both advocates and opponents. It requires that we examine desegregation as an article of our civic faith.

The movement to desegregate public schools appears, in retrospect, to have extended the tradition of the moral reform crusades. In successive waves of emendatory zeal, concerned citizens have tried to recast civic rituals and public morality in ways that have seemed to hold the greatest promise for saving urban society. Strategies have varied, changing as crusaders have learned what has not worked. Experimentation has always been conscious and vigorous. Competition among simultaneous movements has sometimes been stiff. Despite the differences, however, reform movements have been connected by a common goal to teach, urge, or, when necessary, compel certain segments of the population to behave better.

Early reformers developed ceremonies that paralleled those of religious services and churches. The object was to reassert the kind of direct control over individuals' public conduct and private beliefs that reformers thought had been lost. Without some kind of sustained institutional presence, however, these efforts could not provide the sense of fraternity among the members of different classes that supporters hoped could be achieved. Subsequent attempts to create such effects on a part-time basis in the Sunday schools or on a small scale in the case of settlement houses also proved unsatisfactory. The failure of settlement houses to spark a civic renaissance in spite of their avowed secular approach to urban problems and muted moralizing must have been especially disappointing. Though more obviously paternalistic in their mission, the charity crusades mounted citywide campaigns and had the support of paid staff and a complex organization backing them. Yet this movement, too, enjoyed only limited successes and never really captured the interest and loyalty of the lower classes it intended to save. Clearly, any movement to redeem the underprivileged and the city as a whole, even when undertaken on a citywide basis and with organizational support, did not succeed as long as it depended on the voluntary compliance of those targeted for reform.

The growing attention paid to corruption in local governments after the Civil War certainly was a manifestation of the need for something of a more compulsory nature. Local governments provided some of the key public rituals and institutions for drawing a fragmented and potentially volatile population together. Yet these ceremonies and offices were stained by the very immorality and confusion that already had eroded much of public life outside of government. If government was to protect a delicate social order and enhance the benefits of an industrial economy for all citizens, it must be strong, decent, and imbued with as much Protestant efficiency as possible. A related development that also spoke to the need for institutionalized relief was the gradual absorption by local governments, and eventually by the federal government as well, of the welfare services provided initially by private groups.

Each of these reform movements made important contributions to city life at the time they appeared. If nothing else, they illustrated how members of a particularly threatened element in urban populations—the upper class—attempted to cope with challenges to their social status and economic clout even as they were abandoning the cities. The gradual ascension of persons of humble origin into positions of influence no doubt offended them. The extension of political recognition to the masses and the symbolic approval of the customs that this implied drove the better classes to distraction. In spite of their withdrawal from the cities, however, the legacy of some of their crusades during the Progressive era has endured. It is no minor historical irony that upper-class reformers agitated so tirelessly in behalf of strong, centralized government and against government that was closer to the "people." That they also ceded control of the more fundamentalist and popular forms of mass agitation to members of the lower-middle and working classes at the same time proved fateful.

The separation of the upper classes from the purity crusades of the 1890s merely confirmed their growing disenchantment with openly coercive tactics. They came to rely on more subtle and indirect ways of controlling the masses. Yet as the civic ideal toward which these upper classes worked became more abstract, the strategies they adopted to achieve their goals began to lose their impact. The promise of a reconstituted moral and social order based on the supervision of the lower classes by the city's better citizens was forsaken. There was one exception, however, and the public school was it.

Reformers, focusing much of their attention on the city's youth, developed public education while the history of moral reform crusades was still pretty much in its infancy. School attendance was required and exposure to a set of prescribed ideas was mandated by the state. The public school system, a lasting and compelling answer to the question of how to institutionalize the quest for moral reform, became that institution around which new or revived civil rituals and codes of public morality could be most efficiently and permanently fixed.

Although an ambitious project, it was plagued with two overriding problems. The schools, notes one observer, "were called upon to do the impossible: to uphold the myths of the 'classless' community while . . . preparing young people for their future lives in a society based on class divisions." Though apparent in the lower grades, this issue was especially troublesome in the high schools. Once there, students were placed into different curricular tracks. Officials then "undid the damage to democratic pretensions by bringing them back together into a . . . democratic community to eat lunch, take recess, learn their 'civics,' attend assembly, and cheer their athletic teams to victory."[63] Moreover, under the reforms carried out during the Progressive era, caretakers of the school system proposed to conduct this unplutocratic experiment with only limited interference by the public. Opportunities to register one's pleasure or dissatisfaction with educational policies were strictly circumscribed and relegated to ceremonial encounters at school meetings or in the voting booth. Popular control achieved through such mechanisms and manifested "in the form of elected school officials," as citizens came to learn, "does not guarantee efficiency, but it does guarantee political legitimacy."[64]

Here then was the legacy willed to black activists who sought to desegregate the public schools. The issue, as they and their supporters understood, involved a straightforward question about minority children's civil rights. Could minority youngsters be denied the same kind of education received by white children? A precious American ideal was at risk. If denied access to a good education, minority children might not have the opportunity to improve their station in life as generations of immigrant children had done before them. Yet as described, this view of the public schools resulted from a rather selective reading of city history and probably bore as little resemblance to education in rural areas. Many immigrants were able to use the schools for self-improvement. Many others did not. Still, there is no denying the powerful grip of this ideal and its hypothesized connection with desegregation on several generations of civil-rights advocates.

One frequently can dismiss arguments against desegregation as so much gutter sludge and be confident that the intellectual content and emotional appeal have not been exaggerated. Over the years, however, critics of desegregation have raised issues that get closer to touching the historical significance of this reform than many of its strongest defenders have ever dared to go. The most crucial issues can be summarized quickly in two familiar questions. Should children, black or white, travel long distances to attend schools to correct something they had no hand in creating? Are we, blacks as well as whites, to pay a price for something done to slaves more than a century ago? In the face of such compelling questions, all the grand allusions to universal brotherhood or references to the broad remedial powers of the federal government under the Fourteenth Amendment wither. Yet they are simple questions, once the history of moral reform crusades in cities is reviewed. Obviously, the answer in both cases must be yes. The traditional goal of such movements has been to purify and redeem the city by leading residents to a finer understanding of their responsibilities to it and to one another. If the commonweal has been violated in some way, there must be an accounting. The role of the child in such a process is critical. Generations of reformers have tried to beat the brutish tendencies from urban society and especially its poor and "morally bankrupt" adults by capturing the minds and spirits of their children. However cruel the experience may have seemed to those forced to live through it, somehow both they and the city as a whole were to have been better for it.

School desegregation, seen in a broader historical context, has comparatively less to do with justice or the alleged rights of minority children than we have been led to believe. That is not to say that the benefits as well as the liabilities of citizenship should not be spread to all segments of the population. Rather, it is only that such considerations have not played an especially prominent role in the history of morality crusades. The question of whether schools should be desegregated focuses on a different set of issues involving the nature and control of public institutions. Traditionally, schools and their related educational rituals have been treated as the best hope for reconstituting public morality. The questions being asked by civil-rights advocates about desegregation, therefore, were similar in many ways to those posed by reformers during the Progressive era. Namely, the question was whether the schools could be shaken from their complacency to help fashion a viable civic religion for an urban society. There was a problem, however. The model for public education created by Progressive reformers did not animate the moral order of cities as they had thought it would. If anything, the institution had grown indolent. Professionalization and centralization were cornerstones of the program for establishing a viable civic religion in the cities. According to recent critics, however, such changes only bloated the administration and made the schools indifferent to the social crisis mounting at their doorsteps. The much heralded structural reorganization of the schools was now standing in the way of a revived public life and civic morality. Desegregation became the means through which the schools might again be able to fulfill their promise.

The flaws in this campaign should be apparent by now. Foremost among them was the role of minority citizens as agitators for reform. Minority civil-rights activists turned the traditional morality crusade upside down by reproaching the upper classes and political community for not helping them reform their own people. The underprivileged themselves and not merely their more prosperous sponsors were initiating a crusade and using coercive measures to achieve their goal. In the past, coercion had always been used on the underprivileged. The upper classes had invited such a change when they ceded control of these strategies to lower-middle and working-class persons during the 1890s. Still, they probably never envisioned themselves being treated in that manner. The use of the courts to promote such a campaign was dictated by the inability of blacks to secure relief through established political routines. This helped to create the appearance that the social order indeed was being turned on its head. Of course, this is an important element in all ritualized rebellions.

A more subtle but equally important flaw in the desegregation crusade was the target of reform. Minority and nonminority proponents of desegregation alike were united in their goal to help minority children acquire a better education. They saw their chance to assist students and to improve the whole community by getting white and minority children together. Some of the common-school advocates of the 1830s also had tried to build more viable public ceremonies and a sound civic morality by bringing different persons together in the schools. Both of these programs for social reform have been based on the idea that the most effective way of changing a public institution, and by implication public life generally, is to change the people in it. Progressive-era reformers shared this bias, but they also understood the importance of changing the structure of the institution itself. How the institution worked, processed demands, and resolved questions of its own legitimacy might frustrate any effort by people to improve themselves and public life.

Somehow this element of the Progressive-era reformer's program for civic revitalization was lost or at least conveniently forgotten. We know that neither social scientists nor jurists, persons whose professions benefited from changes instigated by Progressive-era reformers, have paid close attention to the ways in which school systems actually have interpreted desegregation orders on a daily basis. They, too, envisioned broader institutional changes arising from changes in the people working or studying in the schools. The consequences of ignoring the process by which reforms are fashioned and carried out can only be guessed at here. However, it is clear that many earlier reform crusades failed for lack of attention to such matters.

There have been some noticeable changes in moral-reform crusades since 1800, of course. Foremost among them has been a tendency on the part of reformers to attribute less blame for urban problems to the underprivileged. Greater attention today is paid to larger social conditions as the source of urban problems over which the individual has little control. In the process, there has been a corresponding decline in the amount of responsibility placed on the shoulders of the poor for moderating the effects of such conditions on their lives. The school desegregation movement also illustrates a second important change in urban crusades: the eclipsing of private groups as leaders of reform efforts by government agencies. Philanthropic organizations such as churches still play an important part in reform movements. However, government bodies have taken an increasingly more active role in identifying the sources of urban ills and mobilizing the resources to attack them.

The involvement of government offices in reform activities is significant on a variety of grounds. Regardless of their substantive contributions, such institutional commitments carry two important symbolic gestures with them. First, they implicate and excite the public's interest in a problem far more directly and powerfully than was customary in earlier reform efforts. Under such circumstances, civic rituals are presented with a stiff challenge. Through them citizens must somehow discover an answer to their questions—one that makes sense and one that promises to work. To the extent that civil institutions and ceremonies fail to arrive at such an answer, public life generally is diminished and the credibility of specific civil routines is jeopardized. Conversely, the development of reasonable answers to unreasonable dilemmas through public channels enriches civic life and invigorates government ceremonies. Also, governmental intervention, especially at the federal level, tends to expand the scope of remedial efforts beyond a particular locale or class of persons. It prompts a search for bigger, more representative political jurisdictions, and ultimately moral communities, to involve in the reform movement. Early urban crusades were directed largely at the poor in their own neighborhoods. Later, the cooperation of local governments was solicited so that public-works projects to beautify entire cities could be undertaken. The quest for the "true urban community" of late has extended beyond the city limits. This took place for a time through the efforts of some federal agencies and national civil-rights groups that tried to spark interest in metropolitan desegregation plans. In the case of St. Louis, the city school system also worked toward this goal.

As of today, the pilgrimage in search of this mythical community has been pursued vigorously over at least two continents and taken the better part of two hundred years to reach its current state. Exactly what or, perhaps more precisely, where that state is depends on one's attitude toward cities and reading of American urban history. Basically, one's choices are limited to two options. The first one is based on a wealth of sociological and urban planning theory and reflects the idea that the autonomy and effectiveness of smaller community units have been undermined by "developments in transportation and communication technology." These changes have enlarged the urban marketplace, "increased economic interdependence, and further refined the complex division of labor" already in place. In order to deal with such changes one must have conventions and methods of social control that help to knit these broadened territories and diverse interests into a coherent whole. The most appropriate economic or political unit through which such integration can be achieved is the metropolitan area, or so it is thought. Opposing this position are those who argue that local communities or neighborhoods are the primary arenas within which most people actually carry on their lives and are socialized into the larger world.[65] These communities are vital to the well-being of the city and entire metropolitan region for this reason. Metropolitan boosters take strong issue with these points. They observe the progressive absorption of such areas into larger economic or political planning units and note the growing importance to neighborhoods of organizations oriented toward the metropolitan region.[66] Both factors are taken as signs of the local community's deteriorated position. These critics go on to say that smaller residential units are either enclaves for a backward urban peasantry or temporary refuges for people otherwise committed to an urbane, cosmopolitan way of life. No matter which way one views the issue, people who advocate the use of neighborhoods as the basic planning unit in urban areas appear to be distinctly in the minority.[67]

If the history of moral-reform crusades presented here is accurate, there can be no doubt as to where the quest in behalf of the "true urban community" has led. The imaginary boundary line separating safe areas in cities from those scheduled for reclamation has expanded from the warrens of the poor and spiritually bankrupt to entire metropolitan areas in a little less than two hundred years. This should not be taken to mean that planning activities or reforms initiated at a metropolitan level are destined to be any more successful or inspired than those with smaller audiences in mind. It means only that contemporary urban reformers believe they will be. Of course, the reformers of every age believed the same. If successive waves of urban idealists have been proved wrong, their errors may have laid less with the geographic breadth of their vision than with its content.

Regardless of their ultimate outcome, however, such emendatory efforts are noteworthy because they happened at all. Generations of urban commentators have found cities to be sinkholes of civil indifference and lairs for all the worst forms of communal turpitude one could possibly imagine. Stripped of their customs and meaningful social contacts with their neighbors, urban residents could give full vent to those drives and feelings that civilization was supposed to suppress, if not eradicate. Many of our finest public and private leaders as well as social theorists have shared this view of urban life. In the United States, at least, the failure to discover an ideal communal experience full of warmth and public spontaneity inspired some people to try to re-create it. The schools proved to be a critical institution through which that end might be secured.

5. In Defense
of Desegregation

The style of life pursued by most immigrants to cities greatly contributed to the low esteem in which they were held by more established groups. It also played a part in accentuating their low economic standing. Their social status and social class positions complemented each other. Yet the reformer's zeal was directed far more vigorously at ridding urban society of the immigrant's style of life. Little effort was made to relieve the immigrant of the difficulties presented by an onerous social class system. Indeed, many reform crusades were designed with the explicit purpose of reinforcing a rigid economic order and convincing the poor of its legitimacy.

As inheritors of this legacy, advocates of school desegregation read their history selectively. Like some early proponents of the common school, they accepted the idea that the schools would stand as an institutional commitment to the search for economic and social equality. At the same time, they seemed to ignore more than a century's worth of evidence showing that public schools have tended to reflect rather than remove the inequities inherent in the American economy. Progress in overcoming such inequities, it was thought, would be evolved from the superior academic preparation blacks would receive and the eventual recognition that everyone is more similar than different. To the extent that class barriers were removed at all, equality was to have been derived from disintegration of the barriers of social status that separated white and minority children. The politics of social status took precedence over the politics of social class.[1]

It is my intention in the present chapter to examine further the nature of the struggle between justice and order and, in the process, to offer a credible defense of school desegregation as an article of our civil faith. While it is true that we have no single theory about desegregation, the elements of such a theory have already been examined. In the preceding chapter, efforts to desegregate public schools were presented as an important legacy of early moral reform crusades whose intended purpose was to stop the presumed decay of urban society and to reimpose a sense and degree of control over disorder. During the 1800s, the schools became an important battleground. They were formally charged with the responsibility of preparing the next generation of workers and citizens for the challenges of an industrialized and urbanized world. If there was any hope of changing that world, presumably for the better, it would have to be done through the schools.

The tension that was created while preparing a new generation for the world as it exists and while looking to the schools as a beacon in the struggle to change that world was apparent in the early common-school movement. The issue was not resolved then, and it is no closer to resolution today. In the attempt to resolve it, however, one finds a delicate balance struck between these seemingly contradictory positions. On the one hand, an institution is developed that mimics imprecisely in structure and operation the idealized industrial and bureaucratic order after which it was fashioned and to which the new generation proclaims its fidelity. The institution provides room for growth and the opportunity to amend the social order. On the other hand, there is no rush to repudiate that social order or to take actions that would resolve the tensions inherent in it. What this leaves us with is a process of ritualized crises and reforms whose ultimate effect is to create the appearance of radical change.

Personalizing Desegregation

The deference shown to the prerogatives of school personnel and the presumed perfectibility of their institution is apparent in the package of reforms typically included in a desegregation plan, as well as in earlier school reforms. Well over one hundred different techniques or strategies for achieving effective desegregation have been indexed. The following list contains a sampling of those strategies:

> academic courses for teachers
> attitudinal change
> consistent punishment
> bilingual education
> biracial advisory groups
> busing
> team teaching
> dramatic play
> evaluation of teacher performance
> field trips for faculty
> home visits by teachers
> sensitivity training
> rumor centers
> tutors
> voting for cheerleaders, queens
> orientation to new schools
> public meetings
> principal's role in participatory management

The activities are diverse but are undertaken and fulfilled at the initiative of school personnel. Indeed, the responsibility for framing desegregation policies and building a consensus to support those policies within both the schools and the community is assumed to be in the hands of district administrators.[2]

This tendency is extended even into the sensitive area of increased or improved representation in the policy-making process for traditional "outsiders" such as parents or minority citizens. The establishment of biracial advisory committees to assist school boards is a case in point. The creation of such groups is perceived as a means of "reducing board isolation and improving minority-group influence" during desegregation, and the impetus for such action "should come preferably from within the school administration—either from the board or from the superintendent." These groups should participate in all aspects of desegregation. However, "if an advisory committee is to function properly it needs the respect and confidence of administrators. The administration must feel that the committee is sincerely interested in the schools rather than in taking over school administrative or legislative authority."[3] A rough summation of this position might be that school administrators should be willing to open up their deliberations to a point, but not to the extent that people forget who is *really* in charge.

This idea underscores the argument that school personnel ought to assume responsibility for all aspects of the desegregation process. More importantly, it constitutes an implicit defense of the school system's legitimacy. No one should want or need to impose fundamental changes on the institution just as it is about to experience a dramatic and potentially disruptive reform like desegregation. That alone should serve as a powerful catalyst for organizational change. An institution's caretakers will respond to new challenges by developing fairer and more rational, hence more efficient and effective, ways of accomplishing whatever it is they are supposed to do.

This is a comfortable thesis because it provides a vision of complex organizations as entities capable of self-criticism and correction. However, critics of this approach argue that the numerous actions taken by a district in the name of desegregation offer no such promise to change the ways affairs are conducted. Their contention is that the package of reforms generally included in a desegregation plan may do more to reinforce the existing institution than to rattle its policy-making apparatus to any appreciable degree. The introduction of new programs and procedures in itself is no guarantee that a far-reaching process of organizational change has been undertaken. To support this claim critics could cite a growing body of literature on educational innovation and several case studies dealing in part with desegregation.[4] Additional corroboration for this position is provided in the very program of action typically called for in desegregation plans. Several specific strategies have already been noted. In general, however, the reforms included in such plans are intended to change the institution of public education by changing the persons in it. This attitude, as we saw in the last chapter, has been apparent in many campaigns to improve the schools.

It seems that desegregation planners are in good company when they suggest strategies that are intended to change the way people think, believe, or behave.

Such tactics are popular with persons trying to produce changes in public and private organizations other than school systems. Unfortunately, it appears that altering or reforming persons in those contexts is an ineffective way of bringing about institutional change.[5] Efforts to modify the actions or attitudes of people directly or through the influence of their peers often can fail to secure change. Many experiences with school desegregation could be used to substantiate this point.

By no means am I implying that efforts to change the persons attending or working in schools are useless or not well intentioned. Rather, in taking such actions some questionable assumptions about human nature and the way people survive in large organizations have been made. One assumes that people will change their behavior or beliefs when provided with new information or experiences outside their work environment. It is expected that the insights they acquire will be used once they return to their routine schedule. Moreover, it is hoped that workmates will benefit from their exposure to these new ways of thinking and acting.[6] One supposes that the eventual outcome of these individual changes could be a change in the operation and goals of the whole organization. It is a grand scheme and a comfortable view of how to change a complex organization. The responsibility simply is delegated to the membership or client population. If they gain insight into their tasks and themselves through training, surveys, peer counseling, transfers, or even the removal of a colleague, then enlightened self-interest will take over and institutional change is guaranteed. The process of change may be bumpy and some individuals may suffer for a time, but institutions will be reformed and all of society will benefit.

This is a hefty task with which to charge an individual or even a large group. Yet that is precisely what advocates of desegregation propose to do when they call for busing, teacher transfers, less racist textbooks, and more egalitarian classroom or discipline procedures, among other things. These are, I hasten to add, the same reforms that opponents of school desegregation have been contesting for nearly thirty years. What is so odd about all of this is that representatives of both positions have been waging a war over reforms that are unlikely to transform the schools or larger society except in outward appearance. Both the advocates and the opponents of desegregation either ignored the organizational context within which these reforms were to take place or confused changes in persons with changes in the schools. In any event, they behaved in ways that protected the institutional integrity of public education and denied the possibility of undertaking a more thorough critique of its role in sustaining an economic and social order that many find unacceptable.

The problem with approaching the chore of organizational change as an exercise in building new people or overhauling old ones is that there is no guarantee that new skills will be learned or that lessons will be effectively conveyed to the workplace by reformed individuals. Indeed, these weak attempts to recast organizational routines might have just the opposite effect. Without clear sanctions or efforts to ensure compliance on the part of an organization's staff or clients, people might treat episodic bursts of reforming zeal as nothing more than temporary disruptions in their schedule. If attempts to change individuals are to have any impact on the organization, then the reforms must be nested in the structure of the organization, the way it processes claims against itself, rewards and punishes its members, and directs labor. In short, one can not hope to reform the people in an institution without also changing the organizational context within which they work. Organizational routines can be perceived as comfortable sanctuaries within which rational persons will seek refuge during periods of trial and stress. Under such conditions it seems prudent to mark the path to enlightenment clearly.

Whether one is sympathetic to one or the other of these perspectives of organizational change does matter. Those who view organizations as rational creations and actors in an open social environment believe that school systems work for a more efficient and just society. Those who describe organizations in nonrational terms argue that school systems are likely to push for or enforce reforms only to the extent that such measures do not interfere with their preferred missions and routines. An institution operating under these principles could help achieve greater justice and efficiency in society, but as an afterthought rather than by design. It would be a more stable institution in the sense that its personnel would be protective of traditional goals and less willing to introduce new procedures, even if such changes might guarantee a more "rational" and just social order.

Reform as the Moral Equivalent of War

When former President Carter spoke of energy conservation as the "moral equivalent of war" he was greeted with as much enthusiasm as accorded unsuccessful snake handlers. Yet the idea that a warlike readiness for sacrifice or bold initiatives might be inspired without the destruction or bloodshed of war is not unknown to us. From wars on poverty to crusades against vice and ignorance, we have been a people driven by a vision of our own perfectibility. It is, moreover, a vision consistent with the idea that institutions are a source of individual and collective redemption. In the case of public education, bureaucratization was thought to be not only compatible with democratic values but also a spur to democracy and economic prosperity.[7]

These ideas constitute important themes in the civics of public education. The development of complex school bureaucracies was seen more as the driving force behind the movement for better schools than as a result of that movement's success. As one of the most important monuments to urban reform, the task of the schools was clear and the responsibility immense. Educational systems were to bring together representatives of heterogeneous and rapidly growing populations. Schools were to serve as laboratories or working models of the organizational and industrial world children would someday occupy. Inside the schools, teachers were to equip youngsters and often parents with the skills needed to achieve some measure of economic security. Each element of the public educational enterprise was to complement and to reinforce work going on in all other areas. An immediate goal of school personnel and their supporters was to limit the opportunity for social and political anarchy while ensuring that officials would be responsive to clients' needs. Long-term goals included spreading democratic ideals and softening the more insulting trappings of inequality.

Community leaders were prompted to develop new institutional supports for a society they feared was in imminent danger of collapsing around them. In bureaucracies they thought a rational order conducive to planning had been found. Building an educational institution that lived up to their ideals became a consuming passion. As we saw earlier, however, it also provided a convenient excuse for avoiding some fundamental questions about the way wealth and political power were distributed in cities.

This, of course, is a central tenet in the arguments of those who see public education as a conservative force in the conduct of economic and political affairs. There is no serious disagreement over the conditions that led to the formation of large public school systems; these individuals have read the same history of social reform as those who see schools as a liberating force, and all are familiar with the failed efforts to reconstitute city life that preceded the growth of public education in cities. Both factions agree that the expansion of educational opportunities resulted from a calculated effort to arrest expressions of political and social discord in urban areas. However, the people who view public education as a conservative force consider the bureaucratization of public education to have been less an impetus to that growth than its outcome. In fact, during most of the nineteenth century, "city schools . . . lagged behind the progress of other large organizations in their division of labor and expert direction. School administration in cities [was] . . . organized essentially as it was when the cities were villages."[8]

This seemingly trivial difference over the role and timing of bureaucratic growth in the public schools has several important implications for our understanding of educational reform and the deference to school administrators evident in desegregation plans. Far from being the cutting edge of democratic reform, the expansion of bureaucratic principles in school administration was seen as an effective way to reinforce the class divisions of an industrialized society. In a period of "cities and the growth of great industrial combinations," wrote one nineteenth-century observer, "precision, accuracy, implicit obedience to the head or directive power, are necessary for the . . . production of any positive results." Most school leaders might not have agreed with this sentiment. However,

> in the second half of the nineteenth century they worried most about the aggregate social and political functions of schooling. On all sides were threats to the fabric of society, the authority of the state: mobs and violence; corruption and radical ideas in politics; vice and immorality . . . conflict between labor and capital . . . In a disorderly society, schoolmen argued, the school must itself be a model of order, regularity, obedience . . . a prototype of a conservative republic.[9]

The sense that city residents were lost and far from any civilized outpost was apparently shared by many people, but no more poignantly than by professional educators. Neither mute nor organizationally illiterate, these individuals sought to restructure the delicate relation between those who governed and their clients in ways better suited to the demands of a new age. The principle of direct representation that had guided the conduct of public business in and out of the schools no longer seemed appropriate. The legislative model of government based on that principle had proven unwieldy and too easily manipulated by groups with parochial interests. Officials needed to be insulated from a noisy and intrusive public; the public needed to be protected from itself. To meet these needs in the schools the principle of direct representation was subordinated to two complementary ideas: neutral competence and executive leadership.[10]

Taking the administration of the schools out of politics and turning control over to a central office with trained experts emerged as proposals in some places before the Civil War, but it was not until afterward that these ideas became popular. Decentralized lay authority was replaced first by decentralized professional authority. Control over the schools was fragmented among a number of different bodies.[11] Only later did school officials manage to consolidate their control over the entire administration of the schools and the process for making and enforcing educational policies. The intended effect of these changes was to limit contact between school officials and the public. Though sometimes frustrated by local boards and elected officials, the goal of insulating school personnel from the public was gradually realized. Proponents of centralization could drop their pretense for democratic principles and come out of their oligarchic closets, as could the individual who said that he should as soon think about democratizing the "treatment of appendicitis" as speak of "the democratization of schools." "Democracy," he went on to add, "is a principle of government; the schools belong to the administration; and a democracy is as much entitled as a monarchy to have its business well done."[12]

Weaning people from the idea that they had a right and responsibility to participate in their children's education was not an easy chore. Training people to behave as if they were incompetent was long and difficult, even if ultimately successful. That this process accompanied efforts to introduce a new, distinctly modern organizational form to public education was unfortunate, but no accident. The bureaucratic model from which contemporary school systems were fashioned was used as a weapon against the perceived erosion of order in the cities. It was not used so much to change the social and economic order of cities as it was to change the people who seemed to represent a threat to its new political and economic realities. It was not used to help apprehend a future filled with greater rationality and equity but to acquire a firmer grip on a burgeoning industrial world and the changes it had set into motion.

A child growing up in any nineteenth-century American city could not see "work-family-religion-recreation-school as an organically related system of human relationships," as his rural counterpart allegedly could.[13] The provincial quality of education under those conditions could not be replicated in cities and would not have prepared urban youngsters for the more dynamic world in which they lived. School systems had to be more responsive to the changing circumstances of urban life and, as much as possible, mimic the order obvious in factories and other complex organizations of the day. Yet the open and rational organization envisioned for urban school systems proved to be too open and not rational enough for many upper-class sponsors. Such people abhorred the informal politics that flavored contact between the schools and ethnic groups. Nor did they care for the way in which representatives of those groups used bureaucratic devices like merit classifications and lines of authority to gain some measure of control over school affairs. Ways had to be found to change the leadership of boards of education, reduce their authority, and protect the professional educators who actually ran the schools on a daily basis.[14] In order to ensure a democratic way of life, the control of school systems would have to be remanded to bureaucratic monarchists.

The ascension of an executive elite did not result in politics being removed from educational matters. As historian David Tyack has noted,

> The centralizers . . . were arguing for a . . . system of politics in which power and initiative flowed from the top down and administrative law . . . took the place of decisions by elected officials. They wished to destroy the give-and-take bargaining of the ward system [and] . . . centralize control . . . in a bureaucracy buffered from popular vagaries.
>
> [The professionals] found corporate systems of decision-making to their liking . . . not only because of their scope of coverage, but because of their coercive potential.[15]

Popular participation was discouraged under the guise of improving educational offerings and fostering individual opportunity for students. Yet all students have not been assured of at least the chance to acquire those skills they would need to survive in a competitive world. Indeed, many continue to experience problems in the schools because of their membership in one or another minority group. What has been found instead is that the abandonment of districts to professional administrators has brought on a period of unprecedented institutional expansion and a severe limitation on the number and range of issues discussed publicly.[16]

Sense cannot be made of the growth of educational bureaucracies or their insulation from public scrutiny by alluding to democratic principles and notions about fair play or justice, seductive as such ideas are. One must look to the changing character of social order in nineteenth-century American cities for an answer. Central to that history was the diminishing control exercised directly by urban elites over the conduct of public affairs. Throughout that century members of the upper classes gradually relinquished their proprietary claims to a set of tools for mobilizing community residents. Control over the nature and uses of civil violence, local government, labor, and even mass movements slipped into the hands of less esteemed city residents. It was not stolen or wrestled away from the city's better elements so much as ceded by them. Representatives of the lower orders applied some of the lessons learned in the factory or in politics and built impressive labor organizations and city governments.

Changes in the politics of labor and governmental affairs compelled upper-class activists to moderate the tone of their reform efforts in arenas such as public education where they still had hope of maintaining or reasserting their dominance. What had begun as a purely defensive gesture to ward off the blight-ing influence of poorly reared and impoverished children was transformed into a progressive movement to fill everyone with democratic ideals and hope for economic security. The organizational growth of school districts was consistent, at least in theory, with the push for more rational and equitable ways to deal with a heterogeneous student body. At the same time, it served to block any immediate attempt on the part of the laboring classes or their allies to expand the focus of their bureaucratic insurgency to the schools. It also tended to confine their activities to the local school and to types of community organizing much different from those needed to operate a complex institution on a citywide basis.[17]

Representatives of cities' less well-to-do citizens were not permitted to gain control of school bureaucracies and, hence, could not use those organizations to pursue their own brand of progressivism. Instead, they were forced to react to administrative initiatives legitimated by a citywide board of education for which they had little use and with whose members they had little in common. They were offered a choice, in effect, between posing as opponents of educational reform and being co-opted through local school associations. Neither option was attractive. Nevertheless, looking back on these changes, it is easier to see why the only effective institutional pressure brought to bear on segregated districts usually came from distinctly nonlocal organizations and the federal government.

On Winning and Losing in Desegregation

Who, then, has won or is winning the great desegregation crusade? Perhaps it would be more in keeping with the spirit of the preceding discussion if we asked who the good guys and the bad guys in the battle over educational reform really are. These are difficult questions to answer. My inclination, however, is to argue that there are no good or bad guys in matters of educational reform and that this is especially true in the case of desegregation. Advocates and detractors of desegregation hoped and feared, respectively, that educational institutions could be used to achieve great social changes. Both implicitly and uncritically accepted the early propaganda of the common-school movement. The democratic ideal of treating any child as every other child's equal was something either to aspire to or better kept in civics books. This ideal was, in any event, accepted as a premise in campaigns to desegregate the schools or to keep them segregated.

People on both sides of this controversy ignored the history of successful attempts to insulate the schools not only from the influence of the lower orders but from high-minded citizens as well. Moreover, neither side seemed familiar with the role of the schools as the one institutional sanctuary for stability in a changing and disorderly world. Nor could they have recognized desegregation, at least in the North, as an opportunity to act out the urban morality play of decay and reformation for cities with burgeoning populations and industrial plants. Industrial dispersion and a white-collar revolution in the job markets of many metropolitan areas combined with the growing class and racial homogeneity of central cities to make such a connection untenable.

Desegregation could not serve northern cities as a device for redirecting explosive growth into more satisfactory channels or giving citizens something that would provide solace during a period of rapid change. Yet it could and did serve to rekindle some of the dynamic spark in cities where politics had grown stale along with an increasingly homogeneous class structure that industrial capitalism and the federal government had helped to secure. The widespread diffusion of jobs and people from central cities after World War II had made it easier to neglect, if not ignore, those persons and problems left behind. Indeed, this was only the latest expression of disconcern on the part of well-to-do persons for the welfare of communities they were leaving behind. Their withdrawal from certain types of reform efforts in the nineteenth century, for instance, coincided with their physical retreat to secure neighborhoods and the suburbs. The exodus of jobs and people during the postwar period may have been larger and may have included people who were not so prosperous, but it was not a new phenomenon. In one sense, then, the failure of desegregation in the North could be viewed as a sign of the broader failure to revive civic rituals and to enliven the basis of a civil religion that late-nineteenth-century reformers had worked so hard to establish.

The tension that once existed among the diverse elements of city populations has been dissipated somewhat by the diffusion of these different people across a much larger territory. With this dispersion went the necessity and the urge to exercise and experiment with civic rituals in order to resolve differences. It is not that public rituals have failed to inspire us and are being violently repudiated.[18] It is that they have been used to sedate us and are simply being abandoned.

The basic dilemma in public education today is that its traditional crises have all been sanitized or removed. Contrary to the impression left by opponents of desegregation, school officials have not ceded their authority to make educational policy on most occasions. Their right to conduct school affairs has assumed the status of a social fact. Exceptions do exist, but they are largely confined to instances of "insubordination—refusing to carry out an order rather than failing to carry it out."[19] The conduct and punishment of Boston's Board of Education is a case in point. In general, however, the hope of late-nineteenth-century reformers that the school system might be protected from the public has been realized. The problem is that such people subsequently lost their personal interest in those schools as they moved from the cities or sent their children to private institutions. The principal identifiers and resolvers of civil crises built and insulated a public institution to manage an "unruly" population, and then they left it unattended.

In the wake of their exodus was an increasingly homogeneous population of youngsters from working- and lower-class backgrounds who, regardless of their color, often were unfit to assume roles as workers and citizens competently. More than ever before such children need to be literate in order to compete successfully for jobs. Unsuccessful students no longer can be assured of industrial employment as could their grandparents or even their parents. They must be prepared to move into office, sales, and other white-collar jobs that require the kinds of skills that were once demanded of only a comparatively small number of persons. In short, educators today are being called upon to fulfill the mandate of the common-school movement by producing literate and informed persons for a world that finally is capable of accepting them. Yet at this crucial time the institution of public education lacks the political credibility, initiative, and types of students needed to carry out that mission. Faith in the rituals wrapped up in this public institution is approaching its nadir.

There is the potential for great irony in all this, however. Specifically, the same relentless search for security that helped to exacerbate these problems might now contribute to their resolution. The principle involved is simple enough. The caretakers of any organization will tend to behave in ways that will preserve the basic character and proficiency of that institution. This may be accomplished by continuously adapting the organization to its environment or expanding the locus of its control. Attempts are made, so the theory goes, to extend the principle of rationality to a turbulent environment or to push it to limits not previously tested.[20]

The application of this principle is apparent in the development of the public schools, but no more boldly than between 1890 and 1920, a period when many new responsibilities were assumed by the schools. With the institutionalization of the quest for moral reform and civic revitalization, it should not be a surprise to find the institution and its caretakers behaving in such a fashion. They and their allies must conduct a search for student populations of sufficient diversity in order to justify the revitalization of public rituals and civic idealism that have been central to the growth of public education for more than a century. The legitimacy of their search and encroachment into others' territories is predicated on the idea that the mystical union of the classes can still be achieved through rituals associated with public education.

Metropolitan school desegregation is the most obvious and perhaps the most appropriate way in which this principle could be realized today. This does not mean that metropolitan desegregation is any more likely to achieve great changes in this society or its people than any of the other reform crusades previously described. One cannot expect metropolitan desegregation by itself, for instance, to prod leaders into thinking more seriously about metropolitan government.[21] The Supreme Court decision that the eleven school districts in Marion County and Indianapolis should not remain separate and distinct after most other government functions were consolidated in 1969 shows us that the process may work the other way around. However, the debate over desegregation should prepare citizens of a larger region to acknowledge the existence of problems and their potential role in addressing these problems. This service has been provided before in the history of urban reform crusades, and it is important.

The push for desegregation in the South is an especially useful illustration in this regard because it anticipated some of the issues implicit in arguments over metropolitan desegregation. There was, for example, the attempt by nonlocal institutions to extend both the idea of educational equality and their own power into new territories. Although it caused a good deal of discord at the time, the intrusion of principles like equity and greater efficiency into the administration of educational policies may have been a blessing of sorts. These principles actually complemented the region's explosive industrial and urban growth, acquainting its citizens with the kinds of problems confronted by a more heterogeneous population and preparing a generation of young people for the social and economic realities of a competitive and integrated work setting. More often than not, desegregation in the South also unified white and black districts in the same county, thus helping to avoid the quarrels over equitable taxing and educational services witnessed today in the North.[22] That an institution best described as a "lazy monopoly" might rekindle the kind of civil renaissance it helped to extinguish is, if nothing else, an intriguing idea.

Change without Disorder?

The history of urban moral-reform crusades reflects the close association between social change and disorder as well as a discernible growth in the geographic breadth of reform efforts. Thus, that school districts would initiate desegregation planning on a metropolitan scale does not seem quite so absurd. Such a move no doubt would be greeted with considerable noise and resistance by many parties, including members of the district's own staff and board of education. It also could generate sporadic disorder in the form of protests and street violence. All of this might seem inconsistent with an institutional culture based ostensibly on rationality, civility, and the rule of rules. Moreover, such a step probably would not produce the far-reaching social changes that nineteenth-century reformers had hoped to secure through the schools. To my knowledge, for instance, there has been no permanent reconciliation among different social classes as a result of desegregation, whether on a local or metropolitan-wide basis. If our earlier assessment of reform crusades was fair, however, then we should not be surprised by such failures. Indeed, many of the reform crusades seemed little more than soothing palliatives and "holding actions" that covered the retreat of middle- and upper-class persons to safer places. (As today, many of these people sent their children to private schools.) The art of facilitating change without disrupting basic class divisions in metropolitan areas inched toward perfection during the nineteenth century. Now we must try to understand how a balance was struck between the two institutional drives that acted as catalysts for this process: change and orderliness.

Although there is nothing novel about this idea, the means by which it was realized has remained something of a mystery. Fashioning a compromise between order and justice is possible only to the extent that the integrity of the challenged institution is preserved. Changes in authority or in the basic mission and principles of an organization, as we noted earlier, are quite rare. Control over the apparatus through which institutional planning and coordination are realized is not relinquished willingly. Moreover, the looseness of most rules that guide bureaucratic practices often enables administrators to bend and recast even the most ambitious reforms.[23] Some accommodation to demands for change is possible nonetheless. Observers of reform efforts have noted that "outsiders" or subordinates are sometimes offered a chance to help shape policies on extraneous issues. There are times, however, when the scope of their responsibilities is broader and the impact more substantial. On such occasions an interesting trade-off occurs. The organization is influenced by the novel petitioners and its behavior is modified. At the same time, the organization's legitimacy enjoys at least some modest growth in the eyes of its clients or membership because of the display of flexibility.[24]

There is no reason to believe that either the organization's leaders or its petitioners understand the nature of their bargain or set out with a clear idea to achieve such a rapprochement. All that matters is that the authority of institutional managers and the legitimacy accorded their rule become devices for controlling and directing conflicts. In order to fulfill such an important role, the "fictional" quality of authority and legitimacy must be rendered visible through commonly accepted rituals. Only in this way can the unanticipated and poten-tially chaotic exchanges of combatants in conflict be transformed into ceremon-ial encounters between tolerant, even if openly hostile, competitors. The trick is to create images of compliance and changes in behavior—reducing displays of conflict and redrawing lines of authority—while maintaining the sanctity of the institution and avoiding social chaos. This is no mean task, and the price for failure can be severe, but no more severe than when the parties do not accept each other's "ceremonial compliance" as a sign of submission.

The implications of managing fundamental conflicts in this fashion are espe-cially important. In the words of one student of conflict, such management helps "to understand how conflicts of interest may be reconciled with the implicit cooperation involved in such ritual encounters." It also helps to account for the special treatment accorded those whose behavior represents an affront to estab-lished rituals. Thus, refusing to carry out an order becomes a "ceremonial violation" and carries with it particularly nasty sanctions, at least in comparison to those that result from the failure to carry out an order.[25] The justification for meting out disparate punishments is simple enough. Refusal to show appropriate deference to approved ceremonies does much greater violence to the fictional inviolability of an institution than does incompetence. In most instances, heresy is a far greater crime than stupidity or sloth.

Desegregation as Couvade

A crucial test of a society's strength is whether its members are able to develop techniques that enable them to manage serious conflict among them-selves. Of course, what constitutes a "serious" or "fundamental" conflict will differ in each society. In every society, however, one finds obvious differences in the ways certain types of persons are treated. Discrimination is a basic fact of organized life. Power, wealth, and status are never distributed uniformly among the individuals and institutions of a society. The customary allocation of such resources creates tensions and dilemmas that cannot be ignored. Custom, ac-cording to an observer of African tribal life, "establishes certain conflicts be-tween men, and may thus produce quarrels among them." It can also help fix the times and places where it is appropriate for such conflicts to be expressed. Just as important, however, "custom also brings into work mechanisms which inhibit the development of the quarrels and which exert pressure for settle-ment."[26] People create customary means of dispelling, defusing, or otherwise coping with the problems and contradictions they build into their own social order. That these techniques do not always succeed or may not cover all conceiv-able problems is less significant than the fact that they exist at all and succeed as often as they do.

Many outlets are peculiarly individualistic in nature. Gambling and excessive consumption of alcohol are two that come to mind when thinking about our own society. Other methods of temporary escape may involve violent acts and several people in a relatively direct way. There are other culturally prescribed techniques for dealing with such pressures, however, that entail a communal effort. Cultural anthropologists, as noted earlier, refer to this sort of communal behavior in "primitive" societies as "rituals of rebellion." The temporary crisis that rituals of rebellion create in the natural order of things is in fact a legitimate and time-honored way of condemning certain despised practices while reaffirming their significance in everyday life.

That it would take some sort of crisis to expose deep-seated prejudices or inequities probably would not surprise or distress most persons. The notion that intermittent outbursts might only enable upset people to vent their anger so that they could quickly return to their assigned roles, though, is quite another matter. It seems to those who have studied such phenomena that rituals of rebellion are peculiar to societies in which very little change occurs. A typical event might involve a memorable but brief display of bravado and violence against men by women acting out a rite through which the men's dominance as protectors and providers in the tribe is perpetuated. This kind of ritualistic posturing, some argue, has few parallels in the institutionalized conflicts of our own dynamic society. The physical and social mobility of persons in industrial societies make such ritualistic protests less likely as well as superfluous. Conflicts in advanced societies are not elevated to the realm of the mystical or religious, the argument goes. They are exhibited and resolved through more secular channels.[27]

Actions taken to address the contradictions of an industrial world would be merely ceremonies. They would lack the supernatural spark that allows us to believe in their ability to "affect our prosperity and unity" as a people. They could not work magic because the values at risk would not be "put on a mystical plane where they could not be questioned." This is crucial because "once there is questioning of the social order, the ritual of protest is inappropriate, since the purpose of the ritual is to unite people who do not or cannot query their social roles."[28]

It is the absence of serious debate over the legitimacy of a given social order and the demystification of the procedures used to raise tough questions that apparently distinguish ceremonial conflicts from rituals of rebellion. Nevertheless, a study of the latter could inform analyses of social change and conflict in our modern world. Change may be ubiquitous, but it need not be as shattering an experience as imagined. Nor does it mean that there is not great persistence in our social world in spite of changes occurring in it.[29]

No doubt there are substantial differences between "primitive" and "advanced" societies and their citizens. Among them probably would be the nature and severity of the questions people raise about the legitimacy of their social order. The profanation of techniques used to address those questions might also be included. I think, however, that it would be an error to draw too clear a distinction between the ritualized rebellions of tribal societies and the alleged ceremonial nature of conflicts in the modern industrial state. It is not at all clear, for instance, that the basic contradictions built into our own economic and political order have been addressed any more seriously than those of less advanced societies. Nor does it seem that challenges to our social order have been resolved in ways that have threatened its legitimacy and long-term stability. If this is true, there may be greater similarities between these ways of managing conflicts than we have believed. It might be that we, too, have found the creation of temporary crises a satisfactory way of exposing some of our differences without tearing apart a social order that affords a certain measure of security and prosperity for everyone.

The ritualized rebellions of tribal societies offer people an opportunity to transform familiar tensions with poorly defined causes into something explicable and at least temporarily remediable. The continuity of tribal life permits, perhaps requires, people to develop a regular way to express their dissatisfaction without disrupting established routines in any permanent fashion. Some argue that this could not happen in a society characterized by such complexity and energy as ours that makes a habit of the unexpected and offers a poor choice for those looking for continuity. Even in industrial societies, however, there is no reason unexpected problems could not also be rendered more comprehensible and subject to the influence of rituals. A world accustomed to the unaccustomed would seem to be especially receptive to magical explanations about why certain persons or institutions are struck down by one or another natural or man-made malady. Our penchant for ascribing the cause of many personal problems and blessings to the intervention of indefinite pronouns is proof enough of the continuing role that mystery plays in our daily lives. The sociological snake oil that accounts for societal evils through veiled references to a "system" shows that there is an institutional analogue to the mischief created by a "them."

A modern world is no less susceptible to or no less in need of magic and mystery than those we dismiss as being primitive. The basic dilemmas and inequities built into our own social order are no more explicable than those touching the people of New Guinea and perhaps in greater need of being described so that we might better appreciate the rituals we have developed to cope with them. This accomplished, we could demonstrate not only the great persistence of social relations in our world but also the limited threats to their legitimacy conveyed in ritualized conflicts.

The history of moral reform crusades in cities shows how mystical notions about the community were an integral part of rituals created to maintain order in the face of change and the chaos it presumably wrought. Ways were sought to re-create or, somewhat later, to fashion a new sense of fraternity among people thrown together in a world over which they had little direct control. In its own way, it was a world that must have seemed every bit as capricious and, at times, cruel as that known to small, isolated bands of hunters and gatherers. More importantly, it was a world into which people endeavored to reintroduce a measure of spirituality and communal purpose lost in the rush toward an ill-defined future. Urban reformers tried to adapt methods of bringing people together that were used in small communities, but they failed. They also experimented with new conventions and ideas about progress more tailored to the special demands of city life. In this, they seemed to fare little better. Their search ended with efforts to create a new moral order that was intended to transcend the parochial interests and sectarian jealousies of the city's various classes, races, religions, and ethnic groups. The imagery and characterization of these efforts were abidingly, if not strictly, religious. The mystery of the city was to be captured in the mystical union of its people, a union symbolized in the power of its great buildings and in the solitude of its parks. The city itself was a living entity that gave spiritual sustenance to those who occupied it.

That these efforts failed is somehow less important to us than the fact that they were made at all. The creation of a permanent civil religion that would have bound us together spiritually while ratifying our physical and social separateness was a lofty, but fundamentally flawed, goal. Yet the public ceremonies instigated in its name did provide a common point of reference for airing and overlooking our differences. The institutions fashioned over the course of a century to facilitate that reconciliation worked, even if they provided no effective means to resolve those differences. Therein lies the basis and art of ritualized crises and reforms.

Conflicts over desegregating schools provide firm examples of ritualized crises and reforms in our contemporary society. Resistance to desegregation among both disillusioned and mean-spirited Americans has been growing for years and shows every sign of finally cresting. At issue in their critique of this reform is not whether desegregation can work. Clearly, sometimes it has worked and sometimes it has not. The problem is that after three decades of experimenting with desegregation we still are not sure either how or why desegregation succeeds or fails. In a nation of mechanics and technicians, this is an unpardonable sin. Equally damaging, perhaps, has been the failure of jurists, scholars, and school officials to advance a coherent and plausible explanation of what desegregation is and what it can achieve. Their inability or unwillingness to develop programs and theories that might help bridge the gap between high-minded principles and hoary administrative problems has contributed to this situation. People might have been willing to accept difficult solutions to their problems. They could not accept such solutions in the absence of a reasonable justification for their sacrifice.

Yet we know that most courts do not initiate reforms that threaten the decision-making prerogatives of local school officials or a community's economic and political routine in the long run. How then are we to make sense of officials' disdain for these reforms? Popular discontent by local citizens, frequently nurtured by public officials, can account for some of the school personnel's willingness to avoid proposed desegregation reforms. Yet if citizens have ceded as much responsibility to school authorities as most observers believe they have, then intermittent displays of disenchantment by parents cannot explain away all or even most of the official resistance to desegregation we continue to witness. On the one hand, we find some school personnel and critics of desegregation complaining—often with equal measures of bitterness and accuracy—about the difficulties they must endure because the courts have forced them to act in one way or another. On the other hand, incidents recalled by parents and others frequently reveal a pattern of cumulative disregard on the part of school personnel in satisfying the intent of desegregation policies, if not the letter of the law. Given this model of behavior, a plausible explanation for the postures assumed by professional educators and their supporters against judicial or federal intervention in desegregation cases could be difficult.

There is no contradiction between the dramatic objections of school officials and others to desegregation and their actual behavior, however, if one appreciates the parallels between desegregation and certain rituals practiced by some primitive tribes on the occasion of a child's birth. Referred to as couvade, the series of prescribed acts of self-denial and isolation from the other tribesmen that prospective fathers undergo often incorporate some show of sympathetic labor pains for everyone's benefit. These exercises in collective and self-delusion offer an opportunity for the father to reaffirm his fidelity to the tribe's rules even though he does not suffer the pains that accompany the birth process. The other tribesmen are thus provided with a fairly routine way of reasserting their control over each other and the primacy of the tribe's welfare that does not threaten to undermine the stability of tribal routines in any permanent or fundamental way. It is as if the fact of birth—like the fact of segregated schools—requires some response, albeit a ritualistic and stylized one, in order to satisfy a larger communal interest.

That the father does not experience the real trauma and changes that come with birth is irrelevant. What matters is that he creates the impression of having done so and that others accept these acts as signs of his conformance to some standard of right conduct or higher authority. The desegregating district, like the histrionic father, can act as if it were laboring under a system of pains and penalties, bringing about some profound change, and satisfy the rules set before it without achieving the changes that adherence to the rules was to have ensured. It can submit itself to purification rites that include filing government reports, changing policies, and transferring students and employees without compelling its members to honor the code of conduct implied in those acts. Officials need not sacrifice their control over the daily routines that determine either what their organization does or the likelihood of substantial changes in its conduct.

Comparing school desegregation to a couvade experience provides us with a direct and easily recognizable means of explaining how we have managed to "punish" offending school systems that have segregated minority children without jeopardizing their ability to perform assigned tasks. What supporters of desegregation either fail to appreciate or care not to acknowledge is that school systems, like any other form of social organization, are set up to accomplish certain things and to attend to some problems while paying substantially less attention to others. In our common ignorance, we somehow have come to expect a complex institution to readily adapt to a collection of detailed and frequently contradictory changes in policy. And we have done this without assisting its caretakers in the difficult process of reforming decision-making routines and avenues of political influence that led to the framing of unconstitutional practices in the first place. Busing, calls for metropolitan desegregation and quality education, and even sporadic displays of violence become issues that various parties manipulate to the ultimate benefit of those whose primary concern is to fend off perceived threats to the authority of school officials over the formulation, implementation, and evaluation of educational policy.

Suggestions that local officials be permitted to construct and carry out their own desegregation plans by relying on established political routines may only reinforce their monopoly over educational policy making and lead to the specter of so-called second-generation desegregation problems in the schools. Enacting such plans under the aegis of the courts could compound the problem further by legitimating the very procedures that first led to the development of unconstitutional policies. Of course, such a desegregation process would possess those traits apparently desired in ritualistic crises and reforms.

Desegregation crises and reforms are significant events in that they provide a medium through which some of our most serious disagreements can be expressed and coped with in a customarily prescribed fashion. Rituals organized to exhibit rebellion against an established order give vent to a society's contradictory values and practices without requiring a real effort to make them more consistent. The rebellion is licensed, even encouraged. Its exaggerated tone and content give expression "in a reversed form to the normal rightness of a particular kind of social order."[30] Conflict can be a source of unity and strength for a community. Conflict also can tear apart a community. Ritualized crises and reforms provide a means through which some balance is struck between these very different outcomes. It is here that the ritualistic crises and reforms associated with desegregation make their most enduring and important contributions.

Conclusion

The choreography of ritualistic rebellions is inspired by the problems we choose to address and limited by the issues we hope to ignore. In the struggle to compose a workable yet civil order, ways had to be discovered to preserve the economic vitality of cities without seriously altering the basic relations among their several classes, ethnic groups, and religious communities. Conflicts were unavoidable, but the nature and timing of confrontations could be influenced and, in a manner of speaking, institutionalized. What emerged from efforts to order contacts among these different people was a set of beliefs about appropriate public and private conduct and a collection of institutions intended to reinforce and give substance to those precepts.

Far from jeopardizing the integrity of established economic and political institutions, such conflicts are culturally prescribed and help to ensure the legitimacy of our civic rituals. The apparent threat to the legitimacy of these rituals is a crucial element in the success of ritualistic conflicts. However, the principal, if implicit, concern of involved parties is to protect an institution's authority and the credibility of its conduct. Social scientists have observed this phenomenon in a variety of contexts and described it in equal diversity.[31] The most popular of these sociological bromides—"buffering the technical core"—captures nicely the analgesic effect of such conflicts upon important institutional practices and contradictions built into our social order.

It is quite literally the case that the durability of these traditions is tried in combat. This, in a sense, is what sociologist Anselm Strauss means when he states that there are no final agreements on authority or limits on negotiations over it. These limits are constantly being tested, toyed with, or ignored. Sometimes they are temporarily or even permanently altered through such contests. Almost certainly, they are refined. More often than not, however, "silent" bargains are struck over such matters, and certain nonnegotiable limits on questions of authority and institutional legitimacy are imposed. These may remain relatively fixed for some time.[32]

That the "important" things would not be negotiated under these conditions would clearly be unacceptable to some parties. Ritualized conflicts become a means through which such concerns can be raised frequently with considerable passion. More importantly, they always possess the potential to become more than a symbolic challenge to an institution's authority. It is because we are unsure of the moment that they can become more than a symbolic challenge that ritualistic conflicts or rebellions are as threatening and effective as they are. The crises they accompany serve to make the painful, unnatural reality of change an acceptable, if at times only temporary, fact of life. School desegregation would seem to be a good example of how ritualistic conflicts and reforms work in this way.[33]

What matters, of course, is that ways be found to stretch or amend the limits of an institution's authority without violating the latticed integrity of the community it serves. Ritualistic conflicts and reforms are the tools we have developed in order to negotiate a path between those who wish to confront the basic inequities of our system and those who would maintain inequitable conditions whatever their cost. The crises, of which these conflicts and reforms are part, create the illusion that far-reaching change is being demanded and delivered. At the same time, little is being done to ensure that the codes of proper conduct implied in such changes are actually being modified.

What was accepted as meaningful social change at one point may be viewed in retrospect as having been trivial and mundane. Both assessments would not only be valid but would also testify to the importance of ritualized conflicts and reforms in weaning us from one comfortable notion about social order and introducing us to another. The symbolic crisis that captures our attention and yields to painful resolution helps us avoid or at least render more manageable the problems of composing order in complex organizations: unpredictability and ossification. It is no great achievement when people create devices through which conflicts can be initiated, pursued, and terminated. It is a matter for celebration, however, when those same conflicts are so ordered as to enable everyone to recognize and accept symbols of victory or defeat and to resume a more congenial pattern of social intercourse.[34]

Much of the imagery crucial to the instigation and termination of ritualistic crises is derived from our political traditions and, in the case of desegregation, especially from the courts. In these arenas, symbols for right conduct are forged and defended, and rules for ending our disagreements are worked out. The problem with conflicts, even the ritualistic ones, is that they always contain an element of uncertainty. The ways in which groups can begin or end formal disagreements are relatively few in number, but not fixed. Given these concerns, a good deal of attention will be paid in the next three chapters to the way ritualistic conflicts surrounding desegregation were structured in St. Louis. Who was allowed to participate and who was not? Which issues were germane and which went unstated? Which reforms were permitted and which were ignored? How was compliance measured and who measured it? When was the ritualistic confrontation among the parties officially terminated? What happened afterward?

To the extent that decisions over such matters are made with an eye toward encouraging only modest changes, the implementation of reforms should be left as much as possible to the offending institutions. School systems need to control the pace and character of the implementation process, if the symbolic challenge to authority implied in desegregation is not to be allowed to blossom into a full-blown assault on rights and privileges. Only when a district stridently and obviously refuses to comply with an order—pitting its authority against that of a court or federal agency—is it likely to have its own credibility questioned and its procedures monitored closely.

The ill-defined period of time that commences with the planning for desegregation and ends with a declaration that a district has achieved a "unitary"—nonsegregated—status is most treacherous. No one can be sure exactly how various parties will behave. The most obvious threat, of course, is to the school district. Its policies and practices related to the treatment of minority youngsters have become suspect. School personnel must work to control the involvement by "outsiders" and to keep their attention focused on those matters prescribed by the courts or federal agencies. At the very least, there must be an increased number of ceremonial encounters between school staff and other parties. What, if any, matters of substance are dealt with on those occasions depends largely on how well structured the conflicts have been up to that point. Beyond the threat posed by these new or unwanted participants, school officials must worry about keeping the district in working order during a period of considerable stress. Relations between the central office and its several schools may be modified by a desegregation order and the programs the order brings. How this new arrangement is made more tolerable and consistent with standard school practices is a serious matter. A related source of problems centers on events within each school and its classes. Here, too, the ability to innovate may be limited by poor communication, insufficient resources, or the sheer orneriness of school personnel.[35]

How successful a district is in introducing symbolic reforms can be cataloged by noting the changes made in policies and administrative procedures. Most of the reforms should involve "personal" rather than "structural" changes. Changes in the nature of rewards and sanctions or the way they are distributed should not be evident. Changes in who has the authority to make such decisions are also unlikely. Instead, ritualistically prescribed changes in school attendance, dress, speech, beliefs, and personal conduct—things that have little to do with determining school policy—should be emphasized. When a sufficient number of these indicators have changed for the better, then the institution is said to be reformed. There are other examples one might think of in which institutional reclamation is achieved through the redemption of its membership. School desegregation is simply one of the most obvious.

There is an unmistakable urge to blame all of this nonsense on a small group of persons dedicated only to the maintenance of their own power and prestige. Such persons no doubt exist in all organizations and, at least within certain limits, can do a fair amount of mischief. Yet there is no conspiracy among officials to do so. They devise no plan to hoodwink the public or to present reforms that are little more than symbolic sops to one group or another. If there is a conspiracy, it is one in which we all share responsibility and collaborate—willingly. If there is a plan, then it is one that has evolved over hundreds of years and now exists as part of our cultural baggage. The notion that there may be a conspiracy and plan is attractive; it appeals to our sense of mystery and need for magic.

Still, it is flawed. In order to accept it, one must assume that there are "good guys" and "bad guys" and, furthermore, that the "bad guys" are a whole lot smarter or sneakier than the "good guys." My own experience suggests that neither assumption is tenable. This impression was supported during numerous visits to schools and community meetings and was confirmed in many interviews with officials and citizens alike. Commenting upon the political acumen of his superiors, one midlevel school administrator pleaded with me to accept the reality that "those guys really weren't *that* smart." I think he was right.

What follows, then, is an exploration into the uses of ritualized conflicts and reforms in two midwestern school districts. If one looks to these cases for signs of desegregation's inherent validity as a tool for transforming American society, one will be disappointed. It is, instead, a description of how complex organizations and the people they serve work to manipulate the conditions under which they must fight each other so as to minimize the carnage that can come with institutional change. If the reader sees this process as an attempt to renegotiate the limits of institutional power and the authority of the public in the conduct of its own affairs, I think he or she will be better served.

6. Desegregating the Ferguson-Florissant Reorganized School District

The bureaucratic monarchists who oversee the operation of urban school systems help to perpetuate an economic and social order that many people complain about but are reluctant to overturn. Educators also manage to perpetuate their own control over a complex organization, however, that is supposed to act as a forum for the expression of new ideas. It may not be possible for an organization to fulfill both these tasks simultaneously. It is possible, though, for the organization and its caretakers to make it appear that both are being accomplished successfully. Like the fabled tortoise, school systems manage this feat by projecting an unassuming, even deferential, image before the public while doggedly, if unimaginatively, pursuing a single goal. In a world that finds rapacious profiteering distasteful, an organization combining both sloth and greed as operational tenets has a distinct advantage over its competitors and predators.

Progress of a sort can be achieved by this type of organization, but it cannot be measured by changes both inside the institution and in its accountability to the public. If the history of public education is taken seriously, then progress is to be measured by the growth of the institution and its expansion into a larger territory with many different people. We know from previous reform crusades that the rationale frequently used for reform efforts was to bring a broader and more heterogeneous population under the civilizing influence of the reformers. This goal was not secured easily. Groups mobilized for and against proposed changes. How they conducted their campaigns and their ultimate success was determined in part by the resources—money, manpower, allies—available to them.

The legacy of reform efforts consists of three complementary achievements. First, advocates of reform gradually reduced the level of fragmentation in the delivery of vital public services and consolidated the authority to address urban problems in large institutions. Second, advocates of reform were able to maintain and, indeed, to capitalize on the degree of fragmentation within the polity. The formal barriers to administrative centralization could be overcome by appealing to the public directly, through nonroutine channels, and by avoiding the difficult task of recasting the entire political infrastructure of cities. Opponents of reform, particularly in the area of education, might succeed in stalling the introduction of proposed changes. In the end, however, they were unable either to stop reform efforts or to exert substantial control over them because of the fragmented political and organizational bases from which they operated. Third, and finally, advocates of reform managed to downgrade serious questions about the unequal distribution of money and power in their communities. By avoiding conflicts over more fundamental divisions or problems built into their social order, both the reformers and their opponents were able to achieve modest changes while ensuring the continuity of regular commercial and political life in the community.

How the legacy of moral-reform movements has been articulated in the St. Louis metropolitan area was first discussed in Chapter 3. Some of the basic changes occurring in the area's economy and population since 1950 were identified. Also noted was the failure of existing political routines and public institutions to address problems created or perpetuated by these changes. Efforts to consider some of those problems through nonroutine channels began in earnest only after regular political channels proved to be ineffective. School segregation provided a rationale for even raising these issues at all. We know, however, that problems related to the unequal distribution of wealth in the St. Louis metropolitan area have been raised only partially or only in the context of a few school districts. Moreover, the proposed solution to the inequities heretofore identified has touched only a portion of the schools and students in those few districts.

Debate was fierce over the plans involving those districts and the more recent contest over metropolitan desegregation. Nevertheless, the process of changing St. Louis into a modern metropolitan area has proceeded without interruption. Discussions about desegregation have contributed to this process, of course, by keeping the public's attention focused on St. Louis as a metropolitan area with metropolitan-wide problems. In keeping with the tradition of urban reform crusades, however, the underlying tensions revealed in our social order as a result of urbanization are no closer to resolution today than they were a decade ago.

Campaigns to reform life in urban areas fill a public vacuum created when existing organizations cannot or will not respond effectively to changing economic and social conditions, though the success of these efforts is guaranteed only if they are adopted into regular political life. Historically, success has been expressed through the creation of great institutions that are supposed to address problems without spending a lot of money. It also is crucial that this process of institution-building be viewed as beneficial, as nonthreatening, and as inevitable as the process of city-building that spawned it. For this reason, if for no other, what goes on inside the institution being created or, in the case of desegregation, rebuilt matters a great deal. The public's perception of the reform and institution-building process must be that it is working well or better than expected. Otherwise, we could not suspend our judgment on the worth or legitimacy of the institution in question. The all-important norm of civil inattention that shields a person or organization from undesired scrutiny might be abandoned.[1] Suddenly, the unthinkable could become the possible.

A crisis, such as that thought to be brought on by desegregation, increases our sensitivity to the conduct of an institution. At the same time, it provides the institution with a measure of freedom or discretionary power that might not be enjoyed during "normal" periods. The latitude of action given to the institution's caretakers may increase during a crisis simply because unreasonable conditions and unforeseen events sometimes require harsh or unpopular steps to be taken. A crisis also may make it more difficult for citizens and potential critics to suspend the norm of civil inattention. We are inclined at such times to allow for a greater margin of error in the conduct of our public institutions, just as we are inclined to give persons under a great deal of stress "the benefit of the doubt" for their indiscretions.

School desegregation may test the limits of civil inattention, but it dare not be permitted to break them. The crisis surrounding the creation and implementation of a desegregation order is kept under control through the efforts of both supporters and opponents of reform, although they are not aware of it. Were they cognizant of this fact, the mystery and drama of their culturally prescribed crisis might be exposed and jeopardized. In any event, they do manage to contain the crisis and sustain the norm of civil inattention behind which the process of institution-building is allowed to progress. They do this, as has been noted before, by worrying about changes that have a comparatively meager impact on the long-term operation of the school system. Changes affecting the assignment of students and staff or their satisfaction with a new setting are far from trivial for the people involved. However, such changes do not in themselves alter the basic configuration of power within a district or between a district and the public.

If I am correct, the crisis created by transferring students and school personnel or by introducing other "desegregation-related" reforms allows district officials to accomplish things they might not otherwise be willing to propose.[2] They need not take advantage of this opportunity, of course. Nor may they be aware that they are doing so when they do act. Still, school administrators know that under the best of circumstances it is difficult to close schools, fire staff, or increase the amount of funds for education from local sources. Such things may be more feasible if they are called for under a court order. The normal pressure officials expect may be dampened dramatically because district officials' hands were tied. Thus, as southern school officials learned during the 1960s, there may be some real financial advantages to desegregation. Such advantages or savings may be essential for urban districts that have lost many students and a good portion of their tax base.

There are political advantages to be realized as well for the district that complies, however hesitantly, with a desegregation order. School officials may use the court order in order to push through new educational programs that have no necessary relation to desegregation but can be included as part of a desegregation plan at someone else's expense. The most likely sources for this kind of indirect subsidization would be state and federal agencies. Officials might also move beyond mandated personnel shifts and initiate more general programs for reducing the number of school staff or redefining their job description. The connection between such changes and desegregation may be tenuous at best; but the crisis occasioned by a desegregation order may make it easier for officials to do things of a politically sensitive nature with little political cost to themselves.

One should not expect to see all these alleged advantages being realized in every desegregating school district. Not all districts, for instance, have experienced substantial drops in enrollments and increasing pressure to close schools and dismiss staff. Such problems are more likely to be observed in urban areas like St. Louis. That Missouri districts must work from a balanced budget and obtain the support of two-thirds of the voters in any large tax referendum also increases the chances that the "desegregation crisis" might be used to accomplish things that cannot be secured through routine politics. Finally, one might look to segregation cases in places like the St. Louis area for examples of efforts to use desegregation to demonstrate the feasibility of metropolitan governance and reform. Some of these things will become more obvious as we analyze aspects of school desegregation in the Ferguson-Florissant Reorganized School District.[3]

Some Benefits of a Desegregation Crisis

Our sense of what constitutes a crisis in a desegregating school district would lead us to look for great and manifestly painful disruptions to educational routines and the authority of district officials to make and carry out policies. To the extent that these things do not happen as desegregation occurs, the district and plan in question would almost universally be declared a success. Another important factor in determining the success of a desegregation order would be the degree of cooperation or noninterference by "outsiders" with the district's operation. Our conditioned understanding of desegregation crises would have us expect actors outside the school system to seize upon the opportunity to influence educational policies or to carry out some type of mischief. A desegregation crisis would be minimized to the degree that such outside interference could be contained. I have argued that such a view of desegregation crises is both insufficient and probably wrong. It most certainly reveals a bias—one well grounded in American urban history—in favor of maintaining the prerogatives and insularity of school systems and their caretakers. It also is a view that has little room for the alleged curative powers of a good knock-down-drag-out fight among committed partisans. I have taken the position that such battles are neither all that nasty, nor terribly threatening to the stability of a public school system. They may, in fact, serve to enhance the long-term stability of the institution. Successful desegregation, under this alternate view of crises, might inspire fights that school officials and their supporters could win. More importantly, perhaps, such a desegregation crisis might contribute to broader economic and social changes in an area by drawing attention to the problems being created.

School desegregation in the Ferguson-Florissant Reorganized School District bore little resemblance to the crisis we have been taught to expect. Opportunities for a crisis certainly were there. Judicial orders merging districts for the purpose of desegregation are rare, and this was the first time that suburban districts had been consolidated for this reason. Administrative and teaching staffs had to be merged, debts settled, differences in tax bases and salaries reconciled, and new lines of influence forged within the district and between the district and the public. Then there were the standard problems associated with desegregating the student bodies. All the conditions disposing a district and community toward a desegregation crisis were present. Every rule, role, and relationship in the district could have been questioned and modified under the guise of a desegregation order. Yet they were not, and the crisis proved to be less severe than had been anticipated.

What one found instead were efforts by all parties to limit the number and types of issues subject to public deliberation. Authority to handle most problems was placed in the hands of administrators from the old Ferguson-Florissant School District. The court, as we shall see, expressed little interest in reviewing the conduct of the district. Attempts by outsiders—especially parent groups—to influence the desegregation process met with little success. The merger and desegregation order were a success, however, as far as the court and general public were concerned.

The apparent success of this court-ordered plan extended beyond its quiet introduction and the perpetuation of administrative control over educational matters. In the great tradition of reform movements, "progress" was achieved by consolidating the authority to pursue social change in a larger organization serving a larger and more heterogeneous population. No mere theoretical exercise, the practical benefits of reducing the level of fragmentation to this public service were obvious from the start. Money was saved when schools were closed under the court order. In fact, the reorganized district closed more schools and released more staff between 1975 and 1982 than any other district in St. Louis County. Reductions in both instances were about 25 percent. Enrollments for the district dropped approximately 38 percent during the same period. The court order made it easier to accomplish these savings. Exactly how much easier is difficult to say. However, most other county districts have not done as well in responding to decreases in their enrollments.[4]

Politically sensitive changes or changes involving the imposition of administrative prerogatives have always faced resistance of one or another kind. Reformers, even reluctant supporters of reform, often have turned to nonroutine ways of amending the public agenda when the barriers to change seemed too numerous or impenetrable. On such occasions, reformers took advantage of political fragmentation by keeping opponents from different territories from banding together or even identifying each other. This was comparatively easy to do in the present case. Opposition to the court order—other than that expressed in court by the three districts—was expressed by at least four groups and several community or political leaders who seemed to have little in common.[5] They also seemed to disband rather quickly after the order was upheld on appeal. The most pronounced resistance to the desegregation order by whites came from Berkeley parents who successfully petitioned the court to reduce the enrollment of minority children in several schools. However, resistance to the district's handling of the order came largely from minority citizens who complained about the treatment of black youngsters in several schools, especially the high school to which Kinloch's students had been sent. This resistance failed. The inability of black parents across the district to join together on a sustained basis was a factor. Geography played a part in this, but so did social class antagonisms among blacks. The poorer black families from Kinloch and Berkeley were all but voiceless. The basis for effective political mobilization against district policies had been stolen through the merger. I suspect, however, that this was felt more strongly by black parents.

The failure of grass-roots action in this case extended even into the ranks of groups whose members supported desegregation or at least wanted to make this plan work smoothly. One group, the Association of School Integration in Smooth Transition (ASIST), was biracial, and its membership consisted of local residents, businessmen, clergy, and educators. ASIST held monthly meetings at members' homes, where persons reportedly talked about the fears of black children and otherwise held pleasant seminars about race relations over coffee and cookies. The organization disbanded several months into the first year of student desegregation and had no impact on the desegregation process. A second group, Action Against Apathy, was composed of white middle-class housewives who had been involved in efforts to help black youngsters attending schools in the old Ferguson-Florissant School District. Their offers of assistance in this case were refused for the most part. The group was allowed to conduct a workshop at the high school scheduled to receive Kinloch's students, but attendance was not mandatory, and, according to teachers who did participate, it was not heavily attended. This group had no discernible role in the desegregation process after the workshop.

One can think of plausible reasons offers of free assistance might be rejected from groups like Action Against Apathy or even a university-based group. Perhaps there was no need for the specific services being offered or the groups in question had been proved incompetent. Money certainly was not the issue because officials spent considerable sums on a range of technical consultants who put on "dog-and-pony-shows" not dissimilar to those that had been offered for free. I think the district's rather rigid approach toward citizen involvement can be better explained by its officials' desire to maintain control over the entire desegregation and merger process. Paraphrasing one administrator, they decided "whom to bring in, when, and for what reasons." This was a commonly held attitude among officials whose response to virtually all public activity was to seek protection behind the veil of privacy provided by the court. In this manner school officials were able to resist encroachments by "outsiders" while satisfying the legal guidelines imposed on them. Informal negotiations among "fellow professionals" at the county, state, and federal level led to agreements over the nature of the merger and desegregation plan. And this pattern of bargaining and accountability became the basis of all subsequent discussions about the plan's implementation.

More will be said about how citizen involvement was kept to a minimum a bit later. For the present time, it is enough to note that administrative consolidation was successful in part because the polity remained fragmented. Whether the school system would or could prepare students competently was never considered. Of course, one of the benefits of having public disputes over things like busing is that one can avoid more sensitive matters related to education as well as other social and economic changes. Several of these issues—maintaining independent school systems and ignoring racial segregation in county residential areas—were discussed earlier in the book. However, there were other ways in which this merger and desegregation process contributed to the building of a modern metropolitan area. First, it demonstrated that a consolidation and desegregation plan involving several districts could be carried out peacefully and could realize monetary savings. Second, districts that complied with a court order might face little interference with their regular operating procedures and political activities. Third, cooperative districts might be spared the expense and trouble of being involved in a longer and more bitter dispute over mandatory busing and consolidation with the city school system. County districts participating in a voluntary busing plan with the city had much smaller increases, and sometimes outright reductions, in legal expenses compared to districts contesting their role in segregating the city schools.[6] Finally, the merger and desegregation process has shown people the futility of resisting big economic and social changes in their metropolitan area.

Of particular interest here is the way that the school plan complemented the drive to expand Lambert Field, the area's major airport and neighbor to Berkeley and Kinloch. Plans to keep the area's major air terminal in Missouri were predicated on the expansion and modernization of the existing facilities. Arriving and departing flights already passed right over homes in Berkeley and Kinloch, rattled dishes, and interrupted conversations with painful regularity. Early proposals to extend the airport's runways called for the demolition of hundreds of homes and three schools.[7] There has been no demolition of the schools as of 1985. Berkeley's junior high has been closed, and the elementary school is scheduled to be closed after the 1985 school year. The high school still is in operation as a part of the Ferguson-Florissant Reorganized School District. That Berkeley already had lost its school system gave its citizens one less basis upon which to fight the airport expansion. On the other hand, the expansion makes it easier for Ferguson-Florissant officials to justify the maintenance of their school facilities and actually enhances their tax base. The latter benefit will be realized after an industrial park is built in Kinloch with the help of the airport on land acquired as part of the expansion program.

Organizing Support for the Plan

The significance of what did and did not happen to public education in the merged districts must be placed in the broader context of metropolitan development in this region. The contribution of this case to the process of metropolitan growth cannot be overstated. All the parties to the suit behaved in a way that reduced the chances of widespread disruptions to educational and political routines in the three districts. At the same time, they were establishing a precedent for the subsequent handling of a bigger, if no more ambitious, plan to draw the county and city closer together. Whether the parties to this suit understood or even speculated about the broader implications of their actions is irrelevant. Most of them probably did not. What matters is that they behaved in a fashion that made it possible in the long run to facilitate, however grudgingly, the creation of closer ties between the city and county. This kind of reluctant collaboration, as we have noted, is an important part of ritualized rebellions.

People complained bitterly about the prospect of a merger and desegregation plan involving Kinloch, Berkeley, and Ferguson-Florissant. The defendants in the case pursued their legal challenges as far as they could. Yet they also took the precaution of working out among themselves the broad outline and some finer details of a merger and desegregation plan. This is the plan that the federal court accepted early in 1975. After appeals to the court order were rejected, the plan was implemented with little fanfare and even less noise from the public.

It was a lean plan, written with the idea that both busing and interference with school officials' discretion would be kept to a minimum. The court was able to dispense with most of the grittier details of putting together a school system. State guidelines were available to make sure that bills were paid and titles to various properties were transferred appropriately. The court, having already approved of a busing and student transfer plan, had little to say about racial discrimination except that it was no longer to be practiced. Steps were to be taken to make everyone feel at home in their new schools. Most of the court's attention was directed toward district governance and especially the composition of the new board of education. Four of the six seats were to go to members of the Ferguson-Florissant body. Kinloch and Berkeley would each have one representative.[8] The Biracial Advisory Committee, composed in part of former board members from each district, was mandated. That committee was to assist the board of education in all matters related to the desegregation plan. It should be noted that arrangements for both these bodies had been described in the plan submitted by the state and St. Louis County Board of Education to the court in 1974.[9]

A concerted effort was made by district officials to gain the acceptance of area citizens for the plan once the appeals process had been exhausted. Administrators met with public and private leaders from the area, major civic and religious groups, local realtors, and media representatives. Apparently convinced of the administrators' professionalism and good intent, these people and groups generally stepped aside and left district officials alone. School administrators also held a series of meetings with groups of parents in order to answer their questions about the plan and reduce the level of tension in the community. Administrators characterized these meetings as "tough" or "difficult." Yet they also believed that parents had walked away thinking that their children would be safe and would receive a good education. Whatever anxiety parents felt by the time desegregation began in September 1976, it was not enough to prompt them to resist the plan's implementation.

In light of this response, officials saw no reason to sustain their previous level of activity with the public. Subsequent contacts with citizens over the desegregation process were confined almost exclusively to meetings with the Biracial Advisory Committee and the Emergency School Aid Act Advisory Committee that was established to oversee the solicitation and spending of federal desegregation aid under the Emergency School Aid Act (ESAA). It, too, was composed of people with a history of working in and for the schools. As we shall see, school officials used the court and federally mandated monitoring bodies to legitimate their preferred policies while controlling the groups' access to information needed to make reasoned choices among available policy options. One result was that when problems did arise in the plan's implementation no one was capable of pointing them out or compelling officials to change their policies. Had the court not inadvertently added its credibility and support to district administrators' efforts to structure and limit the public debate over desegregation, the end result probably would have been nearly the same. To be sure, the court provided a symbolic buffer between the system and its constituents, but district personnel had carried on their own aggressive and largely successful effort to convince people and interested groups that they could be trusted to treat all youngsters well. For those who came to doubt the sincerity of the administrators' pledge, there was little that could be done.

There was one other substantial way that continued support for the desegregation order was guaranteed. It involved the selection of officials from the old Ferguson-Florissant School District to direct the newly merged district. An implicit agreement among officials from all three districts to support such a move was apparent in the recommendations made to the court in 1974 by the state and county boards of education. The Kinloch and Berkeley school districts would be brought into the Ferguson-Florissant School District. Former administrators from Kinloch and Berkeley were relegated to posts with comparatively limited responsibility. One became head of public relations and another was put "in charge" of desegregation, although he reported to administrators from the old Ferguson-Florissant School District. In the judgment of the superintendent's old staff, the subordination of Kinloch and Berkeley administrators was necessary because they "were not prepared to handle a big district."[10]

Little doubt existed that Ferguson-Florissant officials intended to maintain their preeminent role as district policy makers. Some calls to old Berkeley and Kinloch administrators were relayed through the offices of Ferguson-Florissant officials. Many phone conversations were tape-recorded without the knowledge of the party calling into the district offices.[11] The widely held suspicion was that the calls were monitored in order to determine who was calling the Berkeley and Kinloch people. The best explanation identified for this kind of control was that Ferguson-Florissant officials were trying to gather intelligence on potential troublemakers from Berkeley and Kinloch, since it was assumed that they objected to district policies. Whatever the motivation for this activity, however, it had a chilling effect on the willingness of many staff—not just those from Kinloch or Berkeley—to discuss problems with the desegregation process openly and thoroughly. Of course, it also had the effect of reducing the chances that the public and the court would be apprised of potential difficulties. The formal record of the district's performance would remain unblemished in the absence of a major outbreak of violence in the schools or community.

There was nothing hasty, unpremeditated, or necessarily wrong in any of this. Those involved in the merger and desegregation process had every reason to expect that educational routines might be disrupted, perhaps severely so. They took steps to ensure that the problems associated with creating and desegregating a new district would be kept to a minimum. People working through established institutions imposed or introduced a degree of order into the process of rebuilding the three districts. Questions of justice or about putting the same old administrative foxes in charge of a remodeled chicken coop were suspended so that the business of conducting public education in the area might proceed. Raising such questions might have served only to interrupt the more important task of building a bigger and more efficient school system.[12]

Structured Ignorance

An important element in all ritualized rebellions is the avoidance of lingering problems that no one is especially keen on discussing. Structured ignorance is an important corollary to structured crises. In the case of school desegregation, many problems are kept from public view in a bureaucratic limbo that protects as well as deadens the institution. This is both a necessary and unfortunate consequence of ritualized crises and reforms in public education.

The dilemma is how to distinguish problems that arise naturally out of any effort to do something new from problems that emerge because of administrative incompetence or meanness. The frequent recurrence of a problem or its severity might be important signs that something is wrong. Another indicator that people are ignoring or avoiding more serious problems also has a long history in urban reform crusades. It is the inability or unwillingness to see problems as a group or collective phenomenon rather than as a consequence of a person's poor qualities. Common to the way that district personnel handled the difficulties of new minority students was the attitude that the problem was in each child. The child's eventual success would depend on his willingness to drop bad habits learned at other schools or at home and to adapt to the better routines of his new school. There was no recognition among many administrators that the problems of this new student population were group—not individual—specific. Hence, they could not understand that the solutions needed to address those difficulties might involve at least some changes in the institution's routines and policies.

Twice during the 1976–1977 school year, staff from the University of Missouri–St. Louis Center for Metropolitan Studies (project staff) met with district administrators and submitted detailed reports of problems that had been identified with the district's desegregation plan. The reports were based on information gathered from site visits at the school receiving junior-high and high-school students from Kinloch and discussions with school staff, students, parents, and other interested citizens from across the district. Recommendations on how school officials might address those problems were presented, and alternate solutions were discussed by everyone present. District administrators stated that the findings only indicated the occurrence of a few isolated incidents and added that unless the names of the complaining parties were divulged—these parties had been promised anonymity—they would disregard the observations entirely. Several officials later stated in confidence that the difficulties noted in the reports were entirely accurate and that nearly everyone in the central office had been greatly upset and angered by the needs assessments. Included among the problems noted in these sessions were:

1. an apparent pattern of disparate suspension rates for black and white students (and several instances of physical abuse or neglect of black students),

2. the inability of many black youngsters to participate in extracurricular activities because of transportation difficulties or discrimination,

3. the use of prejudicial materials and language by some teachers in the classrooms,

4. the lack of provision of educational services by the staff of an educational center located in Kinloch,

5. the perception of black youngsters that they were not wanted at their new schools,

6. the reliance of white staff on black staff to have ready-made solutions to problems involving black students,

7. a distrust on the part of Berkeley and Kinloch residents of school staff and the procedures used to communicate with parents, and

8. the absence of any effective oversight of district programs related to the desegregation effort.

It seems that the treatment of minority youngsters was designed to keep them quiet, if not out of the way. Criticism of their educational training up to the time they began attending schools in Ferguson-Florissant was merited in many instances. The facilities in Kinloch generally were inferior. The course selection was poor. Students had a lot of free time during the school day and apparently chose to spend much of it on nonacademic pursuits. Unfortunately, these criticisms were elaborated into a wholesale condemnation of their social customs and a convenient rationale for their every failure in the new district.

Students who did ask for help during that first year usually did not receive it. A number of those same youngsters eventually dropped out of school. Some black students were reported to have been encouraged to drop out of school, take a high-school equivalency test, or participate in work/study programs. Other students, teachers complained, simply were shipped off to study halls where they would be out of the way.

The court order had stipulated that every effort be made to integrate the new students in their new school and to incorporate some of their traditions. However, from the day classes began (Kinloch buses were late and high-school students were paraded into classes already underway) to the end of the first year (a survey completed by all students asked them to assess the changes they had witnessed since the arrival of Kinloch students), little was done to encourage Kinloch youngsters to claim the school as their own. A traditional social event was dropped from the school calendar and only hastily rescheduled after black students angrily protested its omission. Black students—not only those from Kinloch—who in previous years had been members of a national honor society were not recognized as such on graduation programs. A choral director stated his unwillingness to use black compositions and gospel music because it was not "real music." A group of twenty black and white youths left a classroom after an exchange of insults and squared off to fight in a corridor. A call for the principal prompted the black students to scatter. The list of incidents such as these was long and covered the entire year.

Reports of problems continued to be received after project staff had stopped making site visits to the school. District personnel reported that a number of black youngsters were failing most of the courses they were taking each quarter. Some were being encouraged to drop out of school or to take equivalency exams. In at least one instance, a student claimed that a teacher had demanded to know why he should be helped to complete his academic work. Reportedly, attempts by some black staff to help resolve such problems were consistently ignored or rebuked. Instead, black staff maintained that they had been criticized for not "handling" minority students in a way that reduced the pressure on white personnel.

Matters related to the study of "black culture" continued to be a sore point. On one occasion, the high school's Black History and American Minorities courses were dropped from the curriculum. There had been no discussion of this change before the Biracial Advisory Committee, and the first time parents learned of it was in an addendum to that school's 1978 Fall course catalog. The principal of the school maintained that the decision to omit the courses had been made by a committee of faculty members and students and that prior to a final decision he had met with all department chairs to discuss the inclusion of deleted materials in other courses. The superintendent also was said to have approved of the changes. Staff informed us, however, that several teachers had met once to consider such a change, but no decision about any courses had been made and no date had ever been set for a subsequent meeting. The discussion among department heads had taken place, but the Black History and American Minority courses were reportedly considered too important to modify in any way. Two other courses (Psychology and Social Change) had been identified as more appropriate targets for deletion or change, if small enrollments and overlapping subject matter were a problem. None of these points, though, was brought up during the several private and more open meetings between school staff and concerned citizens. The only admission parents were able to extract from the principal was that the "plan" to integrate the black studies' materials into other courses was not yet in print; it was "just an oral plan." It also became clear, however, that the lower enrollments in the black studies' courses could be attributed to the manner in which the curriculum discouraged students—black as well as white—from taking courses related to minority experiences.[13]

As a result of these meetings, it was decided that a memo citing the reinstatement of the two courses would be distributed to all students who would be attending that high school next year. It was important that such a memo be sent out as quickly as possible, because the registration period was nearly over by the time the reinstatement decision had been made. The memo was not sent out immediately, however. In fact, it was not until one concerned parent called the principals of all the junior-high schools whose students would be attending the high school in question and then they called the high-school principal for clarification that the memo finally was sent out.

The threat to the Afro-American curriculum was real enough and was perceived by some black parents to be an insult to their history. Many minority students (and poorly prepared white students for that matter) faced a far greater danger, however, from the tracking system that was introduced while the district still was under the court's supervision. Minority students were reported by school staff to have been placed almost as a matter of routine in the "easy" track of classes. Very few blacks enrolled in the "advanced" or "college prep" classes. I have no idea how easy it was for white or black students to move from the "easy" track, through the "intermediate" track, and finally into the "advanced" track.

It was alleged that schoolteachers and counselors did not pay much attention to the attendance of black students. If one missed school for three to five days, a note was sent to the youngster's home. Otherwise, it seems, black students were free pretty much to come and go as they pleased. Absenteeism among black students was reported to be high. So was tardiness. It also was said that they were allowed to sign themselves out because of illness. The academic performance of many black students apparently was so poor that in this high school three types of diplomas were intended to be made available to graduating seniors: the regular high-school diploma, a "precollegiate" diploma, and a certificate of attendance.

It was doubted that many blacks would receive the "precollegiate" degree. An "honors program" scheduled to go into effect at the same time was expected by some staff to make this all but a certainty. The program, as it was originally organized, required a student to enter it in the freshman year. Some expected the entrance requirement to be loosened, however, to enable students to move into the program at a later date. However, the chances are slight that a black or a white student "encouraged" to take easier courses would be able to break into a more difficult track.[14]

For at least some minority students, therefore, conditions seemed to change little. The facilities may have been more attractive and there may have been a wider variety of courses available, but that in itself was no guarantee that students would be encouraged to take advantage of them. If reports received from staff and parents were true, no more attention was being paid to minority students in their new high school than would have been paid to them in their old, inferior, segregated high school.

One cannot ignore the possibility that what was seen and heard during site visits was not representative of conditions at the high school. One also might fear that respondents inflated the stories they told or collaborated with one another in order to present a uniformly exaggerated picture of events at the school. One might especially be wary of reports received after the site visits were terminated. Yet the same reports were received from white as well as black students, staff, and parents, and these reports were consistent with what project staff had observed. They could not be discounted. One might exercise some caution when evaluating a frantic parent reporting how her child was roughed up by his elementary-school principal. It is the same skepticism practiced when being told by an administrator that people are quite satisfied, after witnessing a meeting of ministers and elderly people planning to protest school policies. It was difficult to reject the idea, however, that something was wrong.

Minority Staff Problems

School faculty and staff proved to be especially sensitive to the emergence of a pattern in the little problems they witnessed daily. Whites as well as blacks spoke of their frustration and lack of experience in dealing with the issues raised in a desegregating school. Blacks expressed greater anxiety about the problems they saw because many white teachers and administrators turned to them for answers. They feared what might happen if they failed to give a correct or useful answer to a question. Despite their insistence that they could not provide cogent insights into all aspects of "the black experience," they continued to be asked to perform special tasks in the quest for better race relations. On occasion they were asked to stand by a white administrator chiding a black student "just in case the kid went off."

A number of black staff at the high school found this situation difficult. Some left the district to teach elsewhere or left teaching altogether. One black teacher with an excellent record charged the district with not reprimanding a white superior who had disrupted her classes during the better part of the first year of student desegregation. She also charged that administrators were responsible for long-distance phone calls to her family suggesting she was an alcoholic and on the verge of committing suicide (witnesses overheard school personnel giving out the phone numbers to the school employee who made the calls). The teacher resigned late in the year. Her white superior was not reprimanded for his conduct.

Several of the black staff reported that they (and sometimes their white colleagues) were used to "cool out" black parents with complaints. The "cooling out" might involve promises that officials would look into their complaint or include revelations that the parent's child had been in trouble before. These staff had been advised to make sure that "nothing blows in the community" or that they not "get blacks all riled up." Yet they also stated that on occasion they would violate the orders of their superiors and tell the parents what really was going on. They did not do this often, they maintained, because they knew their jobs might be jeopardized. One black staff member assigned to inform black parents of their child's suspension informed us that his principal had requested that he surreptitiously tape-record those meetings. He refused and later left the district.

Not all attempts by school staff to keep things quiet involved the private humiliation of black parents. Events in one predominantly black elementary school seemed to indicate that white parents also could think of themselves as being discriminated against and powerless. A classified ad in one daily newspaper invited anyone who had "a problem and can't get it corrected" to call a local number. I called the party and learned that several parents had placed the ad in the hope that they might identify others with complaints similar to their own. They claimed that their school's black principal was "prejudiced in behalf of black kids." They supported that allegation with a series of stories about the physical harassment of white children by their black peers at the school. Neither the principal nor the board of education seemed concerned with these complaints, so the parents said they had called both state and federal officials in order to see how to file a formal grievance against the district. The parents maintained that they were told that they would need the names, dates, times, and descriptions of all alleged incidents before any federal official could get involved. This had led them to place the ad.

By the time I had reached them, several parents had contacted them already. Among the respondents were a black mother who agreed with their charges and a white parent whose child did not attend the school but "could not believe that this sort of thing could go on." Based on my own experience, I thought it unlikely that these parents would enjoy any more success with their complaints about black prejudice than their black peers had with their allegations about white discrimination. It is difficult for parents to amass a record of such events as they are occurring, much less after the fact. They have few bureaucratic skills and, obviously, little contact with each other.

If one assumes that reports of problems by staff, students, and parents were not contrived, it is difficult to understand why there is no public record of them. There are at least two related reasons. First, as many problems as possible were handled informally. Typically, according to school staff, parents were convinced that they or their children were the problem. Even if they were not entirely convinced, the chances were good that they would not pursue a complaint against the school. The strategy was especially successful when a highly regarded Kinloch resident was sent out to meet with parents. Her job, according to many observers, was to satisfy the parents that something would be done and to urge that they not get "uppity" in the meantime. Parents said they did not think that their patience was rewarded, but neither did they expect to take any more action against the district. The second way the "public relations facade" was maintained was through the use of court and federally mandated advisory committees and sometimes even federal officials to legitimate district policies. It is to these aspects of administrative control of desegregation that we now turn.[15]

An "Open" and "Nonrational" System

In Chapter 5 some attention was paid to organizational theory. I described some approaches that help account for the behavior of a bureaucracy under a good deal of pressure to change its practices. A desegregating school district certainly falls into that category. Most of what we know about school desegregation from experts such as social scientists and lawyers leads us to expect a school system to behave like an "open" and "rational" organization. Its caretakers respond to demands for change by outsiders and readjust policies and routines in a fashion that helps the organization fulfill its mandate more efficiently and equitably. School desegregation is somewhat unique in the sense that boards often are appointed to ensure that reforms are carried out. The general public is also supposed to have an interest in seeing that these groups are doing their jobs. In other words, there are watchdogs to make sure that the school system is more "open" and behaves more "rationally" than in the past.

The approach taken in this book, and somewhat less explicitly by other observers of educational reform, leads us to expect a different set of responses by persons involved in a desegregation crisis. I anticipate most school systems to behave like "open" and "nonrational" organizations. School personnel respond to some demands for change but never act in a way that might disrupt their long-term control over the creation and implementation of educational policy. Such a disruption might be necessary, however, if the hypothetical goals of desegregation were to be achieved. This, according to our alternate explanation, is not a big concern of school personnel. They seem to be more concerned with potential threats to their job security and status than with the alleged benefits of desegregation for students or society in general. Moreover, their concern for social stability seems to be shared by the general public as well as by those powerful outside forces like the courts thought to be most interested in pushing the reform process to its limits. Groups assigned to report on the progress of mandated changes would not be likely to interpret or to carry out their charge and thus would undermine the authority of school officials and, more generally, the legitimacy of public education as an institution. Their task as watchdogs for reform is to make sure that the school system appears to be more "open" and "rational" than it really is or can be, given everyone's overriding interest in maintaining a congenial and predictable social world. The crisis they all face is ritualistically prescribed and resolved more or less to everyone's satisfaction.

Ritualized conflicts cannot be resolved successfully without a fair amount of official ignorance of problems that continue to plague us or that result from the introduction of highly stylized remedies. In the absence of a record that such problems did exist it would be difficult to justify the imposition of more aggressive remedial actions. The service rendered by some school staff and the monitoring bodies in the Ferguson-Florissant Reorganized School District was to ensure that the official record for desegregation reflected few of the reported problems. These problems did not exist as far as school officials, the court and federal government, and general public were concerned. The system officially had behaved like an "open" and "rational" organization. Unofficially, it had behaved like an "open" and "nonrational" organization.

The Biracial Advisory Committee made a substantial contribution to the phenomenon of official ignorance. It apparently made few site visits on its own and established no procedures through which citizens or school personnel could transmit information about problems (or successes) on a routine basis. Nor had it developed clear lines of responsibility and accountability either to the court or the community that it represented, other than having the minutes from monthly meetings included in the yearly report to the court.

The reports to the court contained a good deal of material. Among the items included were extensive lists of activities and projects supported by federal funds that were to have been undertaken as part of the district's desegregation effort. There was no indication, however, whether the projects in question had succeeded or failed and no indication of their impact on the desegregation process. Neither the court nor the federal agencies ever questioned this significant omission. In fact, one school administrator told project staff that federal representatives from Kansas City had informed school officials that the "evaluator's" position in their initial proposal could be cut out. The district has no official evaluation department. Hence, there was never a formal review of the various programs' effectiveness.[16] In the absence of a more thorough review of the desegregation programs' successes and failures, the Biracial Advisory Committee's proceedings provided the only continuous record of the plan's implementation.

Reading those minutes one gets the impression (an impression that was affirmed by attending a number of meetings) that the group's members relied heavily on district administrators for information about the plan's progress and policy options covering a range of issues. This does not mean that there was unanimity on all issues—far from it. However, as several committee members complained one evening, up to that point the official minutes—which were recorded by school employees—failed to convey just how much disagreement and discord there frequently was during meetings. Even if the procedure for recording and transmitting discussions had been changed as a result of this revelation, it probably would have had little impact on the group's decisions. People sitting on this committee, by virtue of their "advisory" status, had no significant recourse but to accept the suggestions made by administrators on most occasions.

The situation was not much different for the ESAA Advisory Committee. It was responsible for holding public meetings so citizens could review and suggest changes in proposals for Title VII funds. It also was to review curricular changes, participate in the screening process for hiring staff in the eleven schools affected by the plan, and monitor and evaluate each of these activities. This committee, composed of parents, students, school personnel, and civic leaders, had a diverse membership but no more effective power than its court-appointed cousin.

That it too depended upon the leadership provided by district administrators was abundantly clear during the public hearing in which the second year's funding proposal was being reviewed. Parents and residents complained that they were being forced to approve a proposal that they had not seen before that evening, having been told that it would be their only chance to offer suggestions. They also wanted tб know why portions of the document were missing (only a draft of some sections of the proposal had been distributed), and why several previously discussed problems had not been addressed in the papers they were reviewing.

Foremost among these problems was the alleged ineffectiveness of an "educational center" located in a redecorated Kinloch school building. The center was to have served children from across the district, but it was revealed at the meeting that publicity about the center's programs had been distributed only in Kinloch. Furthermore, instead of offering educational programs, the center's staff had provided some of the services normally offered by social welfare agencies in Kinloch, such as taking people to food-stamp centers and delivering toys at Christmas. This angered agency heads—one of whom sat on the ESAA Advisory Committee—but administrators defended their actions. Although all of the center's staff were dismissed before the start of the second year of classroom desegregation (officials privately conceded that it was because of the problems aired at the public meeting), district administrators offered no explanations for their conduct on this or any of the other problems raised by parents. The ESAA Advisory Committee had no discernible impact on the proposal and, with the exception of disclosing that the center had been intended to placate Kinloch parents who had lost their schools and not to serve the whole district, the committee exercised no positive influence over the introduction or handling of ESAA-sponsored programs.

Discussions with U.S. Department of Justice representatives revealed that they were aware of the monitors' poor performance and, indeed, that some problems probably were being hidden from public view because of the way the monitoring efforts were organized. But without documented proof that problems existed or, at the very least, more vigorous complaints from citizens, they were powerless to act. The department itself would make no substantial effort to develop such evidence, but would consider it seriously if it were made available. Nor would the Civil Rights Division (CRD), the department's legal branch, make a recommendation that the Community Relations Service (CRS), the department's section responsible for resolving community disputes through nonlegal channels, be sent in at this time. There was an intradepartmental rule that CRS not formally move into a case without the CRD's permission when lawyers had jurisdiction. CRS representatives did come to St. Louis and conduct an informal field study of the situation. Although the report submitted to Washington contained a recommendation that CRS take some steps to address the problems that had been unearthed, no subsequent actions were taken. In addition, letters sent by citizens asking for assistance were never acknowledged. Part of the reason, as reported by a Department of Justice official, was that the CRS regional office in Kansas City had vigorously resisted getting involved in such a potentially serious and politically sensitive case.

If the Department of Justice's own bureaucratic inertia made it immune to requests for assistance—at least in the absence of massive violence—school officials were not unable or unwilling to exploit the agency's internal pecking order for their own advantage. Before the CRS conducted its field study, for instance, a CRS representative was told by the superintendent that the legal branch had made an extensive survey of the district's programs and given them "a clean bill of health." That statement alone was enough to completely halt the informal investigation being made by the field officer at that time. Upon further investigation, however, it was revealed that the "survey" had consisted of approximately one hundred long-distance phone calls to parents of Kinloch grade-school students regarding their feelings about the desegregation process and the busing of their children. It should be noted that several Kinloch parents and officials were unable to discover anyone who had even heard of such a survey, much less participated in it, and that the Department of Justice, for reasons of protecting the parents' privacy, declined to reveal names. In any case, despite the obvious displeasure of Department of Justice officials at having an admittedly "unscientific and confidential survey" used by the superintendent in that manner, they did not reexamine their assessment of the district's conduct or encourage a closer investigation by the CRS.

The court also demonstrated an unwillingness to inject itself into problems alleged to have arisen out of the district's handling of the desegregation process. Meetings between the judge and several Kinloch residents and civic leaders highlighting some of the concerns they had with the district's policies led to no direct action from the court, save a promise that Kinloch would retain its seat on the board. It was reported that the superintendent expressed dismay over hearing about the concerns second hand. The district's policies were not changed, and to our knowledge the judge took no additional action.

The court's apparent callousness to the grievances of minority citizens appears less so once events surrounding the meetings are considered. The group that met with the judge called itself the City of Kinloch Committee of Concerned Citizens (CKCCC) and had close ties with the school system. Several of its members worked with or for the district. The judge gave the CKCCC responsibility for writing and submitting a minority report after their initial meeting. Successful attempts were made, with the assistance of project staff, to acquire a number of handwritten and tape-recorded messages documenting problems, the names of offending school personnel, dates of alleged abuses of students, and detailed requests for assistance. Before these materials could be sent to the judge, however, they were "lost" by CKCCC members. When parents complained about this loss, CKCCC leaders blamed it on project staff. In lieu of a report the CKCCC submitted a "memo" to the court. Instead of receiving a detailed indictment of school policies and specific personnel, the judge reviewed a re-hashed version of the general concerns he already had heard.

It is small wonder that there was no formal record of desegregation-related problems in the schools. In the absence of any significant oversight by civic leaders and grass-roots organizations, the responsibility for critiquing and helping to amend desegregation policies fell to the court and federally mandated committees. Neither of these groups, however, pursued a course independent from that suggested to them by school officials in most instances. Of course, without their own staff and any operating budgets, they would have been hard pressed to compile a thorough record of what was going on in the schools and to offer credible alternatives to district policies. But their reluctance to move on problems even when informed about them was striking. Part of this reluctance can be attributed to the support granted to district administrators by the white majorities on each committee who might have seen little advantage in doing anything that might have enhanced the position of blacks in the schools. An equally important source of the committees' ineffectiveness, however, was the unwillingness of most black representatives to fight for their lower-status peers. Given these barriers to a full disclosure of desegregation activities, it is not surprising that district officials could argue before the court, federal government, and the media that everything was working smoothly—and could be believed.

A Rationality All Its Own

I spoke earlier in this chapter of the difficulty in distinguishing between problems brought on by a novel situation and those attributable to administrative stupidity in its varied forms. Of course, these are not mutually exclusive conditions. Administrative meanness and incompetence can worsen any problem and dramatize those that come with reforms, however well planned they may be. A desegregation plan places an added burden on school officials. Not only do they risk having their errors publicized but they risk being declared racist as well. No mean point, jurists have spent nearly thirty years debating where to draw the line between behavior that may be offensive but legal and behavior that is racist and punishable.

School personnel also take this distinction seriously—so much so that they are likely to spend a good deal of time convincing themselves that they are not racists, merely misunderstood. One can make an occasional honest mistake. One who is tainted by racism is perpetually bad and requires scrutiny. Behavior that is mistaken ought not to be declared racist and ordered changed. Personnel may rationalize that even if it cannot be excused, it can be pardoned. Thus, the ability to define oneself as mistaken but not racist has great practical value for school personnel. It enables them to behave in a way that discriminates between white and minority students or staff as long as they do not intend to hurt one or the other race. The routine manner in which educational policy is made and carried out is not likely to change much under such conditions.

There were several ways this end was achieved in the Ferguson-Florissant School District. One set of strategies used to address students' academic difficulties consisted of something called Learning Opportunity Teams (LOTS) and, in the desegregated high school, a much-heralded counseling system. A second set of strategies was used to deal with students' social problems. Included here were a districtwide grievance system and a high-school committee composed of students and a faculty supervisor. The most important device, however, was the package of workshops offered to staff as part of their preparation before and during the first year of desegregation. These workshops brought staff together in a relatively informal setting and gave them an opportunity either to gather "expert" information or to share tales of their experiences with other staff.

The major educational and social innovation adopted by the district was embodied by LOTS. These teams consisted of teachers who were hired to provide assistance in the classroom and to serve as consultants to school personnel on interracial problems. Each of the eleven schools affected by the student reassignment plan had a team. Unfortunately, the teams were uniformly unsuccessful. At a districtwide LOTS meeting during the spring of 1977, members stated that they had no idea what their duties were, received little direction from their coordinators, and, in some instances, did not have the training their specialized tasks demanded. The teams were not around too much longer. Funding delays and reductions probably contributed to their speedy abandonment.

School staff at the one high school receiving Kinloch students, while upset at their team's failure, had always believed that their advisement system—pairing a number of youngsters with one adviser for several years—was their academic and social "early warning system." The advisement system had earned high marks several years earlier when the school had been evaluated. Its orientation toward meeting the peculiar needs of individual students worked better for its largely white and more middle-class student body, however, than it did for the large number of poor, black students suddenly thrust into a new school.

Some teachers knew of desegregation-related problems. However, project staff were told by other teachers that they had no personal knowledge of the discriminatory practices about which a number of minority students were complaining to selected minority staff members. Some black students who met with their counselors stated that the sessions were perfunctory reviews of their records, not detailed talks about their problems and aspirations. White students also may have had similar experiences, but many black students complained informally about these problems to project staff. Black staff became surrogate advisers in many instances, though on many other occasions students just got lost in the advisement system. At one point, for instance, a black staff member of the school passed along to their counselors the names of some sixty black youngsters who had expressed their frustrations with the new school. Checking back one month later, he found that not one of the students had been contacted. During the same period, it was reported, nearly a quarter of those students dropped out of school.

The real value of LOTS and the advisement system was that they failed to identify problems. This was terribly important in a district where successful desegregation was measured largely in terms of the absence of widespread or organized discontent. Officials maintained that there were no significant morale or discipline problems, and they supported their contention with survey data purporting that Kinloch students were comparatively happy. The results were summarized in the district's yearly report to the court along with a note that students had made little use of the grievance procedure required by the court.

The grievance procedure submitted by the school district and approved by the court blended the school principals' insistence that some discretion in matters of discipline be maintained and the Biracial Advisory Committee's recommendation that students be assured of receiving equal treatment.[17] The procedure made no provision for students and parents to be involved in its implementation, other than as aggrieved parties. Records of discussions regarding a student's problem were kept irregularly, and then not by an independent recorder but by district employees. Minority staff, as noted earlier, were often assigned the task of explaining to black parents why their children had been punished and discouraging them from pursuing appeals. They were also instructed not to share information regarding alternatives to out-of-school disciplinary measures. All of the proceedings involved with student discipline were controlled by school staff and administrators. There was no external review of the procedures at any stage once the Biracial Advisory Committee approved of the original proposal outlining rules and regulations for students. The discipline decisions made by building personnel were rarely, if ever, overturned by district administrators.

Parents and students were required to submit written explanations of their decision to press complaints. Apparently, this rarely happened. Counsel for the district reviewed these complaints to determine if there was justification for further appeal. Unless counsel for the district agreed that the complaint was justified, the student's right to appeal was terminated. These decisions were handed down without the opportunity for the student to secure legal services. If the district's lawyer agreed that the student's rights had been violated, the student and parents would be informed of additional steps they could take within the system.[18]

In the fall of 1976, district administrators told a group of visiting officials from the Center for Community Justice that they had not publicized all the available levels of appeal for fear that parents would use them. They also indicated they felt that the hearings procedure did not place an unfair burden on the complaining party. District officials said that, although the hearings process was strictly administrative and made no provision for the external review beyond the board of education, few students (probably no more than ten throughout the district for the entire previous school year) had made use of the procedure. Yet it is clear from the way the terms "grievance" or "disciplinary appeal" were defined that the great bulk of students' problems would not have been addressed systematically or recorded in the court's record of district activities. The amorphous character of "racial discrimination" made it unlikely that any given student could have argued the fine points of the law with the district's attorney. This severely limited the chances that complaints about racial discrimination would be processed.

None of these concerns about the hearings procedure would have been critical had student grievances or complaints been handled effectively within the schools. However, the informal manner in which students' concerns were addressed appeared fragmented and inconsistently applied. The high-school student council and even a Biracial Student Advisory Committee set up in response to student complaints were unable to ferret out problems for the school's administrators to work on. At least in the committee's case, it was clear in the first year that the handpicked students did not enjoy the confidence of students having problems. The "nice kids" from both races who sat on the committee seemed more sensitive to this flaw in their group than did school staff. One white student noted that a special effort would have to be made to reach students with problems because the group had no "representatives" from that population. The group did not accomplish this feat with any regularity or notable success.

The committee accomplished some things in later years. Its most notable success was to provide an opportunity for youngsters willing to make desegregation work better to identify one another and to engage in group discussions or intermittent programs. At one point, the group grew from a dozen to nearly sixty students and pursued a more aggressive course in setting up programs within its own school and even among the district's several high schools. Part of the credit for this success undoubtedly belonged to the new faculty supervisors who sought and received some outside funding for their projects. Part of the credit also must go to building administrators who supported the group.

The services provided by the committee are not trivial. In fact, the group was one of the most pleasant surprises to come from this school's experience with desegregation. Nevertheless, it did not fulfill its original purpose of identifying students' concerns and problems so that they might be better addressed by school staff. The group occasionally was called in to work with students who were fighting or were unable to resolve a question involving racial considerations, even though more basic problems were overlooked. Black students' academic and extracurricular performance was generally poor. Youngsters were still "tracked" into less challenging courses or were not helped to acquire better skills so that they might become "untracked."

It is possible, but hard to believe, that many school staff were not aware of the social problems between white and black students or staff. Differences in academic and extracurricular performance are quite another matter. Yet little attention was paid to these more obvious problems when teachers from the high school were brought together in order to assess the first year of desegregation and to prescribe actions to make the second year even more successful. Indeed, staff spent most of their time working through a series of real and "hypothetical" situations "with the potential for racial or prejudicial implications."[19] Most of these situations involved the kinds of social slights and misunderstandings of which so many staff had expressed ignorance.

Teachers were asked to categorize these incidents according to the amount of racist intent they thought the act revealed. The "interracial-situations rating scale" had a range of six parts:

1. Conscious racism deliberately revealed in actions
2. Conscious racism expressed in unconscious actions
3. Unconscious racism expressed in unconscious actions
4. Racist actions caused by lack of experience or unexamined cultural myths
5. Action not racist by intent but easily misperceived as such
6. Humane behavior, free of the potential for racial overtones

The authors of the scale did not maintain that it was rigorously designed or scientific. They were members of the school's staff and led the group discussions. It takes no great genius to see, however, just how difficult it would be for anyone short of an experienced psychotherapist with a detailed case history to render such a judgment on a person's actions. Some of the explanations are silly. All of them encouraged discussants to avoid any analysis of the ways in which their work settings or routines might have led people to behave in a more "racist" fashion.

Here are two "incidents" brought before a group of teachers:

Incident 1: Office assistants selected by the secretary or principal were all white students.
Incident 2: A white coach congratulates black athletes by putting his arms around their shoulders. He only verbally congratulates the white players.

The responses of teachers to these incidents help to dramatize just how difficult it was to respond to these stories in a reasonable fashion. Responding to the first story, a teacher wanted to know whether these incidents "are all about white prejudice against blacks?" A second simply maintained, "We don't select our assistants that way. This incident does not fit our school." A third was still puzzled about the classification scheme and asked, "What is unconscious racism? It's difficult to say how blacks would view this situation. White students might think of it as reverse discrimination." Comments made by other members of this group were similar to these and offered no insight into what was right or wrong about the alleged process of selecting office assistants.

Responses to the second story provided more definitive analyses of that situation. "I can't interpret this as racist," one teacher stated. "All kids may not be treated the same. Each has differences." A second teacher argued that the coach "was trying to overcome his own racism." "Yes," said a third, "it's a conscious attempt to convince the athlete that he is accepted. It's not racist behavior." However, another teacher said that the coach was just a racist who was trying "to cover it up" by being nice to the black players.

These incidents and responses are typical of those heard throughout the workshops. No serious effort was made to elaborate upon any of the teachers' answers. It was not clear from these discussions what should be done in order to improve conditions in the school, although teachers were asked to commit themselves to changing something about their attitude or behavior during the next school year. Indeed, based on these statements, it is not even clear that most teachers thought that there was anything in need of changing. No one ever told them that certain types of behavior were inappropriate or that some routines at the school might have become less appropriate because of desegregation. Nor were staff warned that their indiscretions or mistakes might cause themselves or others problems. Obviously, no basis for changing institutional routines and policies was built into these exercises, and none was ever changed.

Conclusions

The Ferguson-Florissant Reorganized School District satisfied the criteria for successful school desegregation laid down by the courts and federal government. More students attended desegregated schools after the merger among the formerly independent districts. There was little overt disruption to educational routines because of the merger and desegregation. Most importantly, the formal record offered no evidence to support the idea that a bigger merger involving more county districts or the city school system could not be undertaken successfully.

It is no accident that the commonly accepted signs of a desegregation crisis were not found in this case. All the parties involved worked to limit the number and variety of issues open to public debate and scrutiny. There were only two occasions when this arrangement failed, and neither was terribly serious. The first arose near the end of the first year of desegregation. A number of white Berkeley parents complained that too many black students were remaining in that town's schools. These white parents thought their schools also were segregated. They petitioned the court directly and over the objections of district counsel, requesting that some of their black students be bused into Ferguson-Florissant schools. The court accepted their petition. Yet the court later took no action when black parents approached it with complaints about the conduct of educational and administrative routines.

The second occasion arose shortly after the start of the second year of student desegregation (1977–1978). A protest march to district headquarters by some ten to twenty black students from Kinloch was covered by the media. The students and several parents presented the superintendent with a list of seven charges.[20] A meeting was scheduled at the high school. At the meeting the superintendent listened to these and other complaints and told the students to take them to the principal. If he did not satisfy them, they should contact him. After the meeting the district's black liaison to Kinloch was reported to have hollered at the students, telling them to shut their mouths and stop causing trouble. The superintendent was heard to have called the seven points "a pack of lies." Except that it received a little bad publicity, however, the district was not forced to change any of its practices.

Given the experiences of other desegregating districts, these two episodes must be dismissed as relatively minor. If anything, they help to illustrate just how tightly school officials were able to control every aspect of the merger and desegregation process. They worked hard to convince people that the district was run by skilled professionals, and they succeeded. They claimed and reasserted their right to be left alone by the public. The all-important norm of civil inattention that protects us from unwarranted or undesired scrutiny was tested in this case, but it was not broken. The crisis befalling the Ferguson-Florissant Reorganized School District was ritualistically prescribed and resolved in like manner.

Postscript

In the spring of 1983 the superintendent "voluntarily" resigned from his position. He had a bit more than a year left on his current contract. Several members of the board of education threatened to force him out because of the way he ran the merger and desegregation plan. These members and one administrator maintained that schools had been closed or attendance boundaries changed in order to satisfy white parents. The board's president agreed with the superintendent's contention that his resignation had not been rushed because of these allegations. Upon his retirement from the district, he assumed a position as a court-appointed financial expert for the metropolitan desegregation plan. It was reported that one black member of the board of education feared the former superintendent "would indulge in the same sort of 'economizing' at the expense of black students that he used in supervising court-ordered desegregation of the Ferguson-Florissant District."[21] Such fears may have been overblown, but the former superintendent did exercise some influence as head of the court's budget review committee. Indeed, as the remaining parties to the suit continued to bicker about the costs of desegregation, several judges from the Eighth U.S. Circuit Court of Appeals mused about broadening the committee's discretion in settling these questions.[22] This, no doubt, would have increased the former superintendent's stature.

In the meantime, problems related to desegregation in his old district continue. A suit was filed against the district in June 1983 by black parents who maintain that their daughter was placed in a segregated classroom and given unauthorized tests "in retaliation for [their] complaints of discrimination" in the district.[23] This kind of segregation began, the parents said, around September 1980 when the federal court released the district from its supervision. No further action on the suit had been taken as of January 1985. Also being considered in January 1985 was a proposal by the Berkeley City Council to secede from the Ferguson-Florissant Reorganized School District. Citizens of that community were angry because of plans to shut two of the city's three remaining elementary schools in 1985. Such an action, were it initiated, would prompt a good deal of legal interest because of its impact on the whole district's racial balance.

7. Maintaining Old Barriers in a New Metropolitan World

Officials of the Ferguson-Florissant Reorganized School District had taken considerable comfort from the idea that no one would pay particular attention to their "little" desegregation order.[1] They knew that the case against the city school system had generated a good deal more interest and probably would for some time into the future. It was a fairly safe bet, then, that their merger and desegregation plan would not be examined too closely. Events proved them right. The trial judge released them from active review even sooner than many observers expected. They also were excluded from early discussions involving a metropolitan desegregation suit and voluntary student exchange with the city. Yet their apparent success in implementing a merger and desegregation plan might also have proved their undoing.

In June 1982 lawyers representing the city schools asked the court to include the consolidated district as a defendant in future hearings. The primary consideration was that should a metropolitan desegregation order someday be considered, the contribution made by Ferguson-Florissant schools to the area's segregation problem ought not to be ignored. Lawyers from the county district argued that its status as a "unitary district" should continue to protect it from any further legal entanglement in a metropolitan suit or desegregation order.

One board member from the city school system chuckled at the prospect of dragging the county district back into court. He was quite aware that the publicized successes of that district's desegregation plan had been contrived and overstated.[2] Yet he had absolutely no interest in having the district's record reconsidered and criticized. He even doubted that the court would allow such testimony. Instead, he wanted to "march district officials across the witness stand" and have them "brag about the wonderful job they had done." This, he reasoned, would support the city district's contention that an interdistrict merger and desegregation order is feasible. Like the administrators of the county district, however, he considered the proposed consolidation of so many districts to be the greater challenge and potential accomplishment.

A former member and president of the city board of education was even more explicit about the connection between desegregation and the way public education ought to be organized. "I'm convinced," he said, "that the only answer to the delivery of education in the metropolitan area is through a metropolitan

126

school system and desegregation is a tool by which to accomplish that." Disparities in wealth, declining enrollments, and bloated school administrations made it imperative that something be done. Desegregation was the excuse to get those problems addressed. "Right now," he added, "there is probably $25 to $50 million spent administratively that can be [redirected] to the classroom. This is where the fear [of school administrators] comes in. . . . We don't need 40 superintendents and their staffs. We don't need all the separate curriculum development. We don't need all those buildings."[3] However unpopular desegregation was, it could serve as a means to reduce duplication and fragmentation in the delivery of educational services. Such changes would be consistent with the legacy of moral reform crusades, particularly if they were accompanied by the creation of a single, large institution to oversee their implementation.

It is here that the entire desegregation process could begin to take on the character of a grand conspiracy. I have heard this idea expressed in various ways by persons in and outside of school systems. Some are content to make veiled references to a "master plan." Others feel compelled to identify the engineers of that plan. Several groups of people stand out in this regard. The "business elite" ostensibly have the most to gain or lose in any substantial matter involving the metropolitan area. There are "whites" (most likely in general and most assuredly in particular) who would rather see the political base acquired by blacks in the city diluted or dispersed. Somewhat more anthropomorphically, people will speak of the "city" wanting to regain control over the "county." A few dismiss the entire affair as a petty battle among educational warlords trying to expand or retain control over their personal fiefdoms. There certainly is more than a hint of this idea in the preceding paragraph. The important point, however accurate or inaccurate these claims may be, is that these groups contribute substantially to the public's need for mystery in the workings of great changes. This, as we saw in Chapter 5, is a crucial element in ritualized crises and reforms.

The logic of such communal uprisings is not easily explained. Indeed, these crises and the reform crusades that give them substance are beyond any individual's or group's control. This is one reason they can frighten and serve us as well as they do. Another reason is that their outcome is or perhaps must be seen as preordained. In discussing the likelihood of a mandatory desegregation order for the larger metropolitan area, for instance, the board member cited earlier stated, "The attorneys representing the suburban districts have by now done enough research to have discovered the inevitable." Now, he added, "they are stuck with the problem of figuring out how to tell the public."[4]

The process by which the public educates or reconciles itself to a large problem or its proposed solutions is often difficult but rarely tedious. We still have found no satisfactory way of resolving the stresses and strains brought on by urbanization in this country. Nor shall we ever, if the history of moral reform crusades is taken seriously. What ritualized crises and reforms help us to do is cope with the problems we have created for ourselves. In this regard, the "successful" reform movement is one that has made our frail efforts to amend the social order appear as inevitable, nonthreatening, and/or successful as the process of the city-building that prompted them. An "unsuccessful" reform movement would be one that did not allow us to suspend judgment on the ultimate worth or legitimacy of the institution being challenged.[5] Looked at in another way, the successful reform effort allows us to test but not breach the limits we impose on our own civil inattentiveness. Some problems, perhaps the most important ones, remain unaddressed. The unsuccessful movement tends to make us look too closely at ourselves and demands a full accounting for past misdeeds.

The process of desegregating the city school system has been difficult, and it is far from finished. Some districts in St. Louis County already have become actively involved in this process. Whether districts in counties farther west of the city will become involved remains to be seen. Among the other items of unfinished business that will be left after city and county schools have been desegregated "successfully" are two especially tough problems. The first consists of the unequal, some would say unfair, way that the metropolitan area's wealth, jobs, and political clout are distributed among different communities on both sides of the river and among their different people. The unwieldy manner that political responsibility is distributed among hundreds of different government bodies throughout the area constitutes the second major issue that will be left unresolved by any metropolitan desegregation order. We know from past experience, however, that these two problems or conditions make an important, if hidden, contribution to the genesis and conduct of urban reform crusades.

One of the implicit themes in ritualized crises and reforms is the avoidance or dilution of serious questions dealing with the distribution of scarce resources like money or political power. The almost analgesic quality of a ritualized crisis is easily overlooked amid the frenzy and frustration of large-scale conflicts; but it is there nonetheless. Crusades involving public education have become particularly attractive over the years in part because they deal with children and the real as well as symbolic challenge of passing on a culture to a new generation. These crusades also became important, though, because people had learned to substitute school conflicts for the potentially more divisive battles over economic and, in some instances, political inequality that they did not or dared not bring directly before the public.

Divisions among people and political jurisdictions, annoying or unjust as they may seem, can actually promote more "successful" reform campaigns. We saw this clearly in the previous chapter on the Ferguson-Florissant Reorganized School District. Prejudice between the races and among blacks themselves made it more difficult to resist policies initiated by school administrators. Another factor was the merger of the three districts into one unit. Parents from these different communities had no experience in working together and sharing information. School officials were required to develop these skills and were given a clearly defined set of leaders to whom they were accountable. A similar pattern developed in the city's desegregation process. In that case, however, black and white parents did discover some common interests and began the difficult process of cooperating with each other for the sake of their children.

There is no single way in which a reform process must unfold. Nor is it always the case that a community "chooses" to work on problems through the schools that it otherwise would prefer to ignore. Local conditions and traditions prompt persons to experiment with various methods for raising and resolving sensitive matters. St. Louis has found its own novel way to ease through a discussion of some problems common to most big cities and metropolitan areas. The merger and desegregation order affecting Berkeley, Ferguson-Florissant, and Kinloch schools was an element in this process. It may yet turn out to be a crucial factor. More generally, however, St. Louis has witnessed a slow and rather deliberate process of experimentation, initially with voluntary and then with mandatory desegregation orders. This pattern was first evidenced in the city and now is being extended into St. Louis County.

How successful this approach is perceived to be may have little to do with how well race relations in St. Louis progress over the next twenty years. Still, it matters that the individual elements of this process and other relevant reforms be viewed as having been carried out efficiently, fairly, and with little disruption. It is important, for instance, that St. Louis County had a highly regarded system for educating all its handicapped and vocational students long before attention was paid to "magnet" or specialized schools as sites for "voluntary" desegregation that would attract students from different communities. Important also is the apparent successes of the Ferguson-Florissant Reorganized School District in carrying out a mandatory merger and desegregation order. Of more immediate significance, however, is the seeming success of voluntary and mandatory desegregation in the city.

Notwithstanding some highly publicized problems with site selection and enrollments, the city's magnet school program was able to expand both the number of specialized units it sponsored and the number of students from county districts it attracted. The city district's mandatory desegregation plan was implemented with comparatively little rancor. It also had the advantage of fitting comfortably within the reorganized administrative structure that had been put into effect a year earlier. Once again it was shown that desegregation and administrative reform could coexist nicely. Yet the city school system's accomplishment did not stop there. Not only was desegregation carried out relatively peacefully but student achievement scores seemed to rise as well. Competently handled desegregation and quality education had been provided at a time when public schools faced disinterested parents and hostile taxpayers. This was no mean accomplishment; and school officials took great care to keep the public informed of these feats.

The media's role in the city case was far more substantial than it had been in the Ferguson-Florissant Reorganized District's desegregation process. To some extent this was unavoidable. The size, problems, and plans of the city district were much bigger than those of its neighbors. Unlike administrators from the county district, city officials had to grow accustomed to working in a large, if not especially well-lit, fishbowl. They could scarcely afford to complain too loudly, however, because the media remained their only reliable channel for reaching the public.

Desegregation prompted parents to show greater interest in school affairs. The court case provided a forum for predominantly white and black groups to express their ideas on desegregation. It also spawned efforts by some of these same persons to initiate a broader critique of school policies *together.* The implicit threat presented by this admittedly primitive coalition was not expressed in elections for the board of education, though there did seem to be for a time a resurgence of support for grass-roots representation. Instead, the threat was articulated through bodies that were seen as being more independent of school officials' control.

The record of these efforts to reassert some kind of "popular" control over the conduct of public education was decidedly mixed. It was, nevertheless, an important record in light of the declining interest shown by the public for public education over the years. The willingness of people to ignore or to keep their children out of the public schools is more than an embarrassment. It is an act of political rejection and reflects the isolation of the institution within the very community it is supposed to serve. The peculiar politics of desegregation are tied up with the politics of St. Louis in ways that are not at all obvious or understood. What can be said is that desegregation set into motion a process of reconciliation between the public and an educational system that since 1950 had grown increasingly more isolated and self-serving.

As has often been the case in our urban history, the problems of a distinct and maligned population have prompted serious public efforts to make things better for everybody. In the past this entailed changing the people who had the problem rather than improving the conditions of their life. This became harder to do, however, as we became less inclined to blame the victims for causing these conditions and the victims became less willing to accept that added burden. Moreover, "they" have assumed at least some of the responsibility and risks of leading a reform effort. While usurping some of the traditional prerogatives of the "reforming classes," however, they have not escaped the vision of reform those persons had. We continue to perceive desegregation as a means of reforming people rather than an institution. Evident also is the persistent deference shown to school officials on most matters related to the creation and implementation of "appropriate" remedial actions. The emergence of the St. Louis Public Schools as the leader of an effort to build a single desegregated system for the metropolitan area is consistent with this. It was only the most recent step in the desegregation process that, as several officials and board members noted, had been taken "for the good of the system."

Voluntary Desegregation and Metropolitan Development

The question in the minds of many black residents of St. Louis in the early 1960s was when, not if, they would elect one of their own people as mayor. Though still only a third of the city's population in 1963, they looked forward to the time when blacks could no longer be ignored as a factor in the city's public life. One needed to search no further than the public schools to understand their optimism. Nearly half of all students at the secondary level and in excess of 60 percent of all elementary schoolchildren in 1963 were black. Here was one institution where they already had a compelling presence.

Yet it seemed to many blacks that they had not translated their numerical strength into real political and educational gains for their people. "Despite the technical demise of segregation in . . . 1955," argued one law professor, "the overwhelming number of whites and Negroes continue[d] . . . to attend schools which [were] de facto segregated or only minimally integrated."[6] Faculty segregation was even worse. Several thousand black students were bused to schools throughout the city in order to relieve overcrowding at their neighborhood schools. Transported in classroom groups, the students remained segregated at their receiving schools to the point that their eating and recreation schedules were different from those of children who lived in the area.

The district's busing and teacher-assignment policies came under bitter attack by the NAACP and Urban League in April 1963. The board of education, responding in a typically patrician style, appointed a citizens committee whose task was to "evaluate 136 criticisms and allegations" directed against the board and school administration.[7] The committee took testimony and prepared its report amid demonstrations by civil-rights groups and formal declarations of innocence by school representatives. In its report the committee was careful to clear the administration of the charge that it had purposefully "resegregated" the schools while admonishing it for some of the practices that had inspired the racial protests. The committee recommended that bused students be more fully integrated into the receiving school's program and that both attendance boundaries and teacher assignments be altered so as to promote greater integration. It also called for an open-enrollment policy that would allow students to be assigned to schools with available space.[8]

The school board and administration did not share the enthusiasm of civil-rights groups for the report. Over the dissenting votes of its three black members, the board of education upheld the superintendent's opposition to any policy that might repudiate the idea that neighborhood schools were inherently superior. Such policies would have included the mandatory transfer of staff to enhance faculty integration and the alteration of existing school boundaries so that more integrated sites could be created. Board members also opposed fuller integration of bused students into the ongoing programs of receiving schools on the grounds that it was not educationally sound or necessary. The superintendent reminded everyone that the busing program was only a temporary and emergency measure in response to severe overcrowding in Northside schools; the completion of new school buildings would greatly reduce the need for the busing program that had prompted the outcry of civil-rights activists.[9] Voluntary transfers of students and staff were acceptable, and a change in school policy would not be required to implement desegregation.

The board of education and NAACP filed suits against each other in August and September 1963, respectively. School officials sought a decision upholding their busing policy and an injunction against civil-rights groups interfering with student transportation. The NAACP's suit was designed to achieve the goals outlined in the 1963 Citizens Advisory Committee report. Both parties withdrew their suits in October 1964, however, when overcrowding in Northside schools was reduced by the opening of new elementary schools and transportable classrooms. Moreover, the 772 remaining students bused to schools with available space were better integrated into their new schools.[10]

It was not until February 1972 that the entire matter of the district's busing, building, and school boundary policies again came under formal attack in court. Like the NAACP before it, the Concerned Parents for North St. Louis (CPNS) expanded its complaint against the district's policy on busing to relieve overcrowding into a full-blown critique of the system's purposeful acts to separate and treat white and black students differently. Nearly three years of litigation and intermittent hearings yielded a report of fifty pages stipulating those facts and conclusions to which both parties could agree. The points on which there was consensus covered a bewildering array of phenomena: racial enrollments, staff placements, school boundary changes, curricular and extracurricular programs, building construction and remodeling, housing segregation, and population shifts, among other things. School officials agreed that segregation was widespread but denied that they were responsible for it.

Before the court could rule on the case, however, lawyers for the school system suggested that the parties build on the information and trust they had developed to fashion a consent decree. A remedy that was agreeable to both parties could be worked out, they thought, and could avoid much of the expense and bitterness associated with court orders and appeals. The judge gave his approval, and the parties began to draft the decree with some technical assistance by consultants working for the Danforth Foundation. The document produced from these deliberations, issued on 24 December 1975, was heralded as a workable compromise. It called for the school system to take three specific actions:

1. Study ways to realign elementary schools with academic high schools so as to reduce segregation at the high-school level. The plan was scheduled to be implemented in the 1976–1977 school year.

2. Initiate a plan for voluntary and, if necessary, mandatory staff reassignments in order to better integrate school staffs. This plan was scheduled to start in the 1976–1977 school year.

3. Establish a magnet school program to offer specialized curricula to students volunteering to participate in an integrated school program. This experiment in citywide open enrollments would be accompanied by a broader study of ways in which the quality of education in the entire district could be increased. Both programs were scheduled to be implemented beginning with the 1976–1977 school year.

The euphoria surrounding the consent decree was widespread. Media from across the nation studied this "common-sense" alternative to forced busing. Many persons, including the parents who initiated the suit, recognized that a mandatory plan might still be required in the future. For the time being, however, they could enjoy their contribution to a "workable" desegregation order. This kind of negotiated settlement was novel, and it inspired a host of groups to offer their services as "mediators" during the subsequent trial concerning mandatory busing in the city. I will have more to say about this in Chapter 8. For the moment, though, I would like to explore the origins and implications of the voluntary desegregation plan a bit more fully.

A Master Plan?

Nowhere in the consent decree and at no point immediately following its publication did anyone, to my knowledge, refer to the 1963 Citizens Advisory Committee report that had been published more than twelve years earlier. Few members of the board of education with whom I have spoken over the past ten years even recalled that such a report was written. Yet the impact of that report is evident in both the consent decree and subsequent efforts to expand the scope of desegregation in the city and the county.

The authors of both reports acknowledged that segregation was widespread but did not attribute it to the actions of school officials. One might dismiss this as a reasonable concession to the school system as long as it had implemented proposed reforms. However, officials ignored most of the recommendations made to them in 1963 and, with the tacit approval of local civil-rights groups, continued to do nothing to halt the increasing effects of segregation inside the school system. It was only the stubborn efforts of the CPNS that made it possible to push the school system beyond that point. This was the primary achievement of the group. Its members used the judicial system to fill a political vacuum created by the school system *and* representatives of more traditional reforming groups. Beyond approving the consent decree, however, the CPNS made no substantial contribution to its content. That, it seems in retrospect, was the primary achievement of the school administration.

The major provisions of the consent decree were noted above. Two of these provisions—realignment of feeder schools to foster integration at the high schools and staff reassignments to enhance integration—were surprisingly similar to recommendations contained in the report issued by the 1963 Citizens Advisory Committee. The only difference was that the authors of the 1963 report also suggested that elementary-school boundaries be changed whenever possible to increase student integration. That suggestion had been rejected by both the school administration and board on the grounds that it could not be done "without destroying the principle of the neighborhood school."[11] The superintendent hastened to remind the committee that it, too, had declared its support for that concept in its report.

The sanctity of neighborhood schools again was raised in response to the suggested adoption of an open-enrollment policy. The committee may have been contradicting its own stated preference for neighborhood schools with such a suggestion. I prefer to think that it was drawing attention to its own confusion as to how one could develop a sense of being part of a metropolitan community while vowing allegiance to a parochial and segregated institution. The committee wanted neighborhood schools. It also recognized the inherent flaw in hoping that the open sore of segregation might heal without bringing people together so that they might better resolve their differences. "Early in the study," the authors stated, "the committee came to understand that the schools were being blamed in part . . . for problems [they] had not created and . . . could not solve. Further, it shortly became clear that many of the problems which face the schools are problems which pertain to the greater St. Louis area." The solution to these problems, the committee concluded, "lies in the cooperation of St. Louis City and its satellite communities."[12]

A program of cooperation with county school districts was neither legally nor politically feasible back in 1963. Although county school officials certainly took the implicit threat of city and county consolidation seriously, it was a safe suggestion to make at that time. It would have been possible for the city district to undertake a more ambitious desegregation program of its own, but it lacked the desire and political will to do so. Even members of the 1963 Citizens Advisory Committee had been unable to resolve the dilemma of wanting to preserve neighborhood schools while raising generations of youngsters to be more sensitive to citywide and metropolitan problems. So its immediate answer had been to add "the dimension of open enrollment" to that of the neighborhood school.[13]

School administrators rejected the idea that any youngster from outside of a neighborhood ought to be allowed to fill an empty seat so that the school might be better integrated. In 1963 they preferred to maintain a policy of transferring students based on their unique educational or social needs. Nevertheless, the district initiated its own version of an open-enrollment program in a new elementary school only a year after the busing controversy had been concluded. Parents from outside the naturally integrated neighborhood were allowed to enroll their children in this "quality integrated school." The "opening of this school," argued officials in 1967, "was regarded . . . throughout the system as an important *educational* step forward."[14]

I emphasize officials' use of the word *educational* because they have consistently and carefully marketed desegregation in this manner. The aforementioned school, for example, was selected to be a "demonstration" program to "improve teaching proficiency" and to foster the creation of more integrated teaching staffs.[15] This marketing strategy had important implications for district policies. It clearly anticipated the creation in 1976 of magnet schools. The specialized curriculum and "voluntarily" integrated teaching staff and student body of each school mimicked the early experiments of officials with the open-enrollment concept. Not only were the schools available to a comparatively small number of people but each site generally was filled with a combination of volunteers and teachers and students already there as well. It also seemed important for school officials to prove that one might have a quality educational program in spite of desegregation, since it was not expected that desegregation alone could produce favorable academic results for students. If desegregation was to work at all, it would have to make good sense educationally, not just legally. That is one of the reasons school personnel made such a concerted effort to define both the general direction of desegregation efforts and the specific content of programs undertaken because of desegregation.

Another Open and Nonrational Organization

It is obvious that school officials did little to hasten the process of desegregation. It is equally apparent, however, that they had more than a little idea of what to do with desegregation once it no longer could be avoided. The implicit goal in all their desegregation proposals has been to preserve and, if possible, to enhance their control over the enterprise of public education. There were things that some officials and board members said they had wanted to do for a long time. Things such as magnet schools made good educational sense to them. Few persons, on the other hand, could get excited about desegregation. No one was sure how it would turn out or what political consequences it might have. Officials did know that sentiment on the board of education and in the community had been unfavorable or at least consistently unenthusiastic. At the same time, few persons inside the school system seemed surprised when new suits were filed and they were ordered to do something to reduce student and staff segregation. The school board and administration had lacked either the funds or the political will to initiate a host of reforms related to public education. Desegregation called for under the aegis of a federal court provided them with an opportunity to find both.[16]

School personnel, board members, and other informed observers helped me to understand how district officials used desegregation to accomplish things they otherwise could not or would not have undertaken on a large scale. Desegregation was viewed primarily as a means to obtain educational reforms and only secondarily as a way to redress the grievances of black parents and students. The magnet school program is perhaps the best but by no means the only example of this. Staff balancing had been discussed for more than a decade, but the board of education had done its best to avoid addressing the problem of segregated school staffs head-on. Teachers tended not to request transfers to schools where they would be in the minority, and combining the staffs of different schools had yielded little desegregation and some resentment on the part of the teachers' union. School officials and board members also indicated that desegregation provided an "excuse" for requesting badly needed funds for research and development, building maintenance and construction, existing educational programs, and teacher salaries. The development of a middle-school program also is attributable to the desegregation effort and will be discussed a bit later. Still, the best illustration of this phenomenon is the magnet school program and its role in fostering a "citywide perspective" in the community.

Persons in and out of the school system acknowledged that the city's chance for being rebuilt was hurt by divisions within the city and between the city and the county. The parochialism bred and maintained by the neighborhood schools, among other institutions, did not help people see that they were part of a larger community. Yet the district had done little to replace a "neighborhood perspective" with a "citywide perspective" during the 1960s and early 1970s. A good part of the reason for this, some people maintained, was the reluctance of the district to touch anything that might involve "racial goals." Others said that the board of education simply feared the community reaction from blacks as well as whites if it chose to embark on a program of closing neighborhood schools. At any rate, it was not until the board agreed to the 1975 consent decree that any substantial steps were taken to redirect the attention of people toward schools with citywide appeal.

The idea behind magnet schools had emerged with educational reform and alternative school movements in the 1960s and 1970s. Although experimented with on a limited basis in the city, so-called practical education or specialized programs that might attract students from across the district had been deleted in the elementary grades during the mid-1960s. These programs were brought back for the younger children and expanded markedly for older students with the advent of the consent decree.[17] It would be fair to say, in fact, that officials seized the opportunity presented by the consent decree in order to propose a whole series of magnet schools. The consent decree was agreed to on 24 December 1975. A complete proposal for establishing nine alternative schools and spending in excess of seven million dollars for approximately four thousand students was submitted to the board of education only one month later on 29 January 1976.

Most students of organizational behavior would find nothing queer in this accomplishment. They would argue that large institutions, particularly those working in a "disturbed" environment, must be responsive to demands or new conditions and can mobilize substantial resources in order to meet such challenges. One could expect nothing less of an "open and rational" organization, even during the busiest holiday season of the year. There may be something to all of this. Yet I am reminded that this same school district routinely misplaces or loses track of students and valuable supplies, seems at a loss to teach many students anything, and often cannot even get its buses to run on time. I do not doubt that many school officials worked long hours on this proposal during the Christmas break. I only doubt that they could have finished and submitted it to the board of education if much of the thinking about voluntary alternatives to mandatory busing had not already been completed. One might ask whether such planning was not the hallmark of an "open and rational" organization. That it is; but so, too, is the competent handling of existing tasks and the pursuit of reforms that would help the organization discharge its responsibilities better. In many instances we know that the city school system did neither of these things, and we see this most clearly in the case of desegregation and related matters. Time and time again the court record shows that the district simply failed to take the initiative or to do things that would have reduced its liability, even when it was clear from the experiences of other districts that comparable inactivity could get them into trouble.

The creation of the magnet school program and the other elements of the consent decree more closely fits what one would expect of an "open and nonrational" organization, one that puts its own survival ahead of the alleged needs of a changing constituency and world. Of course, it is my belief that all organizations behave in this way. I am not trying to make the city school system accountable for upholding a higher standard of institutional morality and performance. Nevertheless, I have found no one to disagree with the contention of one observer that school administrators merely had reached into a file cabinet, dusted off some slightly wrinkled plans for alternative schools, slapped a busing proposal on them, and called it a desegregation plan. Board members indicated that much the same occurred as officials rushed to tidy up the proposal so that it could be submitted to the federal government for funding. Outside consultants allegedly were brought in to write parts of the early ESAA (Emergency School Aid Act) proposal.

The reliance on professional educators to help shape the magnet school proposal was understandable. School officials were under great pressure to submit detailed technical plans before federal-funding application deadlines could pass. The reliance on regular staff and school consultants for advice on how best to organize not only this program but also responses to other parts of the consent decree seemed to increase as the spring and summer wore on. After all, so much had to be done by September: staff had to be selected, sites prepared, students enrolled, curricula developed, and, of course, bus schedules had to be laid out. Federal deadlines and the start of a new school year notwithstanding, "the big rush," as some parents came to characterize it, became symptomatic of nearly all planning activities related to the magnet school program.

There was, to be sure, an advisory committee established to "determine the type, size, location, and other details of the magnet schools." School officials were quick to remind parents at recruitment meetings that "the programs had been devised, in large part, by [the] parent advisory committee" and were, in fact, programs "that parents had said they wanted for their children." Some of the forty-seven persons selected by the district to sit on that committee spoke more modestly of their contributions to the planning process. At least one member complained publicly about the way the plan had been drafted, arguing that the priorities of the committee were not reflected in the final plan.[18] Others recalled privately, sometimes with considerable amusement, how administrators would let them rank their choices for a particular program or teacher following an interview and then would report the outcome of their poll a week later. Surprised by some of the selections, parents began to compare their notes and sometimes discovered marked differences between the official results and their apparent preferences. To some parents it seemed that school officials had already made up their minds. If the committee's positions were consistent with those of school staff, then they were accepted. Otherwise, they were conveniently and quietly ignored.

Diamonds in the Rough

Opinions regarding the magnet schools reveal as much consistency as the quality of the programs being offered. The NAACP led the attack against the proposed program in 1976, assailing it as a "token" integration plan and a "method of delaying meaningful desegregation." Six years later, the same organization asked the federal court in charge of the case to order the state to open magnet schools in St. Louis County. The city government objected to mandatory busing, but in 1977 its mayor extolled the virtue of the magnet schools before a group of local business and community leaders. "The magnet schools," he maintained, "have the potential of doing much, much more than the original intent." They would help to attract new businesses and residents to the city. "The heat of public controversy over desegregation has created diamonds of educational excellence."[19]

While the educational value of these jewels has not been agreed upon, they have nevertheless gained popularity. Between 1976 and 1982 the number of magnet schools increased from nine to eighteen, and enrollments nearly doubled from approximately two thousand five hundred to five thousand. Several hundred white youngsters from various districts in St. Louis County now attend city magnet schools and, beginning with the 1982 school year, there were several magnet programs in different county schools. It was hoped that these programs would provide an opportunity for more black students from the city to enroll in county schools.

Those in charge of the voluntary desegregation program between the city and county worked hard to encourage districts and parents to support this effort. Yet they expressed great frustration over their inability to get the media more interested. Part of the media's reluctance to pay attention to this development in the desegregation process was summarized nicely by one reporter. He characterized the declarations of the committee as "sugar coated" with little or no substantive content. What is surprising is that no one had thought to search the city's experiences with voluntary desegregation for clues as to what county residents could expect from a magnet school program. Had they done this, many involved with "selling" the voluntary program to the public no doubt would have been upset. However, most ritualized crises thrive precisely because people do not fully comprehend what is going on around them. The absence of complete and balanced reporting may perform a useful service under such circumstances.

What was discovered about the city's magnet school program was stated earlier about desegregation in general. That is, sometimes it has worked and sometimes it has not. When a magnet school has worked well, and this has been the case in a number of instances, it has produced an exciting program with interested students, staff, and parents. This does not mean that a school is perfect or that its program cannot be improved. It does mean that something good and educationally sound is going on there.[20] When a magnet school does not work well a number of factors probably are at work. Included among these factors are the following: poor administration, a poorly conceived program, an inadequately prepared staff, and a location in a "bad" part of the city. Magnet schools that have failed or have earned poor reputations have usually suffered from several of these problems. Some programs have managed to survive in spite of these shortcomings.

Notable in its omission from this list of problems is a reference to the type and caliber of student attracted to the magnet schools. Most children in attendance "chose" to be in that school because they either liked the program or did not want to leave the neighborhood school when it became a magnet school.[21] There were some white children whose decisions to transfer into a magnet school were made on quite different grounds. Magnet school administrators suspected and were able to document at least one case in which an area superintendent had "dumped" some "troublemakers" on them. City officials later suspected that several county districts had been engaged in a similar practice when they had referred youngsters to the magnet schools. This stands in marked contrast to the stricter placement criteria laid down by county districts for black city students in their schools. The end result, in any case, is that students who have attended the city's magnet schools have represented a self-selected group.[22] Relations among these youngsters have seemed cordial, if not always warm and spontaneous. The point is that most magnet schools have seemed remarkably free of the tensions that frequently accompany school desegregation.[23] One school board member characterized the magnet schools' "experiment in social engineering" as a "complete success."[24]

The magnet schools have been less successful as an educational innovation. After attracting students to their programs, the magnet schools, at least as late as 1979, were not able to hold their interest. An unpublicized report on the schools' retention rates show that they fare little better than the districts' nonmagnet schools. Only half of the students who attended magnet schools in 1976 were still enrolled in the same school three years later. Officials did not count students who would have graduated or moved, for instance, from a grammar school to a middle school. There has been a lot of turnover in the population of magnet school students. This might be good because it has offered more youngsters an opportunity to attend an "integrated" school. I cannot believe, however, that it has helped the instructional program or, in the long run, the students' ability to take full advantage of the "specialized" curriculum. Students and their parents may be indicating by the students' withdrawal from magnet schools that these programs do not have that much more to offer beyond what could be acquired in a nonmagnet school.

One can see how this could be happening in several schools. Parents complained for several years about one program in which the academic progress of their children was being literally forsaken for song and dance. A similar complaint was expressed about a new magnet school begun in 1980 for children in grades six through eight. It was to be called an "Olympics Skills" school and was to concentrate on "individual rather than team sports" like tennis, golf, wrestling, swimming, and gymnastics. Supporters noted that similar schools had generated a lot of student interest in other cities.[25] School officials did think it prudent, however, to change the title of the school to the "Athletic and Academic Academy."

Another magnet school changed its program that same year. A major corporation had suspended its support of the original program because, in the words of one district official, "it was dated." Some persons were relieved when the program was finally discontinued, however, because it had failed to produce meaningful results not only in the magnet school but also at several regular schools in the district well before the 1975 consent decree. "The record was there for anyone to see," one administrator complained, "it's just that no one cared to look that hard." In its place was substituted a "Center for Expressive and Receptive Arts" for children up to the eighth grade. This was convenient because it allowed the children who had "chosen" to enroll in the previous program to "choose" to enroll in a new program emphasizing "oral and written language, reading and listening skills."[26] This may sound a good deal like what most schools ought to be doing. It certainly was helpful for the specially trained teachers who had "chosen" to teach in the previous program. Now they, too, could "choose" to sharpen their own oral and written skills. The sentiment of teachers caught in this kind of situation was captured nicely by a teacher commenting on his own school. "We're supposed to be a Business and Management High School . . . [but] we have no management, so all we do is give the kids the business."

It is difficult to say whether children attending magnet schools actually have learned more than youngsters who have not. Their level of academic competence as measured by standardized achievement tests has been higher than that of children who are not enrolled in magnet schools. However, this may have more to do with the characteristics of the youngsters enrolling in magnet schools than with the academic training they receive. These students tend to be among the better-prepared youngsters in the district. This has been something of a sore point among both parents who are or might be involved in a desegregation program and social scientists who worry about things like educational equity.[27]

Many parents of magnet school students have expressed reluctance to question the program's academic content, but not necessarily because they fear being shown up by a "professional educator." It is rather that they are grateful to have their child come home excited about school or excelling at whatever specialization his school offers. Other persons worry that the magnet schools might become "islands of privilege" inside a district in desperate need of funds for all its schools. The "self-selected" nature of the student body troubles them. They fear that magnet schools could be used as a means to keep quiet the most potentially vigorous and concerned observers of school policy. Children from families with more money or who see education as a realistic means for securing a better life may be more likely to enroll in such "special" programs or be encouraged to do

so. They also may do better in school because of their "enriched" circumstances. The few social scientists who have worried about this problem at all
approach it from a slightly different manner. They wonder whether white students might be receiving a disproportionate share of school resources because
they are overrepresented in the magnet schools relative to their numbers in the
whole school population. It is for these reasons that it is difficult to determine
whether magnet-school students do better academically and, if this is the case,
why.

If there was a "social class bias" operating in the decisions of who applies
and gets enrolled in magnet schools, it was hard to see when touring the schools
or talking with parents. In several schools some parents (white and black) could
not enroll their children because they could not write their own names. Many
children received free meals because their parents were not especially well-to-
do. Other children received remedial assistance because they were not prepared
to do academic work appropriate for their age group. Both black and white
youngsters fell into these categories. These youngsters may not have been representative of the magnet school student body as a whole, of course. Unfortunately, there were no data that would allow such a determination.

There was some indirect evidence that magnet school children sometimes did
have access to more or better resources than their peers. During the first few
years of the program, for instance, several principals confided that they had
more "toys" and "supplemental" materials than they or their staff knew what to
do with. Their office closets, stuffed with things acquired with federal funds,
testified to that fact. Extra funds were secured from the state as well. Magnet
school officials were drawn to money reserved for "gifted" children because of
good public relations and financial reasons. With the assistance of district staff,
they were able to produce a list of several dozen "gifted" students that apparently
satisfied the state. That list and the test scores of students who were on it were
reviewed at one meeting. These students frequently scored forty to fifty percentage points below the level formally established by the state for inclusion in the
"gifted" category.[28]

A Pervasive Class Bias or Cultural Lag?

There also is indirect evidence that a "social class bias" may be operating in
more than just the magnet school program. People feared that such a bias might
operate in the personal decisions of parents to enroll their children in the magnet
schools. They were correct. I do not believe, however, that people expected a
similar bias to be built into St. Louis City's mandatory desegregation plan
initiated in 1980, but that appears to have been the case. The data on which this
conclusion is based were drawn from a published study released by the school

system in the spring of 1982. This study contains an analysis of students' achievement in the second, fourth, sixth, eighth, tenth, and twelfth grades in various school settings for the 1980–1981 school year. The intent of the authors had been to compare the academic progress of white and black youngsters during the first year of mandatory desegregation. All the appropriate qualifications regarding single-year comparisons versus longitudinal analyses were made, and the conclusions of the report were models of scientific tentativeness. The authors stated there was "no indication that white students achieved less . . . nor . . . black students more than anticipated as a direct result of desegregation." "At least initially," the authors argued, "desegregation [had] little impact on the achievement of students of either race." Everyone tended to improve their test scores by comparable amounts over the course of the academic year.[29]

It is not important for the purposes of this immediate analysis that city students generally and black students in particular perform less well on standardized achievement tests than their peers across the country. What is important is that white and black students in the magnet schools had substantially higher *pretest* scores on these tests than did their peers as early as the fourth grade. This pattern held for students in all subsequent years for which data were available. Nontrivial differences in the pretest scores of black youngsters attending schools in the integrated and segregated clusters were first evidenced among high-school students; those enrolled in integrated high schools had higher scores even before the school year had begun. Black children who attended integrated and segregated schools did not have markedly different pretest scores up through the eighth grade. Something is going on here that has nothing to do with the instructional quality in any of the city's public schools. There is a selection process occurring. It is most obvious in the magnet schools but extends into the regular high schools as well.

The sorting process for children of the two races was different. For whites it seemed a simple matter of providing the better-prepared students with some option to the regular public schools fairly early in their academic careers. Their comparatively small numbers made this task not too difficult once the magnet schools were opened in 1975. The mandatory plan that went into effect in the 1980–1981 school year expanded this program and formally legitimated its latent class bias. Yet blacks took some advantages from this as well. More academically sophisticated black students also began to find their way into the magnet schools no later than the fourth grade. The second stage of their sorting process did not go into effect until high school. Then the better-prepared black youngsters remaining in the regular public schools apparently were assigned to high schools in the "integrated clusters." The least well prepared black students were left in the segregated high schools. The sorting process for blacks is by no means perfect. Until the eighth grade, blacks in the segregated schools had scores comparable to those for blacks who attended nonmagnet schools that were integrated. In some instances their scores were better, though not dramatically so.

The only plausible explanation offered for the apparent lateness of this second stage in the sorting process for blacks centers on their great numbers in the elementary grades. There were just too many black children to mix with too few white children. It was not practical to seriously consider stratifying black elementary schools according to their students' social class background. By the time students reached high school, however, many blacks had received permission to transfer into predominantly white high schools on the city's Southside. A process of self-selection not dissimilar from that practiced by blacks in the magnet schools apparently had already been taking place when the mandatory plan was agreed to in 1980. That plan merely legitimated the process that seemed to allocate the better-prepared black students to the integrated high schools.[30]

These are strong statements, and we all deserve a fuller account about how such a sorting process could have been put into effect. Those looking for a conspiracy, even among some polyester-clad cabal of school administrators, are going to be disappointed. I do not think there was a "plan" to isolate the least well-to-do black students in segregated or less fancy public schools, though that apparently is what happened. It just worked out that way. This conclusion should surprise no one who has studied the history of moral reform crusades in our cities, however. We know that social class problems were very much a part of these crusades. Such concerns were often well hidden, even from the participants, but they were there nonetheless. We expect in ritualized crises that the "big" questions are answered only in ways that reinforce or conveniently overlook the basic sources of inequality in our communities.

School officials responsible for drawing up the mandatory plan for St. Louis City did entertain ideas about the appropriateness of different types of black youngsters for desegregation. It was thought that desegregated schools might be more stable if they contained black and white youngsters with similar social class backgrounds. Yet it was obvious to these officials that they could not organize the mandatory plan around such an idea because of the overwhelming number of black children in the elementary grades.[31] In the end, the crucial variable in determining which black students would be desegregated was their proximity to the predominantly white elementary schools on the city's Southside. Officials were anxious to keep the distances traveled by children to a minimum and to retain as many white children as possible. Many were worried about what would happen to those students remaining in segregated sites, however, and said that something special would be done for these youngsters.

The planning process was reminiscent of that undertaken for the magnet school program five years earlier. This time "the big rush" was imposed by the

Court of Appeals. Having rejected the trial judge's decision favoring the school system on 3 March 1980, the justices wanted a final plan submitted no later than 2 May. The trial judge appointed an advisory committee on 14 March to help the district. Less than one month later, on 3 April, the district unveiled a draft of the plan. There was no doubt that the justices wanted something to go into effect for the next school year.

Some members of the 1980 court-appointed desegregation monitoring committee had harsh words for the system's plan. Specifically, they wondered why more schools and black youngsters could not be included in the "integrated clusters" and why those clusters were concentrated in the south and central parts of the city. The superintendent argued that he "was following the court's recommendation in proposing only a 30 to 50 percent black enrollment" at schools in the integrated clusters. He did agree with the criticism that too many black youngsters in the northern third of the city would be left in segregated schools. Without a broader base of white youngsters to work with, however, there was little else that could be done.[32] One only can suppose that it seemed prudent to keep busing to a minimum and not to frighten away more white students by busing them into the northern reaches of the city.

The plan that was advanced was probably more practical and politically acceptable than others that could have been proposed. More students than ever before were to attend desegregated schools, and efforts were to be made to help students left in segregated schools by developing "enrichment learning laboratories" for those sites. Notwithstanding the apparent equity of the proposal and good faith of those responsible for it, the plan did in fact have some unfortunate assumptions built into it about the worth or redemptive powers of some black youngsters. Such assumptions are not unfamiliar to those who have studied the organization and impact of earlier moral reform crusades. Nor are the assumptions unfamiliar to any St. Louis resident who has taken the time to read the 1963 Citizens Advisory Committee report.

The authors of that report were concerned, it will be recalled, with finding a way to better integrate bused students into their new schools. They wanted to be sure that in the "integrating process all constructive learning principles," such as ability grouping or tracking, would "be preserved." To this end,

> transported pupils who [were] of the same educational level as those students in the classroom of the receiving schools [were] to be fully integrated into the existing classes. However, the students who [had] some educational or cultural lag . . . must obviously be taught in a grouping appropriate to their educational level.
> This is not to say that Negro pupils are mentally inferior to white pupils. We merely remind the Board . . . that the median scores on achievement tests of transported pupils are generally lower than those of local pupils . . . and that this fact has nothing, per se, to do with race. When pupils are transported to

schools of parallel economic status, the scores of Negro and white pupils are usually not significantly different.[33]

The most effective form of integration, the authors thought, would bring students together who had similar cultural, that is, social class, backgrounds. Mixing students together who had to overcome racial and class differences would be difficult. Any plan that would bring together only students with similar economic backgrounds, of course, would limit the amount of desegregation that could take place. To the members of the 1963 Citizens Advisory Committee, however, this seemed preferable to a plan that would merely expose more students to members of the opposite race.

One can only guess how lasting and pronounced an affect such thinking might have had on subsequent school administrations. There is no doubt that at least some upper-level administrators involved with the planning process were aware of the report's content. What exactly was said or not said in the special planning group responsible for outlining the mandatory plan I do not know. The work of these school personnel was monitored and reported on by court-appointed expert Gary Orfield, however. His report to the court on 2 May 1980 contains a summary of the thinking that went into the decision to leave most of the predominantly black schools on the city's Northside segregated. His words and impressions bear repeating.

> One of the most telling criticisms of the plan . . . is that the plan leaves segregated some of the very ghetto schools where the violations were proved in the first place. To some extent . . . this problem is inevitable . . . All schools . . . could be integrated . . . in a plan if each were assigned 77 or 78 percent black students for the fall. The school board chose, however, a goal explicitly authorized by the Court of Appeals, a goal I believe is much more likely to produce substantial and lasting desegregation—but for a much smaller number of schools.
>
> Another question remains. Even if only a limited number of schools can be involved in clusters, why couldn't some have been included farther North? The answer is that they could have been. There are certainly . . . attractive schools further North. The problem is that this would mean skipping over other, nearer black schools, some in areas that are or may become more residentially integrated as well. Some members of the Internal Committee believed that there would be a substantially greater loss of white students if clusters reached further North.
>
> My position was that so long as the plan reached as many black students and white students as could be accommodated within the specified goal I should not try to second-guess. I do not think that it would have created great additional difficulties to have substituted a small number of schools more to the North in the clusters but I think that the existing clusters are rational and reasonable. They should be approved.[34]

This is probably a fair summary of the assumptions made by members of the district committee when drawing up the mandatory plan. It still leaves the question of how deeply ingrained the social class bias evident in the 1963 report was in more recent administrations. I think that bias was preserved, but not in any way that administrators could be accused of consciously keeping less well-prepared and well-bred black youngsters away from whites. It was more that successive generations of school officials had learned to ignore the social class implications of their programs. Or, they attempted to turn such forces into "positive" channels like building more "stable" schools. Rarely are such factors overtly taken into account during the course of a reform effort, and desegregation in St. Louis has been no exception to this general rule.[35] The 1963 Citizens Advisory Committee report provided one of the few glimpses into this question during over two decades worth of school desegregation activity.

There are pervasive social class biases built into the way public education is organized. About that there can be little debate. Yet these "biases" or "limitations" in public education are so fundamental to the way the institution has come to operate that we cannot or dare not question them too openly and severely. Racial segregation provides us with an opportunity to argue about such inherent flaws in our social order in an indirect and stylized fashion. School desegregation offers us the chance to amend that order while sustaining and even reinforcing its legitimacy in the eyes of its membership. If it were permissible to charge school officials with a crime in regard to the social class bias their policies reflected, it would have to be a crime of nonfeasance rather than misfeasance or malfeasance. Moreover, at least in the case of St. Louis, it would have to be a charge also leveled at the board of education, the NAACP, the U.S. Department of Justice, an assortment of judges, and the two citizen groups involved in the suit, among others. All of these people or groups had a part in raising, or not raising, certain questions to be considered during the course of the trial; all assented, however grudgingly, to the desegregation plan finally approved by the U.S. Court of Appeals. There was no conspiracy to isolate less-well-to-do black students from their peers. There did not have to be. Such is the nature of ritualized crises and reforms.

And What of a Metropolitan Plan?

Citizens opposed to busing were incredulous when in June 1981 Orfield suggested to the U.S. District Court that it order St. Louis County school districts to voluntarily participate in student exchanges with the city. They were aghast when the court issued just such a command less than two weeks later. Had the court approved a "mandatory-voluntary" plan? It was unthinkable! Semantic purists scurried to their dictionaries. Only veterans of the armed services were familiar with the concept of someone being ordered to volunteer for some unsavory task. Yet there it was in bold-faced type on the front page of the daily newspapers. The judge had ordered county school districts to participate in a voluntary desegregation plan with the city school system.[36]

To many persons this merely seemed to be the latest twist in an already bizarre case in which remedies for segregation were discussed before anyone was found guilty of causing schools to become segregated. More cool-headed observers of the case understood the political and legal significance of the court's gambit. A rejection of the court's offer carried with it the poorly hidden threat of being cited as a defendant in a lengthy and expensive legal battle involving a mandatory plan and possible merger with the city school system. Acceptance of the plan meant at least a temporary reprieve from that fate. Most districts rejected the proposal and vowed to fight against "forced busing" for as long as it might take.[37] Several accepted the court's suggestion but only after imposing conditions for their participation. Eleven of the county's regular school districts had eventually joined in the plan by the summer of 1982. Other districts were expected to follow suit by the fall when, in addition to voluntary pupil exchanges between the city and county, several magnet schools were scheduled to open in the county. Further incentive was provided in August when the court outlined the interdistrict merger and desegregation order it would impose if districts did not voluntarily desegregate.

If all of this seems strangely familiar, it is no mistake on the reader's part. The same pattern of threatened legal actions, voluntary transfers, and reliance on magnet schools that was evident in the St. Louis City case had begun to unfold in the metropolitan school segregation case. Many wondered whether the revival of this drama in the county would end as it had in the city. Would the districts maintain their autonomy? Would county school administrators insist on fighting to the last pint of their constituents' blood. Would frantic Protestant, Baptist, and atheist parents have an immaculate conversion to Catholicism in order to enroll their children in parochial schools? Or would they become good Lutherans instead and enroll in its church schools? It was questions such as these that occupied the public and added a bit of flash to a worn story line. However, it was the dull, plodding persistence of the city school system, the NAACP, and the courts that determined just how far this drama was played out. In the meantime, the public was learning to accommodate itself to the painful reality that it was part of a metropolitan community. The public schools once again were providing the vehicle for this lesson to be learned.[38]

The cold and rational course for county districts would have been to accept the voluntary plan but make it more agreeable to themselves. Eventually, this is precisely what they did. More districts have taken this position as they have learned just how little is being asked of them. Indeed, there were some advantages to participating. Many of the three hundred white students from the county who elected to enroll in city magnet schools for the 1981–1982 school year really enjoyed their experiences. Less attention was paid to the 240 black students from the city who chose to attend schools in the county, but the receiving districts have been pleased with the program. Among the reasons for this has been the ability of the receiving district to screen black applicants before assigning them to a particular school or grade level in the school. Less desirable candidates have been discouraged by being told that they must repeat a grade. Students with better preparation and presumably better pedigrees have been placed in satisfactory grades and schools. Some have charged that this has "skimmed the cream" of the city's black student population and has further eroded an already depleted middle-class population from the city schools. Nevertheless, a series of stories published in May 1984 in the *St. Louis Post-Dispatch* indicated that the vast majority of minority students were enjoying their new schools.

Another important reason for county districts' satisfaction with the exchange program involves the money they have received from the state for every black student they admit and every white student they send out. During the 1981–1982 school year this amounted to a figure of $1,250 paid toward the host district's basic fee for educating a student and 50 percent of the remaining balance. "It is clear," noted Orfield, "that every receiving district would be helped financially." In fact, he went on to say, "the financial benefits . . . are so great that any district that declines is saying 'We want to lay off more teachers and close more schools,' or 'We want to pay higher taxes.' "[39] The state, in effect, has offered supplemental aid to financially strapped districts agreeing to a lend-lease program in which children were bartered on the basis of their skin color and, at least in some cases, their social class standing.[40]

The financial terms of this bartering agreement, rather than the mushy concept of a "mandatory-voluntary" desegregation plan, have been questioned in the courts. The U.S. Department of Justice petitioned the Supreme Court in July 1984 to review the financing provisions of the metropolitan plan. In so doing, it joined the state of Missouri in its longstanding protest against the substantial bills the state was compelled to pay in behalf of the plan. The state attorney general, who was locked in a campaign for the Republican party's gubernatorial nomination with the county executive of St. Louis County, insisted that there had never been a complete hearing of the state's culpability in the case. Of course, that hardly mattered to the participating school districts.

There was some indication, however, that culpability had begun to matter to presiding U.S. District Judge William F. Hungate. He had rebuffed part of the city district's effort to expand its magnet school plan even before the federal government announced its concern with the financing schemes that gave life to his metropolitan order. An audit of the city's desegregation bills to the state in June 1984 had revealed, as far as state officials were concerned, nearly $1.5 million in excess charges for the previous school year. It was both obvious and "understandable" to the state auditor that the school system was using the desegregation orders to "obtain as much money for its operation as it [could]."[41] The court, it seemed, was not ignoring this problem and would have to consider seriously requests to change the district's tax rate over the persistent objections of city voters.

The class bias built into the city's voluntary and mandatory desegregation plans nevertheless was being extended into the St. Louis County school districts. Desegregation, it seemed, might be tolerable and even profitable as long as it did not violate time-honored conventions guiding contacts between a community's social classes. This is the crucial point to keep in mind when evaluating both the prospects for a metropolitan desegregation order and its likely impact in St. Louis. The "mandatory-voluntary" approach already in place has its attractions. Like the consent decree in the city, however, it has been untidy and has left too many loose ends. The voluntary goals agreed to by participating county districts eventually may be viewed as an insufficient response. The city school system and the NAACP could press their case. A metropolitan desegregation and merger plan might be required by the courts, but I doubt it. People fear a metropolitan school district, even though there is some indication that a desegregation plan worked out on that scale would retain some conventional and comfortable class biases. How well such a district might educate, run, and respond to community pressure will be considered in the next chapter.

8. Desegregation and the Politics of Educational Quality

Advocates of desegregation may comfortably ignore the hidden social class biases built into their plans to reform urban school systems and residents. No such lapse, however, ought to be tolerated when the quality of educational programs under desegregation is questioned. Yet, as we shall see, that, in effect, is what was allowed to happen in St. Louis City. People expressed a good deal of interest in this topic; but they allowed themselves to be convinced that the district's efforts were not so objectionable as to warrant more aggressive review. The politics of how this compromise was fashioned and its impact on the district's broader concerns are the subjects of this chapter.

The Quality of Public Education

Under desegregation, the quality of education is not strained. If it were, it would be more by accident than by design. The instructional programs of schools simply are not altered so drastically or permanently because of desegregation to make that much difference in the level of student achievement over a period of years. Individual students may thrive or suffer because of their new desegregated setting, but the quality of the program will not. A poorly conceived and administered academic regimen will be just as badly received in segregated and desegregated schools. Desegregation simply makes it harder to hide.

The Ferguson-Florissant case offered an excellent illustration of this point. Officials condemned the educational program of the Kinloch schools in part because it lacked both depth and breadth. Kinloch students had too much free time and not enough tough academic guidance. Yet once inside the better-financed and better-equipped Ferguson-Florissant schools, these same students seemed to suffer from the same problems they had experienced in their neighborhood schools. They ended up taking the easiest courses, they were allowed to wile away hours in study halls, and they were not checked when late or absent. Here desegregation had little effect on the district's or school's educational program.

There are instances in which desegregation is heralded as an opportunity to improve the quality of an educational program. City school officials clearly approached the 1975 consent decree and 1980 mandatory plan with this idea in mind. The primary emphasis in their campaign to link educational equality and desegregation together was on the magnet schools. The record of these schools, while decidedly mixed, did not discourage professional educators or the courts from relying on them to entice county districts into voluntary desegregation. Alternative schools with specialized programs were first viewed as an educational innovation. Desegregation only provided officials with the opportunity to introduce a program they had wanted for some time.

Magnet schools were not the only educational innovation introduced into the city district under the protective banner of "peaceful and effective desegregation." School administrators also sought and received permission to introduce a new grade structure with separate "middle schools" for children in the fifth through the eighth grades. Like the alternative schools with their specialized programs, these middle schools were designed not to work as tools to enhance desegregation but to reach a particular element in the public school population that tends to be overlooked. The time between childhood and the teenage years had been commanding increasing attention from professional educators across the country. St. Louis educators had tried to generate popular interest to support efforts to meet the needs of this age group, but to no avail. When mandatory desegregation came along, school administrators got the court to tell them to do something that they wanted to do.[1] Citizens who had opposed the idea of selling this proposal as a desegregation tool several years earlier could only shrug their shoulders. Court-appointed expert Gary Orfield could only find kind words for the idea and its advocates. "The leadership of the St. Louis district is committed to . . . this very important change at the same time it must rearrange student assignments . . . for desegregation," he stated. The "plan will produce not only desegregation but a more efficient school system with a type of school organization local educators believe to be superior.[2]

It is too soon to say whether the great faith Orfield and others had in these schools will be rewarded. The school system already has reaped substantial benefits from them, however. Funds secured as part of a desegregation effort were spent to expand a small, informal program for sixth, seventh, and eighth grade "rooms" in some schools into a court-ordered mandate to reorganize the district's grade structure.

The "enrichment and extended learning laboratories" established exclusively for students remaining in segregated high schools constituted the third major educational innovation ushered in as a result of desegregation. Students in the first through eighth grades were to have labs for "basic skills, reading, writing and science." The services of these labs were to be appropriate for both "students with deficiencies and those . . . achieving at or above their grade level." For students in all-black high schools there were to be labs to "strengthen skills in reading, writing, math and science." No subtle academic sop, this program was intended to upgrade the quality of education for youngsters in schools remaining segregated. Charles Willie, an authority of desegregation at Harvard, urged the desegregation monitoring committee appointed in 1980 to pay special attention to the labs because those students deserved compensation for "remaining in segregated classrooms."[3]

Members of that group took Professor Willie's suggestion seriously and did look closely at the enrichment labs. In the committee's 16 November 1981 report, particular care was taken to analyze the labs' progress. The members reminded the board that in "several of our court reports last year, and in our meetings with the Board this year, we have noted several problems with the implementation of the enrichment programs in nonintegrated schools." Among the problems were "the lack of consistent guidelines and an established diagnostic [procedure] . . . for teaching labs, limited participation of students in some schools, program conflict with Title I classes, lack of team teaching, insufficient instruction for students working at or above grade level and lack of in-service training for enrichment teachers."[4] These problems did not shrink noticeably in subsequent years.

Their conclusions had not been arrived at sloppily. The 1980 desegregation monitoring committee had administered a questionnaire to all enrichment teachers and principals at nonintegrated schools. A summary of their major findings is reproduced below:

> Most of the enrichment labs we visited seem to be operating smoothly, although many of them are not meeting the Plan's specific directives for implementation: Half of the labs are not providing instruction to students as often as the Plan requires. In 26 (42%) schools, students are receiving as little as one-third to one-half of the lab instruction they should receive; and in 38 (61%) schools, some students receive no enrichment instruction at all. Approximately one-fourth of the labs are not meeting team teaching requirements, and in fourteen (23%) labs which do report team teaching, the classroom teacher's role is limited to supervising and observing students. Many teachers have not employed a diagnostic/ prescriptive model, some because they were not aware of the requirement. This may be one of the reasons why only half of the teachers reported providing experiences for students, at above and below grade level, as the Plan requires.[5]

The committee left no doubt in anyone's mind that the enrichment labs were being seriously neglected.

The committee went on to add, however, that "despite this prevalent lack of compliance," it was "genuinely impressed with the quality of instruction . . . provided in most labs." The problem with the labs was not so much the absence of guidelines ("teachers have apparently developed well planned and often creative programs without them") but rather the lack of training, planning, and resources that had been allocated to the labs and their staffs. Many teachers had no idea what they were supposed to accomplish much less how they were to accomplish whatever it was they were supposed to be doing. Few of the schools had any math or science labs, although the board had some reasonable explanations for this.[6] More generally, though, the labs simply lacked sufficient resources and personnel to complete their assigned tasks.

The board and administration were not pleased with these reports, and neither was the judge who received a special briefing on the labs. The school system's official interpretation of the plan was that schools "could limit the number of students served by enrichment labs" and even "restrict participation to students who are performing below average ability."[7] That is to say, the labs could be treated exclusively as a tool for remedial education at the discretion of a principal. In fact, one board member confided to me that the labs were supposed to be sites for remedial assistance. They were intended to make a kid competitive, not make him into a genius, he said. Nevertheless, the enrichment programs had proved to be a great disappointment, and he predicted that few would be left after the 1982–1983 school year. Whatever their eventual fate, however, the school system promised to correct the more glaring flaws in the enrichment program. This required the extension of additional resources, staff assistance, and more careful monitoring by the district's own evaluation division.[8]

One reason the general public might have found it difficult to become more aroused by detailed discussions over magnet and middle schools or enrichment labs is that such programs are not generally considered "quality education" issues. The public seems better accustomed to thinking about education in more digestible hunks. Its appetite for information about school violence, teacher demands and incompetence, or achievement test scores seems almost insatiable. When people talk about the quality of their children's education it is most often in the context of personal safety, teachers, and level of achievement. It is for this reason, perhaps, that the media seems especially sensitive to these issues. Parents and concerned citizens, however, have been trained to worry about little else.

Violence, Strikes, and Testing

Residents of the metropolitan area were treated to an almost continuous barrage of reports about school violence throughout the desegregation controversy. This is not to say that the attention was unwarranted. Public schools often are disruptive and even violent places to spend one's day, especially in the "inner city." State legislators conducting hearings in St. Louis in 1977 heard disturbing testimony about assaults but also about administrators who "were afraid to report acts of violence or problems relating to drugs for fear that it might reflect on their ability to control the students." Leaders of two teachers' unions in the city and county demanded in 1978 that educators stop covering up incidents of "beatings, extortion and robbery" that had become commonplace in many city and suburban schools. Sometimes racial tensions are the source of fights between students. This was the case at several city high schools for several years. In

1978, for instance, twenty-three students were arrested at a high-school demonstration in South St. Louis. The students had objected to the revocation of smoking and off-campus eating privileges following a series of fights between white and black students inside the school. Then, in September 1980, about two hundred white students boycotted classes one day at a newly desegregated high school after charges of racial harassment allegedly had been ignored by school staff. The problem in this case was attributed to tensions brought on by the new desegregation program. It took a brick-throwing incident and injuries to five black students to prompt officials to change the school's administration, however.[9]

Deserved, too, has been concern over the commitment, qualifications, and treatment of schoolteachers. The superintendent struck a responsive chord among teachers and parents alike in 1978 when he called for a return to teaching children basic skills. "The citizens, the parents, the children expect academic achievement to improve. Those . . . unprepared to meet this challenge . . . should seriously consider other forms of employment." He, for one, was tired of hearing that tests are culturally biased or do not test what is taught. Achievement test scores had plunged over the previous six years. There had been a few signs that scores were stabilizing. Unless the downward trend could be reversed, however, it was unreasonable to expect the public to support the district.[10] He wanted results.

This was fine rhetoric. Although it came at a time when the system had turned to magnet schools with highly specialized curricula, the seven thousand school employees who heard these remarks found hope in the challenge to get back to the basics. Many expressed a sense of relief. Others shared a renewed sense of dedication to the schools. "It's something that needed to be said," remarked one teacher, "I even felt tears come to my eyes."[11] The excitement was palpable. Finally, perhaps, they could get down to the business of teaching.

Three months later they walked off their jobs in a contract dispute with the board of education. Their strike, illegal according to Missouri law, lasted eight weeks, embittered the public, and closed down the schools. The issue over which they struck involved nothing so noble as the desire to clean out the ranks of one of the nation's most inbred teaching and administrative school staffs. It was money. The district's budget surpluses had grown progressively slimmer, and teachers decided that they had better strike before the surpluses were gone.[12]

The strike was ended only after corporate executives pledged up to six hundred thousand dollars on top of the 1.4 million the governor promised to release from funds owed the district after the state took over the city's teacher college. This, as an editorial in a local paper argued, pointed to the need to revise both the amount of money reserved for public education and the taxing methods used to acquire it.[13] More importantly, the state's bail-out of the city school system offered convincing evidence of its political responsibility to the district. It was a precedent that would be expanded upon after the state was held partly accountable for segregation within the city's public schools. The 1979 teachers' strike accustomed local residents and state legislators to the idea that the state might have to find more funds to help its largest and most financially troubled school system.

The strike also dramatized the political vacuum within which the city school system had learned to operate: no local institution or group was considered sufficiently appropriate by both the disputing parties to serve as a mediating agent in the strike. This included the mayor's office, which offered to assist but was rejected by both the school board and the union. Parents eventually tried to force an end to the strike by filing a suit against the teachers' union.[14] Testimony was heard, but there was no judicial resolution to the controversy. Jesse Jackson even flew in from Chicago to pray for an end to the strike. The task of resolving this dispute was finally assigned to federal labor mediators, the only means on which both the school board and the teachers' union could agree.

Teachers did receive their raises. Both they and school administrators, however, paid a severe price for their political impertinence. A law that would have guaranteed public employees the right to bargain on working conditions and wages was defeated in the state legislature during the strike. This gave them no framework through which to pursue subsequent disputes. Even worse, both parties demonstrated a disregard for the public's well-being that at times bordered on callousness. This treatment was not lost on the public, which only five months earlier had been led to expect a renaissance in public education. That the public had been treated to an intramural spat in which it had a serious interest but no effective voice may help to account for the subsequent disinterest shown by people when school board elections were next held. It most certainly helps to account for the public's unwillingness to protest the dismissal of hundreds of school staff in 1982 or to work for the passage of a tax levy that would have saved their jobs, when in 1977 students and parents protested the transferral of 117 teachers to different schools. Only "lukewarm" support by city leaders for the tax measure was evident. One city official summarized the sentiment of local leaders nicely, "There's no connection between the city's school system and its political system," and "until there is, we're not going to take the flak for problems they have."[15]

The unwillingness of school personnel to be held accountable for their actions was manifested dramatically in the teachers' strike. Neither local leaders nor concerned citizens were able to exercise much control over people who ostensibly worked for them or served at their pleasure. The only thing teachers and administrators wanted to hear from the public was its willingness to give them more money. In exchange for these additional funds the school system did not appear ready to make any political concessions; it did intend to prove itself worthy of the revenues and political autonomy by demonstrating its competence, however, just as the superintendent had said it should.

This proved no small feat. Educational laxness, sloppiness, and permissiveness had rumbled through St. Louis as it had in every metropolitan area during the 1960s and 1970s. A minor curricular revolution was left in its wake, but so were lazy and poorly prepared students and teachers. In St. Louis this problem was compounded by massive changes in the area's population, inadequate support for public education at all levels, and an inbred teaching and administrative staff. A high percentage of candidates for teaching positions in the district had been reared in the city and had attended the local teachers' college. Many had eventually become part of the district's administrative staff. In 1976, for example, it was estimated that of one hundred and sixty school principals in the district only four had not graduated from the teachers' college. Spouses, cousins, and friends were all securely nestled in a district that had not yet suffered serious problems with layoffs and early retirements.

For some graduates of the college there appeared to be no clear correlation between a candidate's ability and employment with the district. Politics was the name of the game, and, according to some instructors, it may have been one of the few words many of their students could spell. Cheating, they maintained, was rampant and unnecessary. If students hung around long enough, they were sure to see the same standardized test and pass it. Courses emphasized teaching methods rather than academic content, and perhaps this was the case because many faculty members had no credentials in an academic discipline.

These and other problems notwithstanding, the superintendent and the board were committed to improving the image of public education in the city. Desegregation and the controversies it sparked provided the opportunity they needed to push through reforms. The public, in turn, wanted to know why children receiving high grades in school could not read, write, or do simple mathematical computations, and had achievement test scores that seemed to be dropping into some educational black hole. The board of education and district administrators intended to give them an answer. Not only would they desegregate the schools in a peaceful and efficient manner, but they would improve the quality of public education as well.

The superintendent first noted that achievement test scores had begun to level off during an interview he gave in October 1977.[16] By the summer of 1979, modest improvements were seen in several testing areas, most notably in reading comprehension and math. According to one news account, a school official maintained that this was just the beginning of an upward trend due to the district's new concentration on basic education. He reportedly stated that students could be expected to continue achieving higher scores on the Iowa Test of Basic Skills (ITBS) because of the teachers' commitment to see that they learned more. By June 1980 school officials were even more confident. Although student achievement was still below national norms, ITBS scores had improved for the second year in a row. The superintendent expressed his pleasure with the progress shown by both students and teachers. Combined with the restoration of the state's highest level of accreditation for the district, the superintendent felt "much encouraged about the quality of education in [the] school system."[17]

It was imperative that the momentum gained during these two academic years not be lost during the process of mandatory desegregation in the following fall. During that period, people would be paying especially close attention to the schools, and the board and administration wanted to ensure that the year would be successful as well as peaceful.

Notwithstanding the superintendent's comments nearly two years earlier, many remained convinced that the achievement tests used by the district did not adequately measure what St. Louis students were learning. At least in this sense, the test was biased. The scores achieved by students were artificially low. Administrators acknowledged teachers' complaints about the ITBS in their response to a curriculum study that had been ordered by the court as part of the 1975 consent decree. There were "major academic areas" not covered by the ITBS. Among them were "art, music, and physical education content, English composition and writing skills; science and health knowledge; penmanship, and others." Furthermore, argued officials, "the ITBS does not in any way measure student attitudes, values, and feelings."[18]

Other officials and board members elaborated upon this critique in private interviews and public statements. The ITBS was not geared to urban school populations and was no longer used by many city school districts. It was outdated. It had nothing relevant to the experiences of minority students. It was not a valid measurement instrument. The test could only be used through the eighth grade. It had too many questions. The list of complaints was a long one, and many were sure that a more sensitive test was available. The school system found that instrument in the California Achievement Test, or the CAT, as it is commonly known.

Before the strengths and weaknesses of the CAT are examined, it is important not to let one point get overlooked: people have different opinions as to what constitutes a strong academic program and a "return to the basics" in the public schools. However, it is difficult to imagine most parents accepting art and music, much less penmanship, health, and physical education as major academic subjects. The alleged shortcomings of the ITBS as a fair measure of student values or feelings requires no additional comment. To the extent that the CAT or any other standardized achievement test has tapped student knowledge on these topics, it would be difficult to argue that such information has reflected a "return to the basics." There must be a more satisfactory explanation for the district's decision to choose the CAT and why it was adopted when it was.

Once again, school desegregation may provide an answer. The 1980–1981 school year was bound to be difficult, and the public needed comprehendible signs that the district was delivering on its promise to provide a quality education as well as peaceful desegregation. The CAT helped by allowing students to show their best achievement scores in a decade. School officials knew what to expect when they chose the CAT over several other standardized tests. The district's evaluation division had studied and compared teachers' reactions to the different tests. Based on this information, the evaluation people had recommended strongly that the CAT not be adopted. Besides several technical problems with the test, observed one official, "it was just too damned easy." Students, he added, "were bound to show higher levels of achievement." And that is precisely what occurred.

The district released a report in January 1982 that compared student scores on the ITBS and the CAT. Board members had requested the study, and the evaluation division had carried it out. The report contained two major findings. First, students who did well on one test tended to do well on the other. Similarly, "students who [had] moderate or low scores on one test [were] likely to be placed in the same relative position on the other." Second, "despite their high relationships to each other on an individual basis, the two tests yield widely disparate estimates of student achievement levels in relation to national norms." The CAT achievement levels were "consistently much higher" than those obtained from the ITBS.[19]

More importantly, perhaps, were the graphs presented in the report. The dramatic increase in most CAT scores stood out starkly and diverged sharply from the more gently contoured downward slope followed by most of the ITBS scores since 1970. In fact, there could be little doubt that during the first year of mandatory desegregation the ITBS scores actually dropped in every grade for every test. The highly touted progress evidenced in student test scores during the previous two years had shown a complete reversal. School desegregation may not have had anything to do with this regrettable change. Students may not have been as well prepared to take the ITBS or may have thought it a silly exercise in light of the district's adoption of the CAT.[20] Nevertheless, the ITBS scores had declined, and the evidence was right there in the report.

School administrators did not want the graphs in the 1982 report. In fact, they did their best to get the evaluation division to change the report or dismiss its content before it was released to the board. There are people who claim that they were threatened with losing their jobs. It probably was for these reasons as well as the fear that the report would never be published that someone leaked a preliminary draft to a local television news bureau. Administrators rushed to soften the findings of the report, and they were quite successful. To my knowledge no reporter fully explored the fact that the CAT scores were artificially high. Nor did anyone treat the drop in ITBS scores as a serious matter or investigate the way the district had used the CAT scores. All that anyone seemed to care about knowing was that students appeared to be doing better. Indeed, by May 1982 officials announced proudly that elementary and middle-school students were improving their CAT scores even faster than what was expected according to national norms.[21]

The flap over CAT scores could have been predicted. School officials in Baltimore County, Maryland, had experienced a similar controversy earlier in that same academic year. In this case, however, the entire state had switched to the CAT from the ITBS. Increasing numbers of Maryland students were "getting perfect or nearly perfect scores on sections of the [CAT] and many school officials [said] they [weren't] happy." These increases, maintained the director of testing for Baltimore County public schools, were "solely a function of the test." Officials in the city of Baltimore had pushed for the CAT to be adopted because, like officials in St. Louis, they had found it more fair for urban children. Another county official, however, was more candid about the test's appeal. "Quite frankly," he said, "it's really a battle of public relations, when you're talking about the [test results] that are being published in the paper, or shown to the school board." "As far as programs for kids," he contended, "it probably doesn't matter very much."[22]

This is a comforting idea. Yet I think that the adoption of the CAT was more than a clever but essentially harmless public relations ploy in the case of St. Louis. It has had real consequences for the educational program of some youngsters. For instance, "basic skill scores of St. Louis students . . . improved enough under the California test that up to 2,000 fewer students were eligible . . . for remedial help provided by the federal Title I program" during the 1981–1982 school year.[23] Seventy percent of all St. Louis school students had been eligible during the previous academic year. Only 65 percent were able to make use of these additional resources during the 1981–1982 academic year. I do not know what long-term effects the denial of such resources will have on individual students. One can imagine, though, that youngsters might believe they are doing good work when in fact they are not.

There is something to be said for being reminded about how little things do change sometimes. In the case of the climbing CAT scores, we see a perverse return to the use of standardized tests as tools for making discriminatory public policies. At the start of the twentieth century, American social scientists and public educators turned the IQ test from a device for identifying children with learning disabilities into an indicator representing their inherent ability to learn. This "single, scalable thing in the head" they called "general intelligence."[24] Not only could all children be ranked along this single scale but one could also distinguish those who were destined for greater things from those on whom substantial resources need not be wasted. Black children, among others, tended to score lower on these tests. It was believed that there was no good reason to worry about training these children to be more than they could become. Society was gradually weaned from this idea and later repudiated the policies based on it. It was also recognized that these scores were artificially low, reflecting something in the condition of their lives rather than themselves that led to their poor performance on this and other standardized tests.

One of the reasons the CAT was developed was to make it easier to distinguish children who tend to score at the lower end in most achievement tests. The CAT, being easier than other standardized tests, is more sensitive to variations among children at the lower end of the achievement scale. In theory, after these children are detected, teachers are able to prescribe particular types of remedial assistance. This is an entirely appropriate and worthwhile thing to do.

This apparently has not been the way the St. Louis school system has used the test. Officials have employed the test as a single, scalable measure of how well students, and by extension teachers, have been doing. All children have been ranked along the test's scale, and it is perceived that they have been doing better.[25] Something in the condition of their lives allegedly changed, and their performance on the achievement tests has proved it. The district has been doing a competent job and has deserved the support of citizens and public leaders alike. That such improvements have happened during a period of considerable stress has made the district's accomplishment even more noteworthy.

A complete reversal in the use of standardized tests to justify or defend discriminatory policies is obvious in the adoption and misuse of the CAT. When the CAT was first adopted, it was used to make children appear as if they were learning more than they really were. Results seemed to confirm the contention of school personnel that they were doing a credible job of educating children in a nondiscriminatory fashion. In truth, however, they were not. The effect of their "well-intentioned" adoption of the CAT was every bit as discriminatory in the long run as was the adoption of IQ tests earlier in the century. In both cases, children were being sorted to fit into an existing arrangement of social classes and jobs, and school systems were viewed as performing competently and responsibly.

Reorganization, Money, and Desegregation

Regardless of whether students really had acquired more knowledge, it was important for the district that they appeared to be learning more. So perhaps it was reasonable for the district to play with student achievement scores as if they had no significance except as a public-relations gimmick. The district had difficult problems, and anything that could be done to reduce them was certainly worth trying. The most pressing of these problems included the district's bloated administration and teaching staff, underutilized school buildings, and poor financial condition. These problems are common to most large corporations that find the market for their goods or services shrinking. Some of these corporations have learned to compensate for the lack of interest shown by individual customers by appealing to a broader public audience for assistance. They do this by pointing out the public good provided by their product and the public harm that would be caused by its loss. The difference between these corporations and school systems is that the former tend to ask for short-term subsidies. School systems and other public institutions are required to search for assistance every year. This surely must put a strain on the creative powers of school officials, because people grow weary of being constantly solicited for more money.

No one expressed much surprise when city school officials requested on 1 April 1984 that the desegregation budget be tripled to nearly $100 million in only one year. Yet this was no joke. School desegregation creates a climate in which such appeals are less likely to be viewed as excessive. However, it also carries with it an explicit understanding that something new or at least different will be done in exchange for these resources. For a large company like Chrysler it might mean that administrative ranks are pruned and reordered, less efficient plants are closed, the accounting system is revised, and the product is improved. In desegregation cases attention is paid to the hypothetical improvements that are to be made in the products of a school system—its students. Officials expect that the black 1985 model will go further and get there faster than ever before. It will be cleaner, more sophisticated, and have broader appeal to the public. The white model will lose that air of stuffy superiority to which the buying public had grown accustomed. Yet it will sacrifice none of its power by having become more hip. Less obvious but equally important, however, is the connection between the improved product and changes in the manufacturing process through which it will pass. Such changes are not always required in desegregation cases, but desegregation can make them easier to introduce. At least that is the way it has appeared to work in the St. Louis area.

We saw several examples of this in the case involving the Ferguson-Florissant Reorganized School District. There, a leaner and presumably more efficient administration was put in charge of three formerly independent school districts because of desegregation. Schools were closed and staff reassigned, also as a result of desegregation. Governance of the new district ostensibly was put in the hands of a new board of education whose members were drawn from the three old districts. A new tax levy was ordered by the courts. None of this would have happened but for desegregation. Comparable changes would be required if a metropolitan desegregation order were ever issued.[26] Only in this case a merger would involve all the districts of St. Louis County as well as that of St. Louis City. No one found the proposal especially surprising or intriguing except for what it omitted. Missing was any reference to how the new metropolitan district would be administered. Few doubted that the city district's administrators would have an advantage over those from the county. Not only did they control the area's largest school system but they took the precaution of having their status changed to that of a plaintiff in 1981. The major point, however, is that such a plan would bring about a host of administrative and financial changes in public education that many persons have thought necessary since the 1960s.

Up to this point, the relation between administrative reorganization and desegregation has been less direct in the city. Reorganization efforts have complemented the desegregation process rather than being caused by it. The district's 1979 plan to reduce and reorder its organizational chart converged from three major points. The 1975 consent decree was one of them; internal studies and proposals by "concerned friends" of the district constituted the other two paths leading to the reorganization plan.

The consent decree required staff and some students to be moved, but it also called for a study to determine how schools could be better realigned in order to integrate faster. Implied in such a proposal are alterations in how decisions are made and who makes them. People outside the system had begun making suggestions as early as 1975 about how the central office staff might be reorganized. These concerns were expanded to include the whole district's administrative apparatus in a report issued several years later by a committee appointed jointly by the city's boards of education and aldermen. District officials' own analyses reinforced the need to initiate some program that would substantially change how policies are made and implemented. Some critics of the reorganization effort claimed, however, that the real object of the exercise was to change who made the important decisions and to consolidate the superintendent's control over the district.[27] In any event, representatives of these various parties were brought together in a series of seminars in 1978. District officials worked with the recommendations that were made and issued a proposal for reorganizing the district in April 1979.

Most of the public attention given to the plan focused on the proposal to eliminate forty administrative positions and shift the persons holding those jobs into assignments with less authority and pay. This represented approximately a 20 percent reduction in the number of administrative posts and an annual savings of about seven hundred and fifty thousand dollars. None of the three black members of the board of education voted for the plan, and one resigned because of it. She was the body's president at the time. The Concerned Parents for Neighborhood Schools—one of the parties to the desegregation case— and the U.S. Department of Justice filed suit to stop the plan because it involved a number of school closings and attendance boundary changes "that should have been subject to consultation under the desegregation case ruling."[28] An attorney for the district believed that the board did not have to consult anyone, arguing that "under state laws . . . the Board [has] a responsibility to run the school system, much the way a board of Directors has the responsibility to run a plant." The judge agreed with the board of education. "Given the demographic and financial problems" of the district, he maintained, the two requests for injunctions "plainly [did] not offer promising desegregation remedies."[29] Having only recently found the district not guilty of intentionally segregating the schools, the judge was not going to interfere with decisions made by the district.

Notwithstanding the court's decision, it was clear that the reorganization plan would have an effect on subsequent desegregation proposals. Any proposal that would call for a 40 percent reduction in the number of high-school districts in the system, as this one did, would likely have some impact on which schools could or could not be paired for desegregation. One black parent active in the case reported that she had told the superintendent that this was his desegregation plan. His response, according to her, was that it was not; however, whatever the judge ordered could be fit into this new administrative arrangement. Desegregation had helped to make some form of reorganization possible. Now, it appeared, the course of future desegregation efforts would be constrained at least in part by the kind of administrative structure the district had created for itself.[30]

The lack of money had been an important theme in discussions about reorganizing the district. Similar concerns arose in virtually all deliberations about how best to desegregate the district, if at all. The school system approached desegregation as it would have any other business transaction. According to school officials, the district's cash surplus had shrunk nearly 10 million dollars between 1975 and 1977. This would have left the district with less than one hundred thousand dollars in the bank. If the district was to be desegregated, officials were committed to doing it in a way that would make money for the system.

Desegregation under the 1975 consent decree provided officials with an opportunity to experiment with several cost-cutting devices that were used more extensively in the 1979 reorganization plan. The district was required to balance its staff in every school, ensuring that white and black faculty would be teaching at all sites. This led to staff transfers, cuts, and early retirements. It also produced savings. One board member stated that it was a lot cheaper to hire younger teachers to replace older, racist ones who did not want to move. Furthermore, whenever a new position was created, officials would add some responsibilities to it and make sure the right-colored person got the job. Older positions simply disappeared from the district's ledgers, and money was saved. School closings were also proposed as part of the district's voluntary efforts to desegregate the system.

The problem with suggesting such changes as part of a voluntary plan, however, was that they could be successfully challenged in court. Many interested parties could complain that they should be heard and consulted more closely. Several years later, when the district was "ordered" to act decisively, it closed more than two dozen schools in one evening and saved the district about $2 million a year. One board member said it was "marvelous . . . we closed all those schools in 10 minutes and no one could stop us. If it had not been for the desegregation order, we would have been forced by the community to keep those sites open."

Desegregation was also perceived as a way to make money for the district. It was, in the words of one board member, "a license to steal." Funds received for desegregation and acquired from banks at low interest rates were reinvested in certificates of deposit or repurchase agreements with local banks for markedly higher rates of return. Most federal aid money could not be used in this fashion; but a good percentage of it could be transferred into the district's general fund, which was not so confined. Desegregation money, of course, also underwrote the district's alternative and middle-school programs, helped to improve staff salaries, and made a substantial contribution toward building maintenance and capital improvements at a number of schools. Sites that might not otherwise have been left open because of low enrollments were turned into magnet or middle schools and were kept operating with state and federal funds. There was some concern in 1980 that nearly two hundred and fifty thousand dollars had been spent during the previous two years repairing and renovating the twenty-six schools that were closed under the mandatory desegregation order. However, a bit more than $1.75 million was intended to be spent building "libraries, science laboratories, and facilities for instruction in industrial arts, home economics and textiles" in the district's twenty-four new middle schools.[31] That represented a "profit" for the district of $1.5 million in improvements.

By September 1980 the district had increased its cash surplus to nearly $6 million. This was not much of a financial buffer. Nevertheless, the cost savings and subsidies realized from desegregation and effective investments had helped to keep the district from going bankrupt for a few years. The state objected to its participation in what was perceived to be a scheme to subsidize the public schools through desegregation. The state has made these objections each year since 1980 and each year has been ordered by the court to contribute its share to the city's desegregation effort. Occasionally the state has been able to get the court to reduce its contribution on one or another item described by the district as an "essential" element of the desegregation plan. While this has angered the board of education, the city school district has been largely successful in enhancing its revenues from the state by claiming that expenses are related to desegregation.

Despite the additional sums acquired through desegregation, the district's meager surplus again had dwindled by the end of 1981. This prompted officials to call for a new levy that would have increased the tax rate by 46 percent. As if to dramatize the desperate financial situation they confronted, district officials fired 280 teachers and proposed to transform several high schools into magnet schools. The connection between the system's need for new funds and desegregation as a source of such revenues was inescapable. Indeed, board of education members freely admitted it. The superintendent was reported to have called the proposed conversion the most economical response to continued drops in student enrollments. No one was happy with the plan, and no one wanted to think about the prospect of cutting all employees' salaries or firing 25 percent—some one thousand eight hundred—of the district's personnel if the tax failed.[32] Yet the anticipated deficit of $26 million for the 1982–1983 school year was unthinkable and illegal.

The defeat of the tax levy in June 1982 suddenly made the unthinkable very real. Board members reluctantly chose not to resubmit the proposal for the August primary for fear that it would hurt other tax proposals already on the ballot. In the meantime they prepared a "disaster budget" that called for the elimination of physical education, music and art teachers, school-crossing guards, some libraries and teachers' aides, reduced field trips and building maintenance as well as other support services. School officials gamely tried to convince the public of the need for additional resources. Opponents of the district's desegregation effort did not even bother to mount a campaign against the tax levy. They were confident that people would take the opportunity to punish the district for its racial program. It was believed that the poor condition of the local economy would also make people unwilling to tax themselves more.[33] The critics apparently were correct.

Board members reviewed their options. Some wanted to bring another tax proposal before the voters later in the year. Yet no one really believed that the result would be any different. Other members expected that the district eventually would have to try a different strategy, one that was guaranteed to anger even more people. "The courts have ordered us to make an effort" to raise money, said the board of education's vice-president. "And we've made every effort we can. Now, we can go to the court and tell them we've honestly tried."[34] The court could be approached with a proposal to build a new tax rate for public education in the city on the back of its own desegregation order, but some school officials preferred having the state increase its contribution. The judge had already expressed his willingness to establish a new uniform tax rate for a consolidated city and county school district, however. So, creating a new tax rate in the city in order to sustain an unpopular desegregation program and school system might not prove too unreasonable. For those who still found the idea unappealing, one needed to look no further than the Ferguson-Florissant Reorganized School District for an example of how to work such fiscal magic. Once again, it was considered that desegregation could be used to accomplish what could not be achieved through routine politics.

Refilling a Public Vacuum

It really is not fair to say that routine politics failed the city school system. Such a declaration would be predicated on the assumption that the public schools are an integral part of the city's political operation. They are not. Persons running for positions on the board of education solicit and receive help from interest groups with strong ties to local politicians and even from the city's ward organizations; the mayor appoints persons to complete the unexpired terms of board members who can no longer serve; school officials work closely with local representatives to the state and federal government on matters involving public education. Still, the public school system remains curiously aloof from local politics. As the most politically autonomous public institution in most cities, it is immune from many of the partisan conflicts and intraparty squabbles that plague any political system. Nor is the public school system subject to many constraints imposed by the public on organizations closely tied to the city's political system.

The history of public education in cities reveals that civic leaders have traditionally considered such autonomy highly desirable. Independence from politics also suited the needs of the professional bureaucrats who actually ran the school system and who wanted to protect this institution from the sources of political and social profanation evidenced in other public arenas. The last thing these administrators wanted was to put the patients in charge of the asylum. If the civilizing influence of learning and self-discipline could be felt nowhere else in a city, it would be preserved in the public schools. The creation of a strong, centralized board of education and school administration were crucial elements in this scheme. One also might have added that these bodies were supposed to remain "above politics," at least in the traditional and partisan sense of the phrase.

It was the failure of the St. Louis district to achieve this state of nonpartisan sobriety that led to a resurgence of nineteenth-century evangelism in post–World War II St. Louis. After the war, a number of civic leaders objected to the influence that Democratic politicians were enjoying in school affairs. Indeed, until 1959 political patronage was still a prominent feature in the selection and retention of school personnel. This was especially true in the case of nonteaching staff. Concerned citizens eventually decided to gain control of the school board in an attempt to purge the district of partisan politics. Their campaign began in 1953 with the election of one reformer to the board. Two more were elected in 1955. The plutocratic coup d'etat was successfully completed after a blistering campaign in 1961 and a series of revelations about school board corruption. Five more reformers were elected to the board. The leader of this movement and first reformer to be elected became the board's president. A merit system for nonteaching staff was quickly adopted, and local politicians no longer had any incentive to worry about what happened in the schools. Nor, one must add, could they be held accountable for its conduct and responsible for its maintenance.

This did not trouble upper-class reformers and their supporters. Enrollments were growing. Money would be available for building and servicing new schools. As in earlier reform movements, however, these crusaders had only a narrow vision of what the future might hold. They had apprehended a future in which traditional values and ways of doing things had little relevance. So rather than opening up the district to new ideas and constituencies they sealed it from popular control at precisely the moment when the city was undergoing profound changes. The result was nearly two decades of uninterrupted governance by civic elites and educational bureaucrats.

This rule was not marred by the cynical scent of partisan politics. Instead, the district was subjected to the corrupting influence of its own autonomy and its caretakers' self-indulgence. While progress in the district was at a standstill, everything else was changing. This was most apparent in the district's racial policies or, more accurately, in officials' denial of racial policies. This stagnation was also clear in the absence of changes in the district's curriculum and administrative structure. If the district managed to avoid the many educational fads of the 1960s and 1970s, it also exhibited little interest in adopting reforms that even St. Louis educators thought made good sense. Political autonomy had not produced a system capable of innovation or self-criticism but instead had created a bloated administration, an over extended teaching staff, and a system increasingly more isolated from the people it was supposed to serve. Routine politics in the city did not fail the school system. The district had chosen to cut itself loose from local politics except for a few occasions when it was necessary to perpetuate the illusion that school personnel were accountable to the public.

School desegregation changed all of this. As distasteful as the idea of desegregation was to many school leaders, administrators emerged remarkably fit and pleased by their symbolic humiliation before the courts. Much of the reason no doubt could be found in the opportunities desegregation had provided for introducing new policies and programs to the district. Conscious experimentation on a broad scale was possible for the first time since the end of World War II. A number of the bigger innovations already have been discussed. Smaller changes, such as giving a principal the right to help select his staff and the use of "management by objectives" in planning school programs, were tried first in the magnet schools and were gradually extended to all public schools.

School officials express various levels of satisfaction with these different innovations. Yet there is one area in which experimentation was especially vigorous and for which no one, except perhaps the court's advisers, was willing to claim success. The area was citizen involvement. Arguments over school segregation inspired an unprecedented number of groups to express greater interest in the schools. Most of these groups either took a position on the segregation controversy or pledged to cooperate with whatever plan eventually was ordered. The leaders of several groups hoped to enhance their own organization's stature by creating a role for themselves as "honest brokers" among the various parties to the suit. Other bodies seemed to get dragged into the controversy even though their primary interests were in other areas. The mayor's office and the board of aldermen were clearly in this category. All the groups, however, stood to gain or lose something through their participation. This in itself was a novelty, because the school board and administration had worked to discourage any outside party from thinking about the district as a place where political or financial advantage could be gained. Desegregation upset this contrived state of affairs by once again making it worth somebody's effort to care about what was happening in the schools.

Many people might be surprised by such a finding. Critics of judicially in-spired desegregation plans argue that the courts' intervention into these matters only detracts from the ability of local people to affect school policy. They, along with many advocates of desegregation, take the position that the best plan reflects the ideas of local people working through established political channels. Still, in the case of the Ferguson-Florissant Reorganized School District, such a process left out several important constituencies and exaggerated the influence of school administrators over educational policy making. The inclusion of groups typically ignored by school leaders when making decisions was an im-portant difference in the city case. Just how much of an impact these groups had is open to question. Upper-level administrators in the city held some of the same views about working with "the little people" as did their suburban counterparts. They cooperated with these groups only when they had to. Nevertheless, deseg-regation in the city opened up the district's policy-making process much more than officials wanted.

City school officials were unable to ignore the district's new friends and critics as easily as their suburban counterparts had. A lot more effort had to be expended to keep up with new charges or recommendations made by various groups. Given the unwieldy size and structure of the district, administrators often found it difficult to figure out exactly what was going on inside their own institution. Members of the Concerned Parents for North St. Louis (CPNS) said that this sometimes worked to their advantage. Preparing their case against the district, CPNS representatives would make what even they conceded were some "pretty wild and exaggerated charges" and then would watch school officials try to refute them. In refuting the charges, however, officials inadvertently would give the CPNS data it really needed or a hint as to where information might be found. The CPNS was aided to some extent by school personnel who either would leak important documents or talk about district policies. The Concerned Parents for Neighborhood Schools enjoyed similar access to information about school practices. Its network understandably was better among white school personnel in Southside schools, however. The point, in any case, is that the city school system was a far richer source of information about its own conduct and policies than most officials would have cared to admit.

Parents often knew about things going on in the district long before school board members found out about them, if they ever did. In this sense, the city school system was more "open" to the public than the Ferguson-Florissant Reorganized School District had been. *Open* may be too analytic a term, though, to describe what was going on in this intelligence-gathering system. *Perforated* might be a more accurate word to use concerning how the district subsidized the efforts to criticize or defend its programs. The Concerned Parents for Neighborhood Schools also benefited in material ways from district leaders who allowed schools to be used as fund-raising sites and who, in at least one notable case, were alleged to have contributed substantial amounts of money to defray the group's legal expenses.

All of this activity was carried on informally, however. School officials and board members found no formal mechanism during the 1970s that could channel the energies of the district's friends into projects acceptable to the district's leadership. The existing network of school organizations designed to involve parents with the district and its programs proved unworkable, even irrelevant when confronted with the desegregation process. People who tended to dominate traditional parent organizations were overwhelmed by the controversy unfolding before them. More politically active parents tutored them or, if that failed, tried to lead them around by the hand and show them how to be more effective observers of district programs. Even some school board members were disturbed with the generally unsophisticated and trivial questions posed by parents during periodic visits to schools. Later, as the controversy dragged on, district leaders proposed a new system of citizen involvement. They wanted to broaden the base of community involvement beyond parents whose children attended the public schools or parents who had become "professional activists." This apparently did happen. As yet, however, this new organization has not proved any more successful in refilling the public vacuum created in the schools more then twenty years ago than has any other group.

Elite and Grass-roots Involvement

It has been difficult to find groups to replace the local political organization in the schools. The Parent Congress was replaced by a Parent/Community Advisory Council. Beyond the fact that the Parent/Community Advisory Council membership consisted only of parents, by 1980 it had become something of a nuisance. Parent activists, many of them recruited directly from the ranks of the two groups involved in the segregation case, had begun to make their presence felt. Leaders from each of the high-school districts started to meet at the homes of desegregation proponents and opponents in order to fashion a single agenda to present to the board of education at its monthly meetings. Not long after they began to press their "consensus agendas," the proposal for a new community involvement system was presented to the court and accepted as part of the mandatory desegregation plan.

School officials argued that the change was necessary. Only the citywide Parent Congress, which had been operating since 1968, was eliminated. Other groups whose membership was confined to parents, such as the PTA and mothers clubs, were not disbanded. Even though the concept of broader-based community involvement had been "recommended by an educational task force" before the mandatory desegregation order had been handed down, officials thought that it would help make desegregation work more smoothly in the future.[35] Parents did not like the inclusion of what they perceived to be "outsiders" in a public school organization. The board of education eventually rejected this argument, however, and implemented the new system. Activist parents saw a useful political base, representing several years of hard work, dismissed as an impediment to progress.

Parents had used the lessons they learned from the citywide ESAA Committee and court battle to fashion a broader coalition in the Parent Congress. They knew how difficult it was to bring parents together on an issue as sensitive as desegregation. Leaders from the two parent groups involved in the case had met stiff resistance from their own supporters when they had started to explore areas of mutual concern. Furthermore, unlike the ESAA Advisory Committee on which several of them had served, the Parent Congress touched the parents of all schoolchildren, not just those in the magnet schools. They also recognized that the ESAA committee, like its suburban counterpart, had been too closely controlled by school officials. The Parent Congress eventually became sufficiently independent of the school board to serve as an effective voice for the concerns of parents from across the district. That, in the opinion of several parent leaders, is why it was disbanded.

Discussions with a number of members of the ESAA Advisory Committee about the conduct of that body verified some of the arguments of parent activists and my own observations at many meetings. It was true, they said, that the group did little other than satisfy the federal requirement that parents be involved in the magnet school program. Several maintained, however, that it was their own fault, that they were naive to believe that the district would acknowledge suggestions or that they just did not push hard enough.

"Everything was always being done at the last minute," one former member said. "This was really obvious when we tried to pin [administrators] down on the budget. They'd run it before us the day before it was due in Washington, or we'd get the proposal without the budget." Nevertheless, "we'd vote on it anyway, and it would pass." One member complained about this in a letter to the program's director that left the clear impression that it also had been sent to the "feds." Shortly after the letter was sent, he was summoned for a private meeting with several of the district's highest administrators and "educated" about the "bad judgment" he had exercised. Another member complained privately about the "two sets of books" kept by school officials when discussions at ESAA Advisory Committee meetings were recorded. "There are the minutes that go to district officials downtown, and then there are the 'cleaned-up' versions we receive several weeks later." "Problems which we bring up," she added, "are either put in as part of [the director's] report so it looks like he's doing something about them or [they] have been completely omitted from the minutes." In any event, the official record of the ESAA committee was sanitized in order to make the program and its administrators look a lot better than they really were. Meetings were little more than sessions set aside to complain, and nothing much was accomplished.

One white former member decided to quit the group after it became clear to him that the administration had no intention of taking it or the magnet program seriously except as a public relations tool. An investigation of the "college prep" program at one magnet school was "squashed" by school officials because, he contended, "the program was nothing but 'black studies' and remedial education courses." "White kids," as far as he and several black members were concerned, "were still getting all the [good courses]." What finally prompted him to quit was a pair of decisions about school sites. After a proposed site for one magnet school had been rejected by the committee, the superintendent called him in and asked him why he was "trying to sabotage the program." Construction on the building, it seems, already had been started. The same thing apparently happened with an elementary school that the administration had considered proposing as a site for one of its new junior-high schools. Renovations had begun even before the court had accepted the junior-high program as part of a voluntary desegregation plan. That idea was postponed and ultimately rejected in favor of a "middle-school concept" as part of the 1980 mandatory desegregation order. But the school in question was not forgotten. It became a "middle school."

Both ESAA Advisory Committee members and magnet school staff acknowledged that parental involvement varied greatly among the different schools in the program. Some principals took it more seriously than others; parents who really wanted their children in the program tended to pay more attention to the school. This, several ESAA Committee members noted, was an illustration of the "self-selection" process they thought was occurring but could not document. The original ESAA Committee members themselves were a rather select group apparently consisting of people who represented constituencies the district did not wish to offend. Both of the original cochairs went on to become members of the board of education, as did at least one other member later on. A teacher who served on the ESAA Advisory Committee became head of the teachers' union. At least six other parents eventually served on the Citizens Education Task Force (CETF) and/or the Desegregation Monitoring and Advisory Committee appointed by the court. The ESAA Advisory Committee served as a training center and modest springboard for a number of persons who remained active in school politics. More generally, the desegregation controversy spawned a whole generation of grass-roots leaders for the district, only some of whom worked their way up by serving on one or another of these committees. Others emerged with the support of local politicians who thought it time that the patrician conduct of the school board be challenged. It was, and the leadership on the board, it seemed to some observers, began to swing over to a more pragmatic set of individuals.[36]

Permanent leaders and ties to the city's political system do not yet seem likely. The school board has expressed no willingness to trade even a bit of its autonomy for some support from the Democratic party. This is one important reason school officials eventually went to the court and asked that the tax rate in the city be raised as part of the proposed voluntary exchange program between the city and county. District officials have opened their doors to politicians only during extreme emergencies. The 1973 teachers' strike was one such occasion. The passage of a bond issue in 1976 was another. It was then that the CETF was established by a joint resolution of the board of aldermen and board of education. Composed of persons from across the community—"civic, labor and community leaders, parents, media people, and educators"—it was the forerunner of the district's Parent/Community Advisory Council.[37]

The CETF was intended to reestablish a political base for the city district, although it did have members who were St. Louis County residents. As a mixture of well-connected elite and grass-roots people, the CETF was supposed to increase the district's political capital without any substantial political investment by school leaders. The CETF identified issues and solutions to problems, informed the board of education of its ideas, and mustered support for the school system in the city. It was an advisory committee whose only leverage came from the various constituencies represented on it. The committee did help to get the bond issue passed. However, without any clear understanding of its own mission and unwilling to take a strong position on anything except "a philosophy of education" for the public schools, it quickly died off. By the spring of 1979, its primary benefactor, a local foundation concerned with educational matters, had withdrawn its financial support and initiated its own efforts in the area the CETF had entered only reluctantly—desegregation.

Insofar as the CETF had a hidden agenda, it was to serve as an advocate for metropolitan desegregation. Yet this agenda was so well hidden that even the membership could not find it. The underlying disagreement among the members, according to one of the group's professional staff, "was between those who understood desegregation as *the* issue that needed to be addressed and those who saw it as the quality of public education." Some members who argued against taking any formal action on desegregation admitted in private that they saw it as a major problem. "They saw it," argued the staff member, "but they didn't want to deal with it."

The organization's first director said in an interview that "it was not reasonable to assume that such a group could come to a consensus on anything. Yet they tried." Cleavages within the community, he said, were built into the organization: city people versus county people, whites versus blacks, elite versus grass-roots leaders. It was all there; and the organization became a platform on which all of these divisions found a voice. The board of aldermen began to withdraw its support shortly after the group had been brought together, and for reasons unrelated to anything the CETF would do eventually. Its primary sponsors left the board of aldermen for other political posts, and support for the CETF on that body soon withered. The board of education, for its part, seemed to take the organization seriously only after its director suggested that the group might consider entering the case for mandatory desegregation as a "friend of the court." This upset district leaders, who wanted no more citizens involved in the case. After this confrontation, however, school officials began to share more information and to seek assistance on certain issues.

Relations between the district and the CETF were never especially good, though. In response to the 1975 consent decree, for instance, the school board established nine committees to study the district's curriculum. Some of these committees had functions similar to those of the CETF committees. The perception among CETF members was that the school board was disenchanted with their group and chose not to recognize the work they were already doing. School officials merely noted that they had been ordered by the court to do this work. Nevertheless the effect of the order did not bolster the CETF in the eyes of the community or its own members for that matter.

Several members of the organization reinforced the opinions expressed by the professional staff. Notwithstanding the efforts of the group's director and staff, they argued it was difficult to get people to take a firm stand on desegregation. The CETF decided to serve the community by providing factual and current information about desegregation. It chose to hold a series of citywide and neighborhood forums in order to fulfill that role. Armed with money from the Missouri Council on the Humanities, the group pulled together local experts on desegregation and other race-related topics. Neither the board of education nor the board of aldermen was eager to have the program carried out. The former feared that it might injure the court case or give the public too much information about the district's "deal" in the consent decree. The latter was concerned about getting people "all riled up" in the neighborhoods and the effect that might have on their reelection campaigns. They need not have worried so much about the response of persons to the neighborhood forums. All the damage to be inflicted was accomplished at the first and only citywide meeting in February 1977. There the CETF was introduced to the public, and white parents from South St. Louis first heard that "they might as well get used to the idea of busing because it was coming to St. Louis." Mothers with infants and toddlers challenged that contention vigorously. Within two weeks the Concerned Parents for Neighborhood Schools was formed and well on the way to becoming a party to the case. This was the primary accomplishment of the CETF during its short life.

The neighborhood forums, like the citywide meeting, alerted the public that something was going on. Beyond that it is doubtful that anyone learned much about anything from these sessions. Planned hastily and publicized poorly in the neighborhoods where they were held, the forums attracted few people. An average of twenty-two people attended each of the twenty initial meetings; four sessions were cancelled altogether because no one showed up; two other sessions were shortened because of low attendance. Some people complained that too much attention was placed on the school board's proposal to expand the magnet schools and establish integrated junior-high schools. People also thought that too many "humanists" had been included on the panels. However, it would have been difficult to exclude the humanists, given the funding source for the sessions. CETF members noted that they also had to accept school administrators on the panels as the price for using schools as meeting sites. Citizen complaints that were dutifully solicited at each meeting were compiled but never worked on or responded to. A July "television spectacular" served as a nice conclusion to these efforts by becoming a "shouting match" between representatives of the Concerned Parents for North St. Louis and Concerned Parents for Neighborhood Schools.

The CETF managed to maintain some semblance of activity through the spring of 1980, but the possibility of it assuming a larger role in the mandatory desegregation process had long since vanished. Indeed, by September 1977 its primary sponsor had begun a quieter initiative to draw together all the parties to the suit in an attempt to reach an out-of-court agreement. This already had been tried on a far more modest scale by several project staff. That effort had failed, as would the initiative of the private foundation and its "blue ribbon" panel. Nevertheless, during the lull in the judicial proceedings in 1977 and 1978, there was some hard and heavy lobbying by groups that wanted to repeat the "success" of the 1975 consent decree on a grander scale. It seemed at times that almost everyone who, as one observer of the case described, was "well known" or who "wished to be well known," and not already a party to the suit, wanted to be involved. However, none of the parties wanted to jeopardize its standing in court and a potential "victory" for another jointly resolved settlement. They were more comfortable with the prospect of a more expensive but definitive resolution that would be handed down by the court. They began to change their minds several years later, of course, and worked with a court-appointed mediator to hammer out a "mandatory–voluntary" plan for the 1983–1984 school year.

Overseeing the Mandatory Plan

The Citizens Steering Committee, sponsored by the private foundation, carefully resisted efforts by some parties, including at least one representative of the city schools, to support a metropolitan desegregation plan. Although individual members might have supported such an outcome, they dared not repeat the errors committed in the better-publicized efforts of the CETF. The business and civic leaders on this committee were more cautious. They did not come out in favor of any particular plan and did not invite trouble by including grass-roots people in their group. They already knew that no basis existed for reaching a mediated settlement. So they busied themselves by piecing together a coalition that would urge peaceful compliance with whatever plan eventually was ordered. This effort was successful. A long list of prominent business leaders, corporations, community leaders, and religious groups pledged their support in April 1980 for the peaceful implementation of the mandatory desegregation plan. News reports carried the word that the Citizens Steering Committee was "uninvolved" in constructing that plan. However, a new "citizens" group called the Coalition for Peaceful Implementation was formed to help mobilize community support for the plan. It was backed by the same business groups that had supported the Citizens Steering Committee and the CETF.[38]

The panel appointed by the trial judge to help the district draw up the mandatory plan was composed of people who had been involved in the schools or in the desegregation process. It had at least one labor representative and one person with ties to the business community through the private foundation that had been so active. The chair of the panel was dean of a local law school and a personal acquaintance of the judge. The group's activities were noted earlier; but one element in its deliberations—the proposed closing of schools—helps to point out just how much control it had over the district's own plan writers and school board.

The decision on how many and which schools to close was "the very first thing you have to decide, because then you'll know what facilities you'll be working with," opined the superintendent.[39] One person later said that the superintendent had made a classic error in using post hoc logic. The proposal to close schools should be based on what you want to achieve with desegregation, not the other way around. Desegregation monitoring committee members challenged the need to close these schools as part of a desegregation plan, but it was approved nevertheless. When I asked one member of the board of education about the decision he simply smiled and said that they had behaved like any good business by taking advantage of this opportunity to close some worn out sites.

School administrators were able to put together the package of school closings, pairings, magnet and middle schools, and racial quotas that they desired. Members of the desegregation monitoring committee were pretty overwhelmed by the size of their task as well as the speed with which it had to be accomplished. They had little choice but to respond to suggestions made by school personnel as long as those suggestions were consistent with the guidelines set down by the court. They were on much firmer ground once the plan was being implemented and the committee's monitoring activities began.

A number of people serving on the 1980 desegregation monitoring committee had become rather proficient observers and critics of school programs over the previous decade. Moreover, they were able to utilize their contacts in the schools and neighborhoods more effectively in these roles. Frankly, there was little that escaped their attention. It was often the case that they knew of problems long before the school board did. Combined with some aggressive staff work and a director trusted by the court, the committee mounted an impressive, if not always popular, effort to oversee the district's desegregation program.

Differences between this committee's actions and the monitoring effort during the suburban case could not be more stark. The prolonged court case had given black and white parents from opposite ends of the city a chance to meet, fight, get better acquainted, share some common concerns, and eventually form good working relationships. The district itself was much larger, and the case involving it received much more attention. Citizens serving on the suburban groups that "advised" Ferguson-Florissant officials did not have the advantage or incentive provided by aggressive media coverage. They also had no staff or assistance in visiting school sites. The city committee had the help of the League of Women Voters and graduate students from several local universities in conducting its site visits and surveys. High school students volunteered to do office chores. The information that was acquired and the previous experience of committee members gave the group the independence it needed to assess what was being done in the schools. They were not timid about sharing the knowledge they gained.

The reports submitted to the court were thorough, detailed, and covered a range of topics directly and indirectly related to the implementation of the district's desegregation plan. There was sometimes evident a disturbing dependence on numbers. How many students did this? What percentage of the teachers had those materials? Were buses really arriving on time? Did all the Northside schools have problems with overcrowding? Yet it was the fact that the committee was able to back up its observations with "hard data" that helped to make it as effective as it was. Not only did the committee compare its numbers to those provided by the district, it also had numbers that the district never had thought to collect.

The school board and administration had decidedly mixed feelings about the desegregation monitoring committee. Privately some conceded that the committee routinely identified problems before central office staff could hear about them. Part of the reason for this may be that the committee was identified by some principals as a faster and more effective vehicle for getting problems addressed by the central administration. Committee staff members added that officials do respond quickly to smaller technical or building problems once they have been identified. Before the public, relations between the school system and monitoring committee were cool at best and sometimes hostile, but never in a distasteful or unprofessional manner. Their challenges were conducted through the press and court according to a schedule that coincided with the submission of the committee's reports to the court. Nevertheless, the contest was taken quite seriously by everyone involved.

It was not uncommon for these reports to be thirty or more pages in length, exclusive of the appendices, and to contain reviews of as many as sixteen or seventeen different topics.[40] When there was more going on or when a sensitive problem arose, the committee produced more reports. In short, the committee put to good practice the bureaucrat's favorite strategy of burying the opposition with technical reports that require a response. District officials, accustomed to manipulating others with numbers rather than being manipulated by them, argued that the committee studied topics not germane to desegregation or central to its mandate. Committee members readily conceded that they had moved into areas not directly related to desegregation but that problems like overcrowding and the conversion of sites into magnet schools did have an impact on the district's desegregation program. The committee did acquiesce on several issues, however. Most notable among these were shortages in supplies or texts, building repairs, and special education or "mainstreaming." The committee's reports on material shortages correctly anticipated a massive, year-long delay in the 1983 distribution of school supplies.

School officials and board members were forced to adjust some programs and even to come up with new suggestions because of the committee's complaints. It was the committee, for instance, that refused to ignore the so-called enrichment programs in segregated schools. The attention the 1980 desegregation monitoring committee brought to that program was an embarrassment to the district and angered officials, but strategies to improve the program were developed as a result. An even greater "victory" from the committee's standpoint was the successful challenge to the district's plan to convert several high schools into magnet schools as a device to save money. Public resistance was stiff, but the school board insisted on sticking with the plan. The court rejected it, however, after reviewing the arguments made by the committee. School board members were dismayed by this decision and the precedent it might represent. They had grown accustomed to using the desegregation order as a means to enact novel or politically unpopular procedures. The court's reversal of a bureaucratic initiative might be a bad omen.

Three somewhat academic points about the work and impact of the monitoring committee ought to be raised now. First, students of organizational change will recognize in the desegregation monitoring committee's work an interesting hybrid of strategies discussed in Chapter 5. The information compiled and the reports issued by the group constitute a classic example of the "survey-feedback" method of inducing organizational change. Data about an institution's performance in some area are "fed" back to its directors and general personnel. Organizations behaving like rational systems have some way of incorporating this new information into their standard operating procedures. Yet the district's own evaluation procedures were not thorough. Sometimes both the personnel in that division and their findings were held in contempt by other officials and the school board. The division's work on the CAT and magnet-school programs, for example, often was ignored or repudiated by upper-level administrators because it did not suit their grander schemes for improving the district. More traditional channels for redressing a complaint or noting a problem often did not work. If they had, principals might not have turned so readily to the 1980 desegregation monitoring committee for help.

What made the "survey-feedback" method as effective as it was in this case was its combination with a "structural" change introduced to the system at the same time. This change refers, of course, to the court-appointed monitoring committee. The existence of such a group does not guarantee that anything noteworthy will change, because a district's accountability to the group may be limited or district personnel may find ways to control access to information and powerful outside agencies like the court. The Ferguson-Florissant Reorganized School District provided an excellent example of how this could be accomplished. Its officials' success in this regard should not be taken as a sign that they were smarter or more sophisticated administrators than their city colleagues. Rather, it is that the city's desegregation monitoring committee had far more independence from, assistance by, and political clout with the court than did its suburban counterparts.

Not every "citizens group" in the city enjoyed the success of the 1980 desegregation monitoring committee. Indeed, a strong case can be made that it was as successful as it was only because the members had learned from the failures of earlier grass-root and elite efforts. A number of people who served on the monitoring committee, for instance, had been part of the ESAA Advisory Committee for the magnet schools. It was every bit as unsuccessful as the suburban groups performing the same functions. The city people had seen how the district could use a group such as the ESAA Advisory Committee as part of its desegregation strategy. These people also had used the opportunity, however, to expand their network of contacts across the city and among both races. Citizens in the merged suburban districts never had that chance.

A second lesson to be learned from the monitoring committee's work involved the group's aggressive pursuit of problems not directly tied to desegregation. Issues such as the conversion or closing of schools and even building repairs, its members thought, should be understood to have a bearing on the conduct of desegregation. Implicit in this argument is the same reasoning found in the Denver desegregation decision: constitutional violations discovered in one part of a district may be taken as a sign that a broader problem exists; there is a corrupting influence touching all the district's policies. The trouble with this argument is that it would have opened up districts to a more thorough critique of institutional practices than anyone really wanted to undertake. The legitimacy of the institution had to be preserved. St. Louis's desegregation monitoring committee had begun to make the same "mistake" as the court in the Denver case. It had expanded the critique of school policies to cover a broader range of decisions made by officials than was prudent or necessary to discharge its desegregation-related tasks.

No one bothered to cite the case law on this matter. No one had to. School officials and committee members—with a little help from the court—managed to renegotiate the limits within which the committee would work. This kind of self-discipline is characteristic of ritualized crises. Parties in conflict voluntarily restrain themselves in choices of issues and the tactics they employ. It is a civilized way to beat up on one another without inflicting any permanent damage.

This brings us to the third point. By muzzling itself and yet continuing its provocative analyses of some district programs, the monitoring committee effectively bolstered the legitimacy of the school system. The committee showed that the district could be made more accountable and responsive to the demands of concerned citizens. Granted, it may have taken a federal court to ensure that the district behaved in a more corrigible manner. Nevertheless, on occasion the beast could learn how to heel. This was a healthy sign.

There were other signs that the institution's caretakers might have been willing to put themselves and the district on a shorter public leash. The loss of its population and tax base had compounded the problems encountered by any district compelled to desegregate. The district failed to change when the community around it changed, and it lost much of its public support. Rather than altering its conduct so as to attract people, the district chose to experiment with a variety of organizational tricks to bring the public back on terms agreeable to the district. This strategy failed, and members of both the school board and administration knew it.

Their response to this problem was predictable. In the short run, they considered softening their resistance to electing board members from particular geographic areas of the city. As late as March 1981 the board had voted overwhelmingly "to oppose any type of legislation that would call for board members to be elected by subdistricts." It was agreed that all members should run for their positions in citywide elections. More direct forms of representation might introduce partisan politics back into the district and divide the board up into "special interests" representing only "particular constituents." At that time, three bills were considered in the state legislature that called for some form of direct representation on the school board. After a second year of mandatory busing, an expected rejection of their proposed tax levy, only enough candidates to fill the available positions on the board, and the retirement of the board's original reformer, however, the board changed its mind. By a slim six-to-four margin the board voted to endorse a plan that would provide for at least some direct representation.[41]

In the long run, district officials counted on some kind of metropolitan merger and desegregation plan that might place them in control of a new organization. The school board for such a district would have persons on it who had been elected from different areas in the city and county. However, these members would represent such large and diverse areas that the effect would be similar to that achieved by citywide elections in St. Louis.

As with other elements in this ritualized crisis and reform called desegregation, it is the appearance that change is occurring that is important. The public must believe that progress is being achieved and that there is hope. "This is a crucial moment when we need everyone's help," the school board president said as people were working feverishly to compose a mandatory desegregation plan in 1980. "It's important to get rid of past rhetoric. We must get rhetoric of the future."[42]

9. Some Reflections on the Art of Muddling Through

The role that desegregation plays in creating a new civil order or reinforcing an old one in urban communities has been the subject of this book. Most people, as acknowledged at the outset, probably do not accept the idea that there is a debatable proposition contained in the problem I have posed. Many assuredly have not taken comfort in my treatment of desegregation as a ritual that created only the illusion of change. More conservative observers of educational reform—people who probably object to desegregation on the basis of principle or practical failures—likely have found this a congenial argument. Yet they, too, were willing participants in the culturally prescribed crises and reforms inspired by desegregation. They chased their own tails every bit as much as so-called liberals did. It was a silly race in some ways, full of wasted energy. At the same time, it was a profound and moving display of our cultural heritage in which we strove, however imperfectly, to find some basis for understanding ourselves better. That we did not succeed as much or as often as we might have liked is, from the standpoint of our history as a nation, much less important than the fact that we tried at all.

Conflict has always been a popular topic for social theorists and scientists. Yet the anthropologists provided the key to understanding how tensions between groups can be mollified through some stylistic exchange of insults or blows. Their description of ritualized rebellions in primitive cultures enabled me to make sense of the fuss made over a reform that in itself seemed to make little difference in a community's basic economic or political life. Yet that, it seems, is the primary accomplishment of ritualistic crises and reforms. We make some gesture of concern, a symbolic attempt to heal old wounds, without taxing our institutions too severely or exacerbating the problems that lie at the basis of our disagreement. We move to resolve our differences in short, cautious steps, never taking a definitive action to resolve the problem but also neatly avoiding the chaos that such a resolution surely would bring.

Ritualistic conflicts like those involving school desegregation have made an important contribution to the process of urbanization in this country. It is no coincidence that moral reform crusades began to appear as cities showed dramatic increases in number and size in the early nineteenth century. Nor was it an accident that these same movements facilitated the process of city-building by providing people with a chance to articulate their fears and address some of the dilemmas laid bare by the creation of a new world. More importantly, perhaps, these crusades did not interfere with the growth of cities. The economic, political, and social forces that shaped this distinctly urban world were allowed to proceed more or less unchecked. None of the various reform efforts provoked by the consequences of urbanization had much bearing on the direction or speed of that process. That includes school desegregation.

More recent events in the St. Louis desegregation case help to illustrate this point. A number of bright and well-paid consultants working for one or another of the parties to the metropolitan suit were hoping to settle an important issue raised in this case, namely, to determine whether black children are enrolled in districts that have high minority attendance because public agencies made it difficult for their parents to move into white neighborhoods. If the court had allowed housing agencies to be cited as defendants and the plaintiffs had made a convincing argument, a mandatory plan for the city and county would have been likely. If the defendants had shown that publicly inspired housing segregation has had a comparatively small impact on where blacks "chose" to move, a mandatory plan would have been unlikely.

Let us assume for a moment that the plaintiffs could prove their point. A new metropolitan school district might be created. This much the courts could do. The courts could not, as desegregation advocate Gary Orfield already has acknowledged, do much of anything to change the existing pattern of home ownership and apartment rentals in the city and county. Government agencies would have to take affirmative steps to ensure that future residential decisions were not touched by the motives that shaped the current housing market.[1] Mind you, these are some of the same government agencies allegedly responsible for encouraging housing segregation in the first place. Even if these public institutions accepted this new mandate, they could not change the present distribution of people in various types of housing throughout the area. However, they also might organize future redevelopment efforts and subsidy programs so as to encourage the growth of more racially heterogeneous neighborhoods.

There are only two problems with this line of reasoning. First, we are talking about a metropolitan area with a population that has stopped growing and that has been losing some of its younger white and black residents for some time. This situation could be reversed, of course, but it took a long time for the area to get into this fix, and it will not likely get out of it overnight. The period of recovery will be extended even longer than anyone fears if the young people who buy homes and send their children to public schools do not return quickly and in large numbers. Second, should a miracle occur and these people return, there are few signs that their housing choices would reflect a more enlightened attitude. Indeed, there is good reason to expect that their residential decisions would reflect the same class biases that have been common to every generation of urban

residents. It is for these reasons that this latest desegregation crusade will probably have as little effect on the process of urbanization as have previous reform
efforts.

Other than having no major impact on the process of metropolitan development, the most pronounced effect of desegregation is that it further enhanced
the power of professional educators. This has been an outcome of school desegregation in the St. Louis area, and possibly other places as well. It is evident
that school officials in St. Louis used the crisis brought on by desegregation to
their advantage, welcoming the opportunity to be pushed to do things they
believed were inevitable or desirable. This would be even more obvious in a
mandatory metropolitan desegregation plan. School administrators in the county
would assume the same posture of reluctance concerning desegregation as did
their counterparts in the old Ferguson-Florissant Reorganized School District.
They would let the court order them to take on this responsibility and would
laugh all the way to the state treasury. As one reviews the strategies available to
a lazy monopoly like the public schools, such passive aggressiveness seems
ideally suited to their needs. It is nevertheless a real and serious barrier to
democratic control of this most undemocratic public institution.

Schemes to "diminish" the power of bureaucrats and professionals and to
increase the power of parents and the community generally do not work. Part of
the reason is that "the existing arrangement, in which professionals hold most
operational power and submit to ritual lay control on prescribed occasions, is as
agreeable to parents as it is to professionals."[2] Another part of the reason is that
officials vigorously resist any attempt to diminish their power. One way to curb
some of the excessive power of school officials, some people argue, might be to
encourage organizations with a national power base to serve as public watchdog
over local school systems. Yet this would hurt the very principle of local control
over educational matters that we claim to hold dear. It also would threaten to
impose another bureaucracy—with its own professionals and immunity to popular control—on top of the one people already find objectionable. The cure, in
such a case, might bear "a striking resemblance to the disease."[3]

So What's the Answer?

What could have been done through desegregation to reform the way in which
school districts operate has been considered throughout this book. Most of the
time I have been content to criticize others for failing to look at the issue or take
more affirmative steps to deal with it. I have not offered any solution to this
problem. Supporters of desegregation will argue that they are not naive idealists
but experienced veterans who appreciate the difficulties of reforming big institutions with the law. Yet if lawyers and scientific experts believed that reform
would be a difficult process, why have they been content to prescribe changes

that hold no hope of reforming the way the institution works? Why do we leave the administration of reform to the very people responsible for creating or perpetuating "constitutional wrongs" in the first place? Why have they not done more about the courts' apparent impotence? My solution may not satisfy many persons, least of all me. However, it does go a lot further than some advocates of desegregation have been willing to go in addressing the combined problem of desegregating and reforming a school system at the same time. For some reason I find the idea, as suggested by Orfield, that all one can do is "desegregate as many kids as you can . . . then you put in some educational programs to try and make it work" a suitable companion to the thesis that "the plans that work best are those designed by local officials."[4] Both are calculated to achieve little in the way of "meaningful" social change.

My solution is straightforward. If one really wants to combine desegregation with administrative reform, have the courts dissolve boards of education. Do not dismiss them and hold new elections or reappoint persons who are more sympathetic to desegregation. Do away with them in those districts found guilty of segregating minority students. This would have a chilling effect on everyone with an interest in school affairs. Suddenly, school administrators would have nothing to shield them from an aroused public. The party legally responsible for maintaining a segregated district will have been removed. This is fitting, but not merely because school board members should be held accountable for perpetuating an ugly system of racial segregation; it is fitting because they were too dumb to realize that the professionals running the district and formulating policy also were running them. Strip away that symbolic buffer between the public and school administration and things will snap, crackle, and pop in public education. If you want to inspire lay involvement in public education and reinvigorate the connection between the public schools and regular political community, that is the way to do it.

Liberals ought to be pleased by this proposal because a court could still be used to frame a desegregation order if it chose to. Otherwise, school officials would have to convince the public that their plan was fair. Liberals, no doubt, would also see this democratic renaissance spill over into other areas of educational policy. Desegregation has a way of stirring people from their comfortable complacency. Conservatives might be less pleased by this because their sense of the "regular political community" probably extends no farther than the local elites in an area. The chances are slight, however, that any judge would choose to jump back into the mess that would have been instigated by such an action. This ought to please the conservatives who disapprove of judicially inspired social reforms.

In theory at least, everyone would be happy. Realistically, it is unlikely that everyone would be. The entire system of public education might be thrown into utter chaos by the simple political act of dissolving the board of education. The issue of who is accountable to whom might be reopened. The very basis of order in this important public institution would have to be renegotiated. Officials' authority to suggest and implement educational policies could be questioned at every turn. We all know, however, that this will never happen. Even if this suggestion could be carried out legally, no one would allow the public schools to be exposed to that kind of severe scrutiny. It was my intention in writing this book to help explain why desegregation does not provoke such far-reaching social change.

The challenge of my peers to offer solutions to the courts' apparent ineffectiveness as an agent of social change reveals how they have confused their roles as advocates and scientists. It also suggests that they might have missed the point of the present analysis. No agency, perhaps least of all the courts, was prepared to tackle the onerous and delicate task of reforming another public institution. The same could be said of the public generally. Everyone had more sense than to open the school doors too wide and permit too thorough an inspection of its workings and the assumptions that gave it legitimacy. Nevertheless, all recognized the importance of keeping open some avenue through which the less attractive aspects of our social and economic order could be reviewed, even if nothing was ever done about these problems. That is why and how ritualized crises and reforms are used.

The occasions when courts have been willing to take a more aggressive posture toward school districts—Boston and Cleveland are notable examples—have coincided with officials' reluctance to comply with less rigorous demands. This, as noted earlier, is a more serious crime than the initial offense because it constitutes political heresy and must be severely punished. I would add that in neither of these cases did basic institutional reform take place. Eventually, professional control is reasserted and, in an odd way, further legitimated by virtue of having been so "severely" reviewed. This is something many of my liberal friends simply do not understand, having long ago sacrificed any claim to being scientific critics of the thing they helped to invent. My more conservative colleagues do not seem to suffer from the same malady. They know precisely what it is that they do not like about desegregation, and they find some roundabout and clever way of getting their problem solved. Conservatives talk about busing, white flight, and the sanctity of neighborhood schools and neatly avoid the cumbersome task of finding a better way to run the public schools.

Some of the ways that residents of St. Louis have struggled with this dilemma were discussed in this book. The lessons to be learned from the desegregation experiences of districts in the St. Louis area are tempered by the knowledge that the reform may be handled differently in other places. Not all districts are as fiscally and politically independent as that in the city of St. Louis, for instance. Nor do districts in other states have to struggle with as unsupportive an attitude toward spending money on public education as do those in Missouri. These things make a difference in the way districts approach desegregation and other reforms.[5] Like any good sociologist, however, I believe that there are common themes or patterns in the ways various districts handle the desegregation issue.

For example, officials could not treat their districts as "closed systems" immune to any undesired intervention by outsiders. Their autonomy could be challenged, and some sign of allegiance and compliance to a higher authority could be required of them. At the same time, officials maintain that the districts do not behave as "open systems." They display no willingness to redistribute the authority to make and carry out educational policy to a broader segment of the public. They retain the right and ability to reinterpret proposed reforms so the changes can be made to fit into existing organizational routines. Negotiating may take place with parties outside of the system. Changes in the ways people and groups inside the system are treated or expected to behave may occur. There is nothing "rational" in the object of these exercises, however. They are not designed to change or improve the "products" of the system to any appreciable degree. Nor, as we have seen in the case of desegregation in the St. Louis area, do they make the system significantly more accountable for failures in "quality control."

Desegregation policies may best be understood as a means of managing a district's spoiled constitutional identity. There is a compelling social need not to remove the institution from the community, as is often the case for people who break the law, even though it, too, has violated the law of the land. It is also unwise to limit the contact of the institution with certain parties in the community. This frequently happens in matters related to "tribal" stigmas like race where one or another party is ostracized from the community. Indeed, one could argue that districts are compelled to desegregate precisely because they have been perpetuating such a stigma. What one does in the case of a segregated school system is to renegotiate some conditions under which that stigma is allowed to persist. One reduces the discretion of school personnel and subjects them for a time to a broader range of constraints than those to which they are accustomed. The legitimacy of the institution is never threatened, which would be the equivalent of expelling it from the community. Continued acceptance, instead, is made contingent upon its satisfactory and largely symbolic conformance to guidelines for treating the "despised" population.

Staff and policy changes can be tolerated because they do not undermine procedures through which such decisions are made in any permanent way. Basic changes in administrative routines or political accountability tend not to be imposed because they might undermine the institution's ability to carry on its affairs. The decision not to enforce such changes increases the institution's chances to maintain its corporate identity by allowing it to control what the public learns about its conduct during the period of reform. Information can be disclosed by the institution only under certain conditions. This provides managers considerable discretion over what is publicized, by whom, and when. Officials are still allowed to select personnel—under only limited sexual and racial constraints—as well as train and socialize them into the traditions of the district. School administrators also retain the right to oversee the implementation of changes at individual school sites. This creates opportunities for those changes to be nullified or modified by those higher up in the district's administrative ranks.[6]

Throughout the book I have tried to draw parallels between school systems and other types of organizations. I am hardly the first person to have done this. Noticeably absent from other discussions of this topic, however, is any mention of the ways in which organizations as different as school systems and corporations use and even foment crises in order to achieve their goals. I do not believe that the parallels between public and private institutions collapse once the discussion turns to such matters. Most of my colleagues do. Otherwise, they would have developed long ago an explanation of desegregation that fits comfortably with what is known about organizational change in other contexts.

At the heart of our disagreement is the idea that private businesses and public agencies are not that much alike. Most people seem to believe that businesses are interested in expanding their markets and that public agencies are slothful organizations content to hold on to the territory and the constituents they already serve. It should be clear at this point, however, that the distinction between private and public organizations is rather artificial.

For instance, it is not clear any longer that all businesses lust for the competition of an open market, unfettered by government regulations and supports. The Lockheed and Chrysler debacles demonstrated that private businesses would behave like much-despised public bureaucracies if their share of a market were threatened. These adventures or experiments in federal subsidization were upsetting because they were expensive and they seemed to violate principles of capitalism. In a similar way, desegregation violates cherished assumptions about the way a public institution is supposed to work. School districts can treat desegregation as an opportunity to expand both their share of the student market and revenues from various government agencies. Faced with a difficult and unfamiliar situation, school systems may behave like corporations.

It is the novelty of the circumstances facing both school systems and some corporations that can drive them to become more similar. In their distress each is able to find comfort in public support. It is here that the utility of ritualized crises stands out. A crisis is needed to make the reality of these painful, unnatural events an acceptable, if temporary, fact of life. Such crises also may serve to ratify in principle what may no longer be avoided in a changing world. Emergency subsidies to a few corporations may help alert us to the fact that private industries flourishing in other nations—Japan is a prime example— receive a good deal of support from their governments. What is good for Consolidated Widgets today may not be in the best interest of the United States. However, a crisis may hasten the day when we all see that what is in the best interest of the United States can be good for Consolidated Widgets. The argument for dismantling segregated schools and subsidizing a desegregating school district rests upon the same logic. Ritualized crises and reforms make the logic work.

The notable thing about most of these lessons is that they are not new. They confirm what observers have noted in the conduct of organizational change in other contexts. The novelty in these findings is in their application to desegregating schools districts. Remarkable as it may seem, most observers of desegregation have not treated it as an experiment in institutional maintenance and resistance to change. They have preferred to approach desegregation as an experiment in making better people. The two are related, but not in any way most social scientists and observers of desegregation were prepared to recognize.

Institutional Crises and Unexpected Opportunities

Our ignorance of history and the subtle compromises made in behalf of social order should not be dismissed as racist or shortsighted. We are, after all, finite beings with an understandable reluctance to waste too much time fretting over yesterday's mistakes and tomorrow's missed opportunities. We prefer to march on and leave such concerns to secular wizards like sociologists who, having examined our failings, can offer some measure of hope for the future. This I will endeavor to do now.

There has been much talk lately about educational quality. Reports were issued in May and June 1983 by different bodies with national constituencies, and each decried the sorry condition of public education in the United States. The pessimistic message was balanced somewhat by the fact that many states have begun to require competency tests before graduation from high school. Many states also require additional language, math, and science courses before being admitted to public universities. This is good news, to be sure, but, as the authors of these reports argue, more is needed. Further remedies suggested include pay increases for good teachers, longer school days, and, above all else, a bigger commitment on the part of the federal government to support such efforts. To dramatize the argument, allusions are made to our national defense, economic competition with our friends and enemies, and Sputnik. It is as if we need some foreign bogeyman to show up every once in a while so we have an excuse to do something we should have been doing anyway. The point is that people are speaking of the perceived decline of educational quality as a crisis and are looking to the federal government for some leadership to resolve it.

We have heard this before, and the argument does have some merit. The federal government can command our attention and mobilize more resources than any other single private or public entity. Yet the major responsibility for educating our citizens falls to the states and local municipalities, and there, too, will fall the responsibility for addressing this newest educational crisis.

The federal government can lead, cajole, inspire, and prime. It might provide incentives for states to increase and equalize taxes for public education. (Equal educational expenditures may not be a right guaranteed under the Constitution but are as much in the public's interest as new highways, waste treatment plants, or farm subsidies.) Grants might be offered to states that establish an educational park specializing in math, science, and language for high-school students drawn from across the state. College students with such aptitudes could be encouraged to enter a teaching career for a specified period by providing them with grants or low-interest loans to pursue their undergraduate training or an advanced degree. If our poor academic training in these areas is jeopardizing our national defense, why not create the equivalent of a GI Bill for people willing to serve our country as teachers? Private schools need not be excluded from these efforts. There are a number of innovative programs implemented by private schools even at the elementary grade levels from which public schools could benefit. Furthermore, private schools that serve as research and development labs for public schools could be awarded grants.

The federal government can help. However, its several agencies cannot be expected to resolve this crisis, write the script, stage and direct the cast, and hope that people will be grateful for the effort. We know from history that such crises are more routinely addressed at a local level. People have traditionally fashioned compromises between some ill-defined ideal and their unique customs at the local level, not in Washington. The states, for their part, ought to increase and equalize their educational expenditures. A number of states, Missouri being a notable example, do not support public education very well. If the residents of a state are reluctant to tax themselves for the sake of this vital public service, they have no right to request that the federal government assume that burden for them. Indeed, increased federal aid should not be offered until a state exercises its affirmative responsibility in this area. Such an arrangement already exists in relation to highway construction, for instance, where the federal government matches funds provided by a state up to a given level.

States and municipalities should also have stronger relations with area industries that could help underwrite the expense of a new lab, field experience, or an entire school dedicated to science, math, or the humanities. Competition to get into one of these schools would be stiff and could attract students from across a metropolitan area or a whole state. Cooperating corporations might also provide summer internships for these students, thus confirming for students the connection between school and work (many corporations already do this on a small scale). Such programs would improve a metropolitan area's quality of life, thereby attracting new industries.

All or none of these ideas may hold any promise. The goal in offering them is to encourage a debate that includes the states in an effective way and brings the traditional reforming classes back into the dialogue. It would be tragic if, in resolving the crisis over educational quality, it was defined away as artfully as was the desegregation crisis. Both crises are intrinsic to the process of building and transforming communities into places where any person's child can enjoy the fruits and responsibilities that come with citizenship. In the past this process has been linked to the construction of new or bigger urban areas and to the kinds of employment and politics practiced in those areas. It will be no different in the future, if only because the differences and inequities papered over in the past as we built our old urban world will be there as we wrestle with a new one. Yet we have a chance to move beyond the ritualistic crises and reforms that helped previous generations accustom themselves to a bigger or more geographically dispersed urban community. We have an unparalleled opportunity to apprehend that sense of community conceived originally by advocates of the common-school movement.

Way back then, it will be recalled, reformers spoke longingly of a time and world in which all children would be able to read, write, and understand mathematics. These skills were not commonly held and ought to have been, reformers maintained, if young people were to hold responsible positions as workers and citizens. It was expected that bringing persons of different social class backgrounds together would make this possible by inspiring a dialogue between them and, perhaps more importantly, inspiring well-to-do persons to keep their children and taxes in the public schools. The plan failed, of course, but not merely because people of all types possess a certain snobbish and defensive streak. Such things are constants in our world, and one is not likely to see the demise of private schools any time soon.

The failure of the common-school movement is better accounted for by the nature of industrial capitalism and types of jobs available in nineteenth-century America. Put simply, it was not as necessary then as it is today for the schools to certify large numbers of literate, technically sophisticated students. Over the course of the last 150 years the need for persons with these skills has grown substantially. Today, given the decreasing number of jobs in which one needs little literacy or minimal training, it is essential that students acquire these skills. Otherwise, they cannot hope to compete in the job market and will not learn how to become effective citizens. We must be willing to prepare them for a world that early educational reformers only could imagine. We have the responsibility to fulfill that prophecy if we wish to build the just and orderly society early reformers talked about but in which they were never quite able to believe.

Postscript

It is all well and good for me to say this, of course, since I probably will never be asked to make that prophecy come true. My meager contribution is found on the pages of this book, and too often I have found my own words insufficient to the task I laid out for myself. Making sense of other people's nonsense is tough work. Sometimes, however, you get surprised.

> The young, white man who had come to enroll in my class wanted to ask me a question. It was late in the day, and I wanted to go home. Maybe he would not keep me too long, I hoped.
>
> "You gonna talk about busin' in this class, Dr. Monti?" His tone was pointed but not hostile. "I drive a bus for the metro-deseg program. I take white county kids into the city and black kids back out to the county schools. It pays the bills, if y'know what I mean."
>
> I sat there wondering why I had signed this guy up. "Where's the punch line?" I thought. "When's he going to drop the big one one me?" I did not have to wait.
>
> "God, you oughta hear the way those black kids talk! They're unbelievable."
>
> "That bad, huh?" But I did not really want to know.
>
> "No, no!" He snapped back. "They're that good."
>
> "What do you mean 'that good'?" I asked.
>
> "Just that. I mean they sit there talkin' algebra and poetry for the whole bus ride. It's wild." He paused, then added, "I don't know where they get those kids, but it ain't from no ghetto family."
>
> I smiled. Maybe there was hope yet.

He was right of course. He knew from his daily experience what many observers of the desegregation order had been complaining about. The black youngsters who "volunteered" for long bus rides to county schools were not like their peers left back in the city. County school officials were pleased, of course, but not only because their new charges were nice, bright children. They also appreciated the fact that these black youngsters were filling seats that would otherwise have been empty. Between 1983 and the fall of 1984, the two dozen county districts had shown a loss of 1,479 students. But this loss was more than made up for by the presence of 2,586 black transfer students from the city. These counts are crucial to school officials because they are a major factor in determining how much state aid a district will receive for the coming year. Desegregation was working for the school districts.

Of course, someone had to pay for all this and that someone was the Missouri taxpayer. The state attorney general had resisted the court-ordered plan as long and as hard as he could. Some argued that he held out too long and only to give himself a campaign issue to beat over the heads of his rivals in the upcoming gubernatorial election. This probably was true. It was also true, however, that he managed to call attention to the excessive costs charged by districts to the state for their "desegregation" programs. Millions of dollars were saved in this fashion. St. Louis area school districts have been staging a raid on the state treasury in the name of desegregation. Yet they also had been compelled to watch the legal costs of the court's plan take off as the attorney general continued his quest. He now is the governor of Missouri. Desegregation worked for him. Although he is not overpaid as superintendent, the superintendent of the city school system is scheduled to receive seventeen thousand dollars from an anonymous donor to teach one summer-school course in 1985 at the University of Missouri–St. Louis and to prepare a report on desegregation. Desegregation is working for him.

These arguments are far from over. That probably is a good thing. Some important questions have been raised by the new governor's reluctance to roll over too quickly before the city and county districts. Among them are the following:

> Must the state fund all proposals for "magnet" and special-education programs that are intended to attract integrated student bodies?
>
> How much money should be spent removing the 'vestiges of segregation' from predominantly black schools in North St. Louis? Are special enrichment programs due black youngsters who are forced to stay in segregated schools?
>
> Must the state spend additional millions of dollars to ensure that the city district retains the state's highest level of accreditation? Would the loss of that rating constitute a blow to the court-ordered desegregation plan?
>
> Finally, should the court order into effect tax-increase proposals that would pay for all these programs or should it suspend the state law requiring a two-thirds majority voter approval for many tax-increase proposals?[7]

These are important questions. Answers to them will go a long way in addressing some of the historic inequities built into the funding of public education in Missouri. Someday, maybe some of the children who traditionally have received less support for their education because they were born into poor families that lived in poor school districts will get more help. If the debate over desegregation finally drew us into a serious discussion of such matters, that would be a very good thing. It would be too bad if we could not also discuss savings that could be realized by reducing the number of underutilized schools and overpaid school administrators. But it would not be much of a surprise. After all, desegregation is not supposed to be the answer to all our questions. It is supposed to get us to ask those questions in the first place. Then desegregation works for all of us.

Notes

Notes to Chapter 1: Introduction

1. Louis Masotti et al., *A Time To Burn?;* Lewis M. Killian, *The Impossible Revolution Phase 2: Black Power and the American Dream;* Arthur Smith, *Rhetoric of Black Revolution;* C. Eric Lincoln, *Sounds of the Struggle.*

2. Brewton Berry and H. L. Tischler, *Race And Ethnic Relations,* 149–56; Joseph Himes, *Conflict & Conflict Management,* 200–202, 212–34; Christine Rossell, "School Desegregation and Community Social Change," 136–40; Robert L. Crain and Rita E. Mahard, "The Consequences of Controversy Accompanying Institutional Change: The Case of School Desegregation," 697, 707.

3. Douglas Longshore, "Social Psychological Research on School Desegregation: Toward a New Agenda"; Henry Levin, "Education, Life Chances, and the Courts: The Role of Social Science Evidence"; John McConahay, "The Effects of School Desegregation upon Students' Racial Attitudes and Behavior: A Critical Review of the Literature and a Prolegomenon to Future Research"; David Armor, "The Evidence on Busing"; Willis Hawley, "The New Mythology of School Desegregation."

4. Crain and Mahard, "The Consequences of Controversy"; Martin Patcher, *Black-White Contact in Schools: Its Social and Academic Effects;* David Kirby et al., *Political Strategies in Northern School Desegregation.*

5. Howard I. Kalodner and James J. Fishman, eds., *Limits of Justice: The Courts' Role in School Desegregation;* Charles Willie and Susan Greenblatt, *Community Politics and Educational Change;* Daniel J. Monti, "Administrative Discrimination in the Implementation of Desegregation Policies"; Jennifer Hochschild, "Local Control of School Desegregation through Citizen Monitoring"; Daniel Katz and Robert Kahn, *The Social Psychology of Organizations,* 654–711.

6. David Tatel and William Taylor, "St. Louis Integration."

7. Diane Ravitch, *The Troubled Crusade,* 81, 330.

8. Ibid., 114.

9. Patcher, *Black-White Contact in Schools;* Robert L. Crain, "Why Academic Research Fails to Be Useful"; Levin, "Education, Life Chances, and the Courts"; Hawley, "The New Mythology."

10. L. L. Langness, *Other Fields, Other Grasshoppers,* 48.

Notes to Chapter 2: Justice or Order?

1. J. Harvie Wilkinson, *From Brown to Bakke,* 5, 43.

2. David Armor, "The Evidence on Busing"; David Kirp, "School Desegregation and the Limits of Legalism."

3. Compare Kirp's statements on the appropriateness of court-ordered plans, for instance, to those of Gary Orfield, *Must We Bus?,* 422.

4. Debra Kalmuss et al., "The Impact of the School Desegregation Cases on the Relations Between Scientific Evidence and Legal Theory," in D. J. Monti, ed., *Measuring the Impact of Desegregation,* no. 14, 21–38; Mark G. Yudof, "School Desegregation: Legal Realism, Reasoned Elaboration, and Social Science Research in the Supreme Court," 61.

5. Daniel J. Monti, "Administrative Foxes in Educational Chicken Coops."

6. See, for example, Leila Sussmann and Gayle Speck, "Community Participation In Schools: The Boston Case," 341–56; Joel Aberbach and Jack Walker, "Citizen Desires, Policy Outcomes, and Community Control"; David Cohen, "Reforming School Politics." One observer has noted that officials actually decrease their "solicitation and encouragement of patron involvement" in some districts experiencing growth in their black enrollments. Policies in biracial districts do not seem to differ dramatically "from educational policies in less racially diverse districts" (Ruth S. Jones, "Racial Patterns And School District Policy," 307–308).

7. Robert Alford and Roger Friedland, "Political Participation and Public Policy," 474; Jennifer L. Hochschild, "Local Control of School Desegregation through Citizen Monitoring"; L. Harmon Zeigler et al., Governing American Schools.

8. Kalmuss et al., "The Impact of the School Desegregation Cases"; Brewton Berry and H. L. Tischler, Race And Ethnic Relations, 149–56; Joseph Himes, Conflict & Conflict Management, 200–202, 212–34.

9. Stephen Steinberg, The Ethnic Myth, 214.

10. Jennifer Hochschild, "Incrementalism, Majoritarianism, and the Failure of Desegregation"; Robert L. Crain and Rita E. Mahard, "Desegregation and Black Achievement: A Review of the Research," 20, 25–29, and "The Consequences of Controversy Accompanying Institutional Change: The Case of Desegregation"; Edgar Epps, "The Impact of School Desegregation on the Self-Evaluation of Minority Children," 59, 65–68; John B. McConahay, "The Effects of School Desegregation upon Students' Racial Attitudes and Behavior: A Critical Review of the Literature and a Prolegomenon to Future Research," 81–83.

11. Crain and Mahard, "The Consequences of Controversy," 707; Christine H. Rossell, "School Desegregation and Community Social Change."

12. Rossell, "School Desegregation and Community Social Change," 135.

13. Christine H. Rossell, "The Atheoretical Nature of Desegregation," 95.

14. Willis Hawley, "The New Mythology of School Desegregation."

15. A. A. Garner, Social Movements in America; Anthony Oberschall, Social Conflict and Social Movements.

16. S. M. Lipset and E. Rabb, The Politics of Unreason; Neil Smelser, Theory of Collective Behavior, 270–312; R. H. Turner and L. Killian, Collective Behavior, 245–68.

17. Rossell, "School Desegregation and Community Social Change," 67–69; Crain and Mahard, "The Consequences of Controversy."

18. David Rogers, 110 Livingston Street; Leila Sussmann, Tales Out of School; Marilyn Gittell, Participants and Participation, and Community Control and the Urban School; Paul Berman and Milbrey W. McLaughlin, An Exploratory Study of School District Adaptation; Daniel J. Monti, "Administrative Discrimination in the Implementation of Desegregation Policies"; Charles Willie and Susan Greenblatt, eds., Community Politics and Educational Change; Howard I. Kalodner and James J. Fishman, eds., Limits of Justice: The Courts' Role in School Desegregation.

19. W. Richard Scott, Organizations, 127–32.

20. Kirp, "School Desegregation and the Limits of Legalism"; Nathan Glazer, "Should Judges Administer Social Services"; Monti, "Administrative Foxes in Educational Chicken Coops"; Orfield, Must We Bus?, 422–26; Crain and Mahard, "The Consequences of Controversy."

21. Herbert Gans, The Urban Villagers; Ira Katznelson, City Trenches; Ida Susser, Norman Street; Gerald Suttles, The Social Order of the Slum.

22. Monti, "Administrative Discrimination in the Implementation of Desegregation Policies."

23. Katznelson, City Trenches; Suttles, The Social Order of the Slum; Peter K. Eisenger, The Politics of Displacement; Andre Thieblemont, "Protest Rites at Saint-Cyr: A Contribution to the Study of Military Tradition."

24. Richard Lingeman, Small Town America.

25. Brian Berry, Comparative Urbanization, 31; R. A. Nye, The Origins Of Crowd Psychology; Kurt Wolff, The Sociology of Georg Simmell, 396–401, 409–24; Louis Wirth, "Urbanism as a Way of Life."

26. Robert Park and Ernest Burgess, The City; Paul Boyer, Urban Masses and Moral Order in America, 1820–1920.

27. Gans, *The Urban Villagers;* Suttles, *The Social Order of the Slum;* Donald Warren, *Black Neighborhoods;* William F. Whyte, *Street Corner Society;* Ivan Light, *Cities in World Perspective,* 275–86; J. Abu-Lughod, "Migrant Adjustment to City Life: The Egyptian Case"; C. Fischer, *The Urban Experience;* S. Milgram, "The Experience of Living in Cities: A Psychological Analysis."

28. Edward Banfield, *The Unheavenly City Revisited;* Charles Tilly, et al., *The Rebellious Century 1830–1930,* 61; Stanley Greenberg, *Politics and Poverty;* Daniel J. Monti, "The Relations Between Terrorism and Domestic Civil Disorders."

29. Katznelson, *City Trenches;* Susser, *Norman Street.*

30. Jordi Borja, "Urban Movements in Spain"; M. Castells, "Theoretical Propositions for an Experimental Study of Urban Movements."

31. R. M. Brown, *Strain of Violence;* Eisenger, *The Politics of Displacement.*

32. Randall Collins, "Functional and Conflict Theories of Educational Stratification"; Jerome Karabel, "Community Colleges and Social Stratification: Submerged Class Conflict in American Higher Education"; John Ogbu, *The Next Generation.*

33. Max Gluckman, *Custom and Conflict in Africa,* 83–84, 108, 133–36.

34. J. Milton Yinger, "Countercultures and Social Change." Yinger has presented his own careful analysis of ritualized rebellions as "rituals of opposition." He, too, notes their paradoxical character, acknowledging their challenge to the social order even as they reinforce its legitimacy for most persons. He has sought to show, as I do here, that there are strong parallels between such acts in primitive and advanced cultures. However, he focuses on their contribution to "counter-cultures," that is, groups or movements that reject established norms and values. Both the countercultural group and its "rituals of opposition" can contribute to social change by offering alternate visions of living and believing to society's members. The argument presented here is the logical complement to Yinger's.

35. S. Bowles and H. Gintis, *Schooling in Capitalist America: Educational Reform and the Contradictions of Economic Life;* Collins, "Functional and Conflict Theories"; Karabel, "Community Colleges and Social Stratification"; Ogbu, *The Next Generation.*

36. William Gamson, *The Strategy of Social Protest.*

37. Norton Long, "The Local Community as an Ecology of Games."

38. *Clayton Citizen,* 9 March 1983.

39. Steinberg, *The Ethnic Myth;* Tilly, *The Rebellious Century,* 241.

40. Karen Paige and Jeffery Paige, *The Politics of Reproduction;* Gluckman, *Custom and Conflict in Africa.*

41. J. M. Ross and W. Berg, *"I Respectfully Disagree With The Judge's Order."*

Notes to Chapter 3: In Pursuit of Metropolitan St. Louis

1. No attempt is made here to test the limits of the reader's attention span with an extended discussion of many tables, graphs, and charts that contain data on St. Louis's population and economy. What follows is a brief and general discussion of a much more substantial analysis undertaken by the author.

2. John E. Farley, "Metropolitan Housing Segregation in 1980: The St. Louis Case."

3. St. Louis County Department of Planning, *St. Louis County, Missouri Fact Book 1977.*

4. Ibid.

5. Henry Schmandt et al., *Metropolitan Reform in St. Louis.*

6. George Wendel, "Previous Attempts at Metro Reform in St. Louis."

7. Minutes from the meeting of the St. Louis County Board of Education, 18 February 1958 and 10 October 1962.

8. Minutes from the meeting of the St. Louis County Board of Education, 26 September 1962.

9. Minutes from the meeting of the St. Louis County Board of Education, 10 May 1971.

10. Ibid.

11. David Colton, "The Kinloch Case: A Court-Ordered District Merger."

12. Ibid.

13. This is the way district officials characterized the desegregation plan in numerous private discussions. They took great pains to get the media to attend to the "bigger" desegregation battle being waged in the city. Generally, they were successful.

14. David Colton, "The St. Louis Desegregation Case (City-Only Aspects)."

15. Ibid.

16. Ibid.

17. Jennifer Hochschild, *What's Fair: American Beliefs About Distributive Justice;* Henry Levin, "Education, Life Chances, and the Courts: The Role of Social Science Evidence."

Notes to Chapter 4: Civil Rites and Civil Wrongs

1. Paul Boyer, *Urban Masses and Moral Order in America, 1820–1920*, 3.

2. Ibid., 287.

3. Ibid., 12.

4. Ibid., 11.

5. Charles N. Glaab and A. Theodore Brown, *A History of Urban America*, 66–98; Boyer, *Urban Masses and Moral Order*, 7.

6. Ibid., 26.

7. Ibid., 29.

8. Ibid., 35.

9. Ibid., 39.

10. David Nasaw, *Schooled to Order*, 17.

11. Boyer, *Urban Masses and Moral Order*, 42.

12. Ibid., 41, 46.

13. Diane Ravitch, *The Great School Wars*, 10, 23, 26.

14. Nasaw, *Schooled to Order*, 37.

15. Ibid., 39.

16. Ibid., 49–50.

17. Ravitch, *The Great School Wars*, 81.

18. Nasaw, *Schooled to Order*, 75–76.

19. Ravitch, *The Great School Wars*, 103.

20. Glaab and Brown, *A History of Urban America*, 86.

21. Blake McKelvey, *The Urbanization of America*, 274–79.

22. Boyer, *Urban Masses and Moral Order*, 83.

23. Roger W. Lotchin, *San Francisco 1846–1856*, 188–202.

24. Boyer, *Urban Masses and Moral Order*, 85–86.

25. Ibid., 87–94.

26. Ibid., 96.

27. Ibid., 98.

28. Ibid., 96.

29. Ibid., 115.

30. Ibid., 113.

31. Ibid., 120.

32. Ibid., 133.

33. Ibid., 144–45, 150.

34. Ibid., 160.

35. McKelvey, *The Urbanization of America*, 145, 155.

36. Glaab and Brown, *A History of Urban America*, 172.

37. Robert K. Merton, "The Latent Functions of the Machine."

38. Boyer, *Urban Masses and Moral Order*, 284–92; Glaab and Brown, *A History of Urban America*, 45–65.

39. Boyer, *Urban Masses and Moral Order*, 175, 282–83, 190.

40. David J. Pivar, *Purity Crusade, Sexual Morality and Social Control, 1868–1900*, 159.

41. Ibid., 178; Ronald C. Wimberley and James A. Christenson, "Civil Religion and Church and State."

42. Boyer, *Urban Masses and Moral Order*, 198–200, 214–15.

43. Ibid., 221.

44. Thomas Less Philpott, *The Slum and the Ghetto*, 60–61.

45. Ibid., 71–78; Boyer, *Urban Masses and Moral Order*, 157; Philpott, *The Slum and the Ghetto*, 346, 314–42.

46. Boyer, *Urban Masses and Moral Order*, 156.

47. Philpott, *The Slum and the Ghetto*, 275.

48. Boyer, *Urban Masses and Moral Order*, 254–55, 265.

49. Glaab and Brown, *A History of Urban America*, 243.

50. Samuel P. Hays, "The Politics of Reform in Municipal Government in the Progressive Era"; Richard C. Wade, "The Periphery Versus the Center"; Zane Miller, *Boss Cox's Cincinnati: Urban Politics in the Progressive Era*.

51. Nasaw, *Schooled to Order*, 105–13; Alan I. Marcus, "Professional Revolution and Reform in the Progressive Era: Cincinnati Physicians and the City Elections of 1897 and 1900"; Michael P. McCarthy, "On Bosses, Reformers, and Urban Growth: Some Suggestions for a Political Typology of American Cities"; Richard M. Bernard and Bradley R. Rice, "Political Environment and the Adoption of Progressive Municipal Reform."

52. Boyer, *Urban Masses and Moral Order*, 169.

53. Melvin G. Holli, *Reform in Detroit*, 162.

54. Ravitch, *The Great School Wars*, 111.

55. Nasaw, *Schooled to Order*, 108, 111.

56. Ravitch, *The Great School Wars*, 191.

57. Nasaw, *Schooled to Order*, 124, 127–28, 132.

58. Alice Kessler-Harris and Virginia Yans-McLaughlin, "European Immigrant Groups"; Nasaw, *Schooled to Order*, 138.

59. Ravitch, *The Great School Wars*, 195–230.

60. Joseph L. Arnold "The Neighborhood and City Hall: The Origin of Neighborhood Associations in Baltimore, 1880–1911," 23.

61. William Julius Wilson, *The Declining Significance of Race*.

62. Ravitch, *The Great School Wars*, 243.

63. Nasaw, *Schooled to Order*, 157–58.

64. Ravitch, *The Great School Wars*, 186.

65. Michael P. Smith, *The City and Social Theory*, 29, 219.

66. Roland Warren, *The Community in America;* Richard Taub et al., "Urban Voluntary Associations, Locality Based and Externally Induced."

67. Smith, *The City and Social Theory*, 182, 272.

Notes to Chapter 5: In Defense of Desegregation

1. Harry Bash, *Sociology, Race and Ethnicity*, 219–23; William Julius Wilson, *The Declining Significance of Race*.

2. Al Smith et al., *Achieving Effective Desegregation*, 83–88, 90.

3. Ibid., 92.

4. David Rogers, *110 Livingston Street;* Leila Sussmann, *Tales Out of School;* Marilyn Gittel, *Participants and Participation*, and *Community Control and the Urban School;* Paul Berman and Milbrey W. McLaughlin, *An Exploratory Study of School District Adaptation;* Daniel J. Monti, "Administrative Discrimination in the Implementation of Desegregation Policies"; Charles Wil-

lie and Susan Greenblatt, eds., *Community Politics and Educational Change;* Howard I. Kalodner and James J. Fishman, eds., *Limits of Justice: The Courts' Role in School Desegregation.*

5. Daniel Katz and Robert Kahn, *The Social Psychology of Oranizations,* 653–712.

6. Ibid., 659.

7. Ann Parker Parelius and Robert J. Parelius, *The Sociology of Education,* 116–18, 141; John W. Meyer, "The Effects of Education as an Institution"; David B. Tyack, *The One Best System: A History of American Urban Education,* 6–7, 14–15, 29.

8. Tyack, *The One Best System,* 76.

9. Ibid., 73.

10. W. Richard Scott, *Organizations,* 309.

11. Tyack, *The One Best System,* 78, 88, 89, 93, 102.

12. Ibid., 77.

13. Ibid., 15.

14. Ibid., 173, 126, 131, 141, 145–47, 158–59.

15. Ibid., 146–47.

16. Ibid., 174, 184–86; Steven Bossert, "Education in Urban Society," 300–303.

17. Willis Hawley, "Dealing with Organizational Rigidity in Public Schools: A Theoretical Perspective," 195; Charles Tilly, *From Mobilization To Revolution,* 73–76.

18. Albert O. Hirschman, *Exit, Voice, and Loyalty: Responses to Decline in Firms, Organizations, and States,* 53–54, 108–109; Richard Sennett, *The Fall of Public Man,* 4–5, 273, 37–39, 222–23.

19. Randall Collins, *Conflict Sociology,* 291.

20. Katz and Kahn, *The Social Psychology of Organizations,* 6, 27–30, 78–80, 86, 91; Richard P. Appelbaum, *Theories of Social Change,* 30; David Silverman, *The Theory of Organizations,* 36, 66; Scott, *Organizations,* 176; Shirley Terreberry, "The Evolution of Organizational Environments."

21. National Academy of Public Administration, *Metropolitan Governance: A Handbook for Local Government Study Commissions.*

22. Bossert, "Education in Urban Society," 297–98, 303.

23. Collins, *Conflict Sociology,* 302–303, 307–12, 337, 342–46; Katz and Kahn, *The Social Psychology of Organizations,* 645; J. Kenneth Benson, "Innovation and Crisis in Organizational Analysis," 7; Allen Imerschein, "Organizational Change as a Paradigm Shift."

24. Richard Lempert and Kiyoshi Ikeda, "Evictions from Public Housing: Effects of Independent Review"; Note, "The Wyatt Case: Implementation of a Judicial Decree Ordering Institutional Change," 1338–1379.

25. Collins, *Conflict Sociology,* 291.

26. Max Gluckman, *Custom and Conflict in Africa,* 137.

27. Ibid., 133–34.

28. Ibid., 119, 134–36.

29. Ibid., 136.

30. Ibid., 109–10, 116, 122.

31. Scott, *Organizations,* 177, 188–90; Richard H. McCleery, *Policy Change in Prison Management,* 8, 38–45; Berman and McLaughlin, *An Exploratory Study,* 1, 11–12; Louis Coser, *Continuities in the Study of Social Conflict,* 23; John W. Meyer and Brian Rovan, "Institutionalized Organizations: Formal Structure as Myth and Ceremony," 343–49, 352, 357.

32. Anselm Strauss, *Negotiations,* 224, 259–60.

33. Federal "bailouts" of private corporations such as Lockheed or Chrysler were allowed because of crises in our aerospace and automobile industries. In reality, the assistance merely ratified in principle what already was an established fact: government could become involved in private business, despite the apparent violation of a central tenet of our economic philosophy. This is another way in which ritualistic conflicts and reforms can be used in order to address serious matters without doing long-term damage to our civil faith.

34. Coser, *Continuities,* 19, 23, 37–38, 41, 45.

35. Scott, *Organizations,* 135–63; Lempert and Ikeda, "Evictions from Public Housing," 858–60; Sussmann, *Tales Out of School,* 218–25; Parelius and Parelius, 87–90; Berman and McLaughlin, *An Exploratory Study;* Hawley, "Dealing with Organizational Rigidity," 198–201.

Notes to Chapter 6: Desegregating Ferguson-Florissant

1. Erving Goffman, *Behavior in Public Places,* 83–87.

2. Michael Lipsky and David Olson wrote an excellent book several years ago entitled *Commission Politics* in which they described how public and private leaders "processed" the crisis brought on by racial violence during the 1960s. They argue that the instrumental challenge of civil unrest was defused and reinterpreted through existing political routines and was responded to in a manner more consistent with the supposed mandate of social welfare and law enforcement institutions. The parallels between their argument and my own are noteworthy. This especially is true of their contention that the dramatic programs that were introduced actually accomplished little beyond reinforcing some of the basic inequities that had led to violence in the first place.

3. Project staff were able to observe only the first year of student desegregation in the district and then only in a small number of schools. A limited staff of four persons actually did most of the site visits in both the city and county. Nevertheless, the staff had an impact. By the end of the first year of desegregation in the county district, relations between officials and project staff had deteriorated severely. Access to schools was curtailed sharply in the second year.

The formal mandate under the National Institute of Education contract had been to observe and to intervene into the desegregation processes of both districts. School officials had to promise to cooperate on both counts before the contract was awarded. This proved to be a difficult mandate to fulfill because of the small number of staff and, in the case of the county district, the sensitive observations that had been made about the implementation of the desegregation order.

In effect, the project was booted out of the district, although contacts were maintained with school personnel, parents, and students. Even though it was easier to get "bad news" about the district, efforts were made to discover what good things were being done. Some things reported could not be corroborated, and some involved the personal lives of district staff. Events described in the text do touch on the personal lives of present and former district staff. They are reported here as told by the actual participants.

Informants were promised anonymity, and therefore, except when it is absolutely necessary, the race, sex, and position of the people in question is not mentioned. The necessity of doing this was made apparent on those numerous occasions when district administrators tried to find out who was involved in the complaints while at the same time they were denying the validity of the observations.

4. *St. Louis Post-Dispatch,* 29 April 1982. Reports in the press of controversies over school closings and staff reductions in St. Louis County became commonplace. Sometimes outraged parents managed to stop or stall proposed changes. Most often they did not. The last time any discussion appeared in the press about a school closing in the Ferguson-Florissant Reorganized School District, it involved a modification in the 1977–1978 desegregation plan. Parents objected to the closing, but the court approved it.

5. These groups were the School Anti-Merger Committee, the Committee for the Preservation of Local School Districts, the Ferguson Association of Individual Rights, and Citizens for Local Schools, Inc. To my knowledge, only the last group had a steering committee drawn from all three districts involved in the order. These groups apparently made quite a bit of noise, according to district officials. They never took significant public action in support of their beliefs, however. Their lack of success could be attributed in part to the "panic selling" that occurred in some neighborhoods at that time. There were reports of "blockbusting" in the press, and people expected the merger to accelerate the flight of white parents from the area.

6. *St. Louis Post-Dispatch,* 2 May 1982. None of the districts in the county accepts the premise that each district contributed to the city's school segregation problem. Those participating in a voluntary exchange of students, however, were excused from any direct participation in the metropolitan desegregation case. This included the Ferguson-Florissant Reorganized School District, which has been excused because of its successful desegregation program. Exemptions from city/county busing were granted by the federal court in 1982 to these several county districts. These districts were spared some large legal expenses.

7. *St. Louis Post-Dispatch,* 2 October 1977. Two assistant superintendents were reassigned as principals to two of the remaining schools in Berkeley. The board of education and superintend-

ent gave different reasons for the shift (*St. Louis Globe-Democrat*, 23 June 1982). The former maintained that it would improve communications within the district. The latter saw it as a move to "streamline" the administration. I saw it as an effort to place the superintendent's people in charge of schools that eventually will be closed to reduce the resistance by people who use those schools as rallying points of community protests. These explanations are not mutually exclusive.

8. No guarantee of representation from those communities was made for beyond 1981. That "tradition" may be continued, however, if only because it has not stopped district officials from getting what they want from the board.

9. I have offered a summary of information found in several documents: *The State Board of Education and St. Louis County Board of Education's Plan for School Desegregation Pursuant to Court Order of August 27, 1973,* mimeographed, 15 November 1974; United States vs. State of Missouri, 388 F. Supp. 1058 (1975). The plan submitted by the state and county contained nine options for dealing with Kinloch's situation. The merger of the three districts was one of these options, but it was the only one elaborated in the report. The court did lift one other strategy from the suggested list: the creation of a magnet school in or contiguous to Kinloch that would draw youngsters "voluntarily" from all three districts. It was proposed as part of the district's 1976 modified desegregation plan and approved by the court for public consideration. The proposal, as might be expected, was defeated.

10. The court order only required that the superintendents of Kinloch and Berkeley be retained as assistant superintendents during the 1975–1976 school year when the "administrative merger" of the districts was being undertaken. Ferguson-Florissant officials were under no compulsion to keep them or any other administrator in their position after that time. One of the two eventually became personnel director in the district. The other "elected" to become a principal in an elementary school after the 1976–1977 school year.

Several years later two black staff sued the district because they had not been offered positions as principals. One of the points at issue was whether black administrators had been "demoted" when they moved into the new district. The plaintiffs argued that they had been demoted due to decreases in their job status and responsibilities. The school system's witnesses maintained that the moves had been "parallel," notwithstanding apparent decreases in the titles and sphere of control of those administrators. Black administrators, especially those from Kinloch, may even have been increasing their status by becoming part of a much larger and better district. The trial judge agreed with the district, and the decision was not overturned on appeal.

11. The unmistakable clicking of the tape recorder could be heard if one waited a few seconds after the party at the district office hung up his phone. Several staff members also saw the tape recording equipment.

12. We know from earlier references to the history of urban reform crusades that their success was measured in part by the creation of such public institutions. In the case of the Ferguson-Florissant Reorganized School District, school officials shared this sentiment. They made it clear in numerous interviews that they interpreted the merger as a much bigger problem and contribution than the desegregation plan.

In addition to things like readjusting salary schedules, clarifying tenure criteria, and standardizing curricular and extracurricular offerings in the schools, the superintendent and his staff were troubled by the prospect of dealing with a bloated school administration. They spoke much less tentatively of their ability to carry out a "small desegregation plan."

13. During a meeting with concerned citizens, the principal was reported to have said that the state requires one year of history, and that students can take *either* four quarters of American history *or* four black studies courses. One parent remarked that it was no wonder enrollment in the black studies courses was low, given this choice.

14. If the academic problems of minority students have continued to be ignored by established counseling procedures, these procedures have actively worked against black youngsters who have had difficulties adjusting to the school's social climate since the withdrawal of the judge from the district. Minority youngsters have remained vulnerable to charges by white staff that they are misbehaving, and suspensions of an unspecified length of time have been used against minority students who are viewed as especially troublesome. While some white as well as black youngsters probably do fall into this category, a discussion of this topic during a meeting with citizens prompted an exchange between the principal and a concerned black parent whose child

had been suspended. There are several interesting revelations about the way disciplinary problems were actually handled in the school. Despite the school system's own policies on such matters, the parent did not seem to have had an opportunity to appeal the decision concerning her child. Nor did it seem that the parent even knew that an appeal was possible. She was simply informed that her child was suspended, and that was the end of the discussion. Furthermore, it seemed that unless the student had the presence of mind to make an inquiry in most instances, the parents of children who had been suspended indefinitely received no written explanation about the situation whatsoever.

That disciplinary policies are enforced differently for white and black students was evident from another situation that almost led to a fight between two black students and a group of white students. A black student reportedly entered the gymnasium and made a request to a number of white students to play basketball with them. At least one of the white youngsters called the young man a nigger, and the black student also was told to get out of the area. The confrontation moved into the student commons where a second black student joined his friend as the latter was encircled by the white students. The pair continued to be threatened while two white male administrators stood by silently. A black female staff member walked through the crowd and escorted the two boys to a black administrator's office. One of the two white administrators stated that he did not know what would have happened had the woman not taken the two students away. The second administrator spoke to the black youngster who had been threatened initially. He reportedly said that although school policy stated the name-calling of the sort directed toward the black student required that the offender be suspended, the administrator thought it best to give the white student a second chance. The black student later stated that he would provide his own protection in the future, because he could see that school authorities were unwilling to ensure his safety. In the meantime, however, white students had learned they could break school rules and physically threaten black students with impunity.

15. Monica Wittig, "Client Control and Organizational Dominance: The School, its Students, and Their Parents"; Leila Sussmann, *Tales Out Of School*.

16. It was not possible to obtain numbers on such basics as achievement scores, referrals to special education programs, enrollments in different courses, suspensions, or attendance. This type of information was requested several times by project staff. Each time officials reported that such data either did not exist or that it would be relayed in a short time, but the information was never received. In fact, it may not have existed in a form that would have made comparisons between white and black students possible. The court only requested yearly summaries of school enrollments displayed according to the race of the students. Similar data were presented for school staff.

17. James H. Laue and Daniel J. Monti, "Student Grievances and Grievance Procedures in a Desegregating School District," drawn from minutes of the Biracial Advisory Committee, 2 February 1976.

18. Ibid., 215.

19. Drawn from the "Facilitator Training Packet for Workshop on Racial Implications of Behavior Sunnyside North High School," 3.

20. *St. Louis Post-Dispatch*, 20 October 1977.

21. *St. Louis Post-Dispatch*, 29 May 1983.

22. *St. Louis Post-Dispatch*, 17 January 1985.

23. *St. Louis Post-Dispatch*, 29 June 1983.

Notes to Chapter 7: Maintaining Old Barriers

1. This included the Federal Court judge who had responsibility for the case involving the city school system. The judge had little patience for grand desegregation schemes and detailed orders. The political attractiveness or unattractiveness of his orders was by all accounts no concern to him. He insisted only that a plan be able to work. This attitude was apparent in the Ferguson-Florissant case and in his handling of the case against the city school system. He wanted these

matters settled as quickly and efficiently as possible. He might have been especially anxious to clear his docket of the Ferguson-Florissant case because of the continuing trouble presented by the city suit.

2. This particular board member was well informed about racial problems in the county district. He was aware of specific schools and personnel who seemed especially troubled by the desegregation process and the problems it had created.

3. *St. Louis County Star,* 30 June 1982.

4. Ibid.

5. There are parallels here with William Gamson's work on *The Strategy of Social Protest,* 41–50. "Challenging groups," he finds, tend to be much more successful when they do not try to displace the groups viewed as their antagonists.

6. Ralph Reisner, "St. Louis," 54.

7. Ibid., 55; in addition to the attack on busing and teacher assignment policies was the challenge to the proposed "relocation of an integrated teachers' college from a Negro area to an underused 'white' high school, to free the building for a new middle school." The Citizens Advisory Committee to the St. Louis Board of Education, "A Final Report," 5.

8. Ibid.; Reisner, "St. Louis," 56. I noted with interest one passage in the committee's report dealing with relations between the board of education and "its" administration. Some critics apparently thought that school officials were not accountable to the board. The committee acknowledged this concern while being unable to find any justifiable cause for it (Reisner, 50). It was dismissed as a public relations problem, the committee arguing that "perceptive and prudent timing should be used" in the release of public statements. This was intended to help clarify for the public "just what the order of action is when decisions are made and policies set."

9. Citizens Advisory Committee, "A Final Report," 55–57.

10. Reisner, "St. Louis," 59.

11. Citizens Advisory Committee, "A Final Report," 56.

12. Ibid., 6.

13. Ibid., 5.

14. Instructional Department, "The Status of Integration in the St. Louis Public Schools During the 1966–1967 School Year," 2.

15. Ibid.

16. A "crisis" was precipitated in 1963 by the actions of civil-rights groups and some ritualistically prescribed solutions had been advanced. There was no public declaration that these solutions would be adopted, and there was no satisfactory resolution to the crisis. A good part of the reason for this failed initiative was the unwillingness of civil rights groups to pursue the conflict through ritualistically prescribed channels, namely the courts. The fact that the same conflict and solutions could be "rediscovered" almost a decade later when there was less support for any kind of remedial action or political agitation is testimony to the power and appeal of ritualized conflict and reforms.

17. Among the most frequently mentioned were programs in "action learning and career education," "individually guided education," and centers for "investigative learning" and "visual and performing arts."

18. *St. Louis Post-Dispatch,* 14 January, 8 February, 1 September 1976.

19. *St. Louis Post-Dispatch,* 14 May, 29 December 1976; 22 December 1977; 6 February 1982.

20. An episode involving the Visual and Performing Arts High School offers an example of this point. Teachers in the city's "honors art" program had ridiculed the magnet-school program as a "Johnny-come-lately." The "honors art" program had been around for a number of years and had an excellent reputation. The relatively new magnet school had generated a good deal of interest but had no track record. This changed when the magnet school's students scored significantly higher on a standardized art test than had the "honors art" students.

21. The same things can be said of the teaching staff.

22. Project staff heard on numerous occasions of black youngsters whose place on the waiting lists for one or another magnet school had been "improved" because of political or personal reasons. The same accusation was leveled at the office staff who ran the magnet school program in its first few years.

204 A Semblance of Justice

23. There have been indications in reports issued by the school system that relations among staff at the magnet schools sometimes could have been better. Racial considerations did enter into the picture in several instances. Divisions between older white staff and younger black staff were reported.

There have been episodes where "racial tensions" have spilled over into fights between blacks and whites. There were several nasty confrontations during the 1981–1982 school year at the Naval ROTC school of which the board of education was never apprised. Students were severely beaten. Meetings between outraged parents and school officials yielded nothing. A number of white youngsters withdrew from the school.

24. I would argue that the "social" aspects of the magnet-school program were a "qualified" success. Reports issued by the school system contained data on changes in the attitudes and friendship ("sociometric") choices of students attending the magnet schools. Several of the findings in these reports are fascinating in their own right and might have had serious implications for the mandatory plan in the city had they been considered. Many persons maintain that desegregating high-school students is insufficient and ineffective. They think it is better to place more emphasis on younger children. If the limited data available from the magnet-school program can be generalized, these points may need to be revised. High-school youngsters showed positive changes in their attitudes toward members of the opposite race, while elementary schoolchildren showed no great changes. White elementary schoolchildren tended to choose blacks as members of hypothetical athletic teams; black children tended to choose whites as "friends" for working on academic tasks. Apparently, these children have "positive" thoughts about members of another race but in a way that reveals prejudiced attitudes and biased views. Young adults may not be nearly as closed in their thinking as has been thought.

25. *St. Louis Post-Dispatch,* 13 April 1980.

26. Ibid.

27. William M. Berg and David L. Colton, "*Brown* and the Distribution of School Resources."

28. Parents who sat on the ESAA Advisory Committee that ostensibly advised officials on the content of the magnet-school program spoke one evening of how the funds were used. Officials noted that all students in the school benefited from these funds because the guest speakers or displays brought in with those funds were shown to all students. Then, one parent clucked a bit about her child's performance inasmuch as she had been found to be "gifted." A man across the room innocently noted how his child, too, had been labeled as "gifted." A second woman, somewhat surprised by the apparent convergence of so many persons with good genes, confessed that her child had been so identified. I admit that I stopped counting after the next women blurted out that *both* of her children had been declared "gifted."

29. Division of Evaluation, "An Analysis of the Achievement of Black and White Students in Various School Settings, 1980–1981," 15.

30. The mechanism for achieving this effect would have changed, however, because everyone was placed back into their regular high schools for purposes of being reassigned. Voluntary self-selection for blacks would have been difficult other than into the magnet schools. This leaves the middle schools as a possible site where the sorting process could have begun for blacks moving into segregated or integrated high schools.

31. There was no complete basis upon which to make such statements. Census data would have been woefully outdated, even if anyone had cared to look at them. Moreover, so many youngsters already were attending parochial schools, it would have been quite impossible to draw reliable conclusions about the class standing of those left in the public schools. Officials said that they looked at the number of students receiving federal funds designated for poor children. But this would have told them nothing about the class background of the remaining students in the school. One official did say, however, that some schools were paired on the basis of the students' social class background.

32. *St. Louis Post-Dispatch,* 1 April 1980.

33. Citizens Advisory Committee, "A Final Report," 25, 28.

34. Gary Orfield, "The St. Louis Desegregation Plan: A Report to Judge James H. Meredith, United States District Court," 17–18.

35. There were some veiled but nevertheless harsh references to the types of people living in North St. Louis during the trial. The attorney for the Concerned Parents for Neighborhood

Schools made it painfully clear that the incidence of violent crimes among persons living in black areas was substantially higher than in South St. Louis. Most persons involved in the case dismissed the argument as irrelevant, if not outright racist. There was an indication that the social class background of white students was considered in the mandatory plan. School administrators feared that a group of poor, rural white students at one high school that already had a high attendance of black students would cause trouble when more black students were bused to the school. Officials did not worry a good deal about another Southside high school with a "higher status" white clientele. As things turned out, the officials were correct in both instances.

36. *St. Louis Post-Dispatch,* 23 June, 5 July 1981.

37. *St. Louis Post-Dispatch,* 29 June 1981.

38. City residents seemed more willing to accept this fact. A proposal to add a five-eighths cent sales tax for use by city and county cultural institutions and for economic development programs in the area was defeated on 3 August 1982. City voters approved the measure. County voters rejected it. In the same election, voters across the state rejected a proposal that would have made it easier for school districts to raise additional funds.

39. *St. Louis Post-Dispatch,* 12 July 1981. In theory, school districts could increase their revenues dramatically if they accepted or unloaded large numbers of the appropriately colored child. The incentive to a district stuck in a state that does not support public education very well should be obvious. The city system, of course, also benefited from this plan for every black student it sent out or white child it received from the county.

40. The city school system, in some instances, benefited from middle-class black children who left their private schools long enough to enroll back into their "neighborhood" schools so that they could transfer to a whiter, more affluent school district. A similar tactic was used by white students in the city who wanted to leave their private schools in order to enroll in a magnet school. The Office of Education in Washington objected to this and declared the district ineligible to receive ESAA funds for the 1977–1978 school year. In this case, the board of education argued that these children should not be treated as transfers from a neighborhood school because they would not have transferred back into the public schools at all had it not been for the magnet program. To count them as transfers from a neighborhood school would have greatly distorted actual increases in the amount of racial isolation at the hypothetical neighborhood school. Eventually, this proposal was abandoned and white students faced no barrier to being admitted back into a public magnet school. I point out this obvious discrepancy in the treatment of transferring white and black students only to affirm that financial interests often require the subversion of principles, even in desegregation.

41. *St. Louis Post-Dispatch,* 20 June 1984.

Notes to Chapter 8: Desegregation and Educational Quality

1. It will be recalled that in Detroit the court ordered a similar reconfiguration of grades to be introduced as part of that city's desegregation plan. No one, including the judge, viewed it as a tool to enhance desegregation. In fact, several parties including the defendant board of education noted that this plan would reduce the chances for more students to be desegregated in their city.

2. *St. Louis Post-Dispatch,* 4 April 1980.

3. *St. Louis Post-Dispatch,* 4 May, 18 July 1980.

4. Desegregation Monitoring and Advisory Committee, "Report No. 2," 36.

5. Desegregation Monitoring and Advisory Committee, "Supplemental Report: Enrichment Programs," 12.

6. Ibid., 12–15. The board of education cited three reasons for the absence of math and science labs: many schools had Title I math labs already; middle schools had regular science labs already; and St. Louis has a shortage of math and science teachers. Thus, many more principals elected to install writing labs in their schools. Given the first two points, however, it is difficult to understand why the board said it would consider implementing math and science labs in the first place, at least outside of the high schools.

7. Desegregation Monitoring and Advisory Committee, "Report No. 5," 25.

8. Desegregation Monitoring and Advisory Committee, "Report No. 4," 38–41. The parallels between the city's enrichment program and the Ferguson-Florissant Reorganized School District's LOTS teams are striking. The only difference is that the city was compelled to admit that students were not receiving the services they deserved. It also had to make some effort to improve its performance in this area because of the work of the monitoring committee.

9. *St. Louis Post-Dispatch,* 18 October 1977; 8 January, 5 October 1978; 12 September, 7 October 1980.

10. *St. Louis Post-Dispatch,* 9 October 1978.

11. *St. Louis Post-Dispatch,* 10 October 1978.

12. *St. Louis Post-Dispatch,* 21 January 1979.

13. *St. Louis Post-Dispatch,* 15 March 1979.

14. Parents who met with the union president reported that she said this was a "spiritual strike." Teachers really wanted to make things better for all schoolchildren. However, when she was pushed to state what the union was going after, she said "a one-thousand-dollar raise." These parent leaders considered the invocation of their childrens' needs in the context of this "spiritual strike" for a thousand-dollar raise to be a distasteful, if not exactly cheap, ploy.

15. *St. Louis Post-Dispatch,* 8 May, 18 July 1977.

16. *St. Louis Post-Dispatch,* 16 October 1977.

17. *St. Louis Post-Dispatch,* 19 July 1979; 3 June 1980. A board member and another school official independently offered a second explanation for why these test scores might have begun to stabilize and even improve by the late 1970s. By that time, they suggested, the massive number of residential shifts experienced during the 1970s had already peaked. Students were not quite so mobile and, hence, could grow more accustomed to one teacher and academic program. Their residential stability could have been translated into better scores on achievement tests. A second board member offered some confirmation for this line of reasoning. He said a principal had informed him that the youngsters failing at his school were recent arrivals. Students who had been with the program all along were performing at an average or above-average level. There are data available that could help to test this hypothesis, but they have not been examined as yet.

18. St. Louis Public Schools, "Response to Curriculum Study Report," 6.

19. Division of Evaluation, "Summary Report: ITBS/CAT-C Test Equating Study," 9, 10.

20. *St. Louis Post-Dispatch,* 22 January 1982.

21. *St. Louis Post-Dispatch,* 26 May 1982.

22. *The Evening Sun,* 9 November 1981.

23. *St. Louis Post-Dispatch,* 22 January 1982.

24. Stephen Jay Gould, *The Mismeasure of Man,* 155.

25. An absurd yet logical extension of this reasoning was illustrated in the words of the district's deputy superintendent for instruction as he tried to account for why elementary-school students were improving much more quickly than high-school students. He had argued earlier that the CAT was more sensitive and responsive to what city schoolchildren were learning (*St. Louis Post-Dispatch,* 22 January 1982). Later he argued that elementary pupils made better progress than high-school students because the test was "probably more sensitive to the elementary grades" (*St. Louis Post-Dispatch,* 26 May 1982). If this is true, then it would seem prudent to find an even more "sensitive" and easier test for the high-school students to take.

26. *Clayton Citizen,* 11 August 1982.

27. Scheduled to be "contained" or "demoted" were a number of black administrators with a long history of service to the district. The reorganization plan neatly removed them from their accustomed bases of power and support.

28. *St. Louis Globe-Democrat,* 23 May 1979.

29. *St. Louis Post-Dispatch,* 25 July 1979; 24 May 1980.

30. A board of education member informed me of another connection between desegregation and administrative improvements. He said that desegregation had created an opportunity to put into place an "internal development program" for the identification and training of mid-level school administrators. It really could have been a good program, he implied. Unfortunately, it "died" for lack of leadership. "It got lost in the shuffle" during all the excitement of the 1978–1980 period. I do not want to make too big a point of this. Had it been pursued, however, the

district would have been behaving as social scientists think "open and rational" organizations are supposed to behave.

31. *St. Louis Post-Dispatch,* 13 April, 4 May 1980.

32. *St. Louis Post-Dispatch,* 22 February, 7 March 1982.

33. *St. Louis Post-Dispatch,* 2, 15 June 1982.

34. Arguments about the propriety and effectiveness of judicial intervention in desegregation cases will not be reviewed in great detail here. For a more thorough discussion of this topic see Stephen Wasby, "Arrogation of Power or Accountability: 'Judicial Imperialism' Revisited." This unpublished paper was presented at the 1981 annual meeting of the American Political Science Association. Also read my paper entitled "Administrative Foxes in Educational Chicken Coops: An Examination of the Critique of Judicial Activism in School Desegregation Cases."

35. *St. Louis Post-Dispatch,* 3 October 1980.

36. It should be noted that the board is struggling to find its own political identity. There are more "characters" on the board now than there have been in recent years, and this upsets people sometimes. It is more difficult now to build a majority to support sensitive positions than it was when fewer "grass-roots" people served on it. These persons may find it more difficult to arrive at a consensus, but they have had to face some tough issues in recent years and have not avoided making some equally tough choices.

37. Jennifer L. Hochschild, "A Study of Citizen Advisory and Monitoring Panels Concerned with Civil Rights Compliance in Schools," 19.

38. Once the desegregation plan was implemented, these business groups found more comfortable tasks to undertake. They formed a blue-ribbon committee of civic and corporate leaders to propose a joint "business and public school program to deal with the St. Louis area's severe youth unemployment problem." *St. Louis Post-Dispatch,* 1 March 1982.

39. *St. Louis Post-Dispatch,* 25 March 1980.

40. Among the topics considered were student and staff assignments, transportation, security, discipline, staff and curricular development, community relations, parent organizations, budgets for several programs, building maintenance and overcrowding, supplies and equipment, enrichment programs, special education and other specialty programs, and the metropolitan plan.

41. *St. Louis Post-Dispatch,* 11 March 1981; 5 April 1981; 13 January 1982.

42. *St. Louis Post-Dispatch,* 20 March 1980.

Notes to Chapter 9: Reflections

1. Gary Orfield, "School Segregation and Housing Policy: The Role of Local and Federal Governments in Neighborhood Segregation."

2. Robert Alford and Roger Friedland, "Political Participation and Public Policy," 474; Jennifer L. Hochschild, "Local Control of School Desegregation through Citizen Monitoring," 67–82; L. Harmon Zeigler et al., *Governing American Schools.*

3. David Cohen, "Reforming School Politics," 437–38.

4. *Newsweek,* 15 September 1980; *St. Louis Globe-Democrat,* 4 April 1980.

5. Marilyn Gittell and T. Edward Hollander, *Six Urban School Districts.* This book offers some key insights into the origins of the reform movement that swept up the city school system during the 1950s and 1960s.

6. Daniel Katz and Robert Kahn, *The Social Psychology of Organizations,* 714. Erving Goffman, *Behavior in Public Places,* 42, 91.

7. *St. Louis Post-Dispatch,* 13 January 1985.

Works Cited

Abu-Lughod, J. "Migrant Adjustment to City Life: The Egyptian Case." *American Journal of Sociology* 67 (1961): 22–32.

Alford, Robert, and Roger Friedland. "Political Participation and Public Policy." In *Annual Review of Sociology* 1, edited by Alex Inkeles. Palo Alto: Annual Reviews, 1975.

Appelbaum, Richard P. *Theories of Social Change*. Chicago: Markham, 1971.

Arberbach, Joel, and Jack Walker. "Citizen Desires, Policy Outcomes, and Community Control." *Urban Affairs Quarterly* 8 (September 1972): 65–75.

Armor, David. "The Evidence on Busing." *The Public Interest* 28 (Summer 1972): 90–126.

Arnold, Joseph L. "The Neighborhood and City Hall: The Origin of Neighborhood Associations in Baltimore, 1880–1911." *Journal of Urban History* 6 (November 1979).

Banfield, Edward. *The Unheavenly City Revisited*. Toronto: Little, Brown and Co., 1974.

Bash, Harry. *Sociology, Race and Ethnicity*. New York: Gordon and Breach, 1979.

Benson, J. Kenneth. "Innovation and Crisis in Organizational Analysis." *The Sociological Quarterly* 18 (Winter 1977).

Berg, William M., and David L. Colton. "*Brown* and the Distribution of School Resources." In *The Impact of Desegregation*, No. 14, edited by Daniel J. Monti, 83–98. San Francisco: Jossey-Bass, 1982.

Berman, Paul, and Milbrey W. McLaughlin. *An Exploratory Study of School District Adaptation*. Santa Monica: Rand, 1979.

Bernard, Richard M., and Bradley R. Rice. "Political Environment and the Adoption of Progressive Municipal Reform." *Journal of Urban History* 1 (February 1975): 149–74.

Berry, Brewton, and H. L. Tischler. *Race and Ethnic Relations*. Boston: Houghton Mifflin, 1978.

Berry, Brian. *Comparative Urbanization*. New York: St. Martin's Press, 1981.

Borja, Jordi. "Urban Movements in Spain." In *Captive Cities*, edited by M. Harloe. London: Wiley, 1977.

Bossert, Steven. "Education in Urban Society." In *Handbook of Contemporary Urban Life*, edited by David Street and Associates. San Francisco: Jossey-Bass, 1978.

Bowles, S., and H. Gintis. *Schooling in Capitalist America: Educational Reform and the Contradictions of Economic Life*. New York: Basic Books, 1976.

Boyer, Paul. *Urban Masses and Moral Order in America, 1820–1920*. Cambridge: Harvard University Press, 1978.

Brown, R. M. *Strain of Violence*. New York: Oxford University Press, 1975.

Castells, M. "Theoretical Propositions for an Experimental Study of Urban Movements." In *Urban Sociology: Critical Essays*, edited by C. G. Pickvance. New York: St. Martin's Press, 1976.

The Citizens Advisory Committee to the St. Louis Board of Education. "A Final Report." St. Louis Board of Education, 20 June 1963. Mimeo.

Clayton Citizen. 11 August 1982; 9 March 1983.

Cohen, David. "Reforming School Politics." *Harvard Educational Review* 48, no. 4 (November 1978): 429–47.

Collins, Randall. *Conflict Sociology.* New York: Academic Press, 1975.

———. "Functional and Conflict Theories of Educational Stratification." *American Sociological Review* 36 (1971): 1002–19.

Colton, David. "The Kinloch Case: A Court-Ordered District Merger." Fact Sheet No. 3. Washington University: Center for the Study of Law in Education, 1981.

———. "The St. Louis Desegregation Case (City-Only Aspects)." Fact Sheet No. 4. Washington University: Center for the Study of Law in Education, 1981.

Coser, Louis. *Continuities in the Study of Social Conflict.* New York: Free Press, 1967.

Crain, Robert L. "Why Academic Research Fails To Be Useful." In *School Desegregation: Shadow and Substance,* edited by F. H. Levinsohn and B. D. Wright, 31–45. Chicago: University of Chicago Press, 1976.

Crain, Robert L., and Rita E. Mahard. "The Consequences of Controversy Accompanying Institutional Change: The Case of School Desegregation." *American Sociological Review* 47 (December 1982).

———. "Desegregation and Black Achievement: A Review of the Research." *Law and Contemporary Problems* 42 (Summer 1978): 17–56.

———. "The Consequences of Controversy Accompanying Institutional Change: The Case of Desegregation." *American Sociological Review* 47 (December 1982): 697–708.

Crain, Robert L., and Christine Rossell. *Political Strategies in Northern School Desegregation.* Lexington: Lexington Books, 1973.

Desegregation Monitoring and Advisory Committee. "Report No. 2." St. Louis City Public Schools, 16 November 1981. Mimeo.

———. "Report No. 4." St. Louis City Public Schools, 19 January 1981. Mimeo.

———. "Report No. 5." St. Louis City Public Schools, 11 June 1982. Mimeo.

———. "Supplemental Report: Enrichment Programs." St. Louis City Public Schools, 16 November 1981. Mimeo.

Division of Evaluation. "An Analysis of the Achievement of Black and White Students in Various School Settings, 1980–1981." St. Louis City Public Schools, Spring 1982. Mimeo.

———. "Summary Report: ITBS/CAT-C Test Equating Study." St. Louis City Public Schools, January 1982. Mimeo.

Eisenger, Peter K. *The Politics of Displacement.* New York: Academic Press, 1980.

Epps, Edgar. "The Impact of School Desegregation on the Self-Evaluation of Minority Children." *Law and Contemporary Problems* 42 (Summer 1978): 57–76.

Facilitator Training Packet for Workshop on Racial Implication of Behavior Sunnyside North High School. Ferguson-Florissant Reorganized School District, April 1976. Mimeo.

Farley, John E. "Metropolitan Housing Segregation in 1980: The St. Louis Case." *Urban Affairs Quarterly,* 18, no. 3 (March 1983): 347–60.

Fischer, C. *The Urban Experience.* New York: Harcourt Brace Jovanovich, 1976.

Gamson, William. *The Strategy of Social Protest.* Homewood, Ill.: Dorsey Press, 1975.

Gans, Herbert. *The Urban Villagers.* New York: The Free Press, 1977.

Garner, A. A. *Social Movements in America*. Chicago: Rand McNally, 1977.

Gittell, Marilyn. *Participants and Participation*. New York: Praeger, 1968.

——. *Community Control and the Urban School*. New York: Praeger, 1969.

Gittell, Marilyn, and T. Edward Hollander. *Six Urban School Districts*. New York: Praeger, 1968.

Glaab, Charles N., and A. Theodore Brown. *A History of Urban America*. New York: Macmillan Publishing Co., 1976.

Glazer, Nathan. "Should Judges Administer Social Services." *The Public Interest* 50 (Winter 1978): 64–80.

Gluckman, Max. *Custom and Conflict in Africa*. Oxford: Basil Blackwell, 1966.

Goffman, Erving. *Behavior in Public Places*. New York: The Free Press, 1967.

Gould, Stephen Jay. *The Mismeasure of Man*. New York: W. W. Norton & Co., 1981.

Greenberg, Stanley. *Politics and Poverty*. New York: John Wiley & Sons, 1974.

Hawley, Willis. "Dealing with Organizational Rigidity in Public Schools: A Theoretical Perspective." In *The Polity and the School: Political Perspectives on Education*, edited by Frederick Writ. Lexington: D. C. Heath, 1975.

——. "The New Mythology of School Desegregation." *Law and Contemporary Problems* 42 (Summer 1978): 214–33.

Hays, Samuel P. "The Politics of Reform in Municipal Government in the Progressive Era." *Pacific Northwest Quarterly* 55 (October 1964): 157–69.

Himes, Joseph. *Conflict & Conflict Management*. Athens: University of Georgia Press, 1980.

Hirschman, Albert O. *Exit, Voice, and Loyalty: Responses to Decline in Firms, Organizations, and States*. Cambridge: Harvard University Press, 1970.

Hochschild, Jennifer L. "A Study of Citizen Advisory and Monitoring Panels Concerned with Civil Rights Compliance in Schools." Center for Educational Policy. Duke University, 26 May 1980. Mimeo.

——. "Incrementalism, Majoritarianism, and the Failure of Desegregation." Paper presented before the Association for Public Policy Analysis and Management, October 1982.

——. "Local Control of School Desegregation through Citizen Monitoring." In *Impact of Desegregation*, no. 14, edited by Daniel J. Monti, 67–82. San Francisco, Jossey-Bass, 1982.

——. *What's Fair: American Beliefs about Distributive Justice*. Cambridge: Harvard University Press, 1981.

Holli, Melvin G. *Reform in Detroit*. New York: Oxford University Press, 1969.

Imerschein, Allen. "Organizational Change as a Paradigm Shift." *The Sociological Quarterly* 18 (Winter 1977): 33–43.

Instructional Department. "The Status of Integration in the St. Louis Public Schools During the 1966–1967 School Year." St. Louis Public Schools, June 1976. Mimeo.

Jones, Ruth S. "Racial Patterns and School District Policy." *Urban Education*, vol. 12, no. 3 (October 1977).

Kalmuss, Debra, Mark Chesler, and Joseph Sanders. "The Impact of the School Desegregation Cases on the Relations Between Scientific Evidence and Legal Theory." *Measuring the Impact of Desegregation*, no. 14, edited by Daniel J. Monti, 21–38. San Francisco: Jossey-Bass, 1982.

Kalodner, Howard I., and James J. Fishman, eds. *Limits of Justice: The Courts' Role in School Desegregation*. Cambridge: Ballinger, 1978.

Karabel, Jerome. "Community Colleges and Social Stratification: Submerged Class

Conflict in American Higher Education." *Harvard Educational Review* 42 (November 1972): 521–62.

Katz, Daniel, and Robert Kahn. *The Social Psychology of Organization*. New York: John Wiley & Sons, 1978.

Katznelson, Ira. *City Trenches*. Chicago: University of Chicago Press, 1981.

Kessler-Harris, Alice, and Virginia Yans-McLaughlin. "European Immigrant Groups." In *American Ethnic Groups*, edited by Thomas Sowell, 107–38. Washington, D. C.: The Urban Institute, 1978.

Killian, Lewis M. *The Impossible Revolution Phase 2: Black Power and the American Dream*. New York: Random House, 1975.

Kirby, David, T. Harris, R. Crain, and C. Rossell. *Political Strategies in Northern School Desegregation*. Lexington: D. C. Heath and Co., 1973.

Kirp, David. "School Desegregation and the Limits of Legalism." *The Public Interest* 47 (Spring 1977): 101–28.

Langness, L. L. *Other Fields, Other Grasshoppers*. Philadelphia: J. B. Lippincott Co., 1977.

Laue, James H., and Daniel J. Monti. "Student Grievances and Grievance Procedures in a Desegregating School District." In *"Is That Really Fair?"*, edited by William F. Lincoln and Sandra L. Enos, 213. Washington, D. C.: The National Institute of Education, 1977.

Lempert, Richard, and Kiyoshi Ikeda. "Evictions from Public Housing: Effects of Independent Review." *American Sociological Review* 35 (October 1970): 852–59.

Levin, Henry. "Education, Life Chances, and the Courts: The Role of Social Science Evidence." *Law and Contemporary Problems* 39 (Spring 1975): 217–39.

Light, Ivan. *Cities in World Perspective*. New York: Macmillan, 1983.

Lincoln, C. Eric. *Sounds of the Struggle*. New York: William Morrow & Co., 1969.

Lingeman, Richard. *Small Town America*. Boston: Houghton Mifflin Co., 1980.

Lipset, S. M., and E. Rabb. *The Politics of Unreason*. New York: Harper and Row, 1973.

Lipsky, Michael and David Olson. *Commission Politics*. New Brunswick: Transaction Books, 1977.

Long, Norton. "The Local Community as an Ecology of Games." *American Journal of Sociology* 64 (November 1958): 251–61.

Longshore, Douglas. "Social Psychological Research on School Desegregation: Toward A New Agenda." In *Impact of Desegregation*, edited by Daniel J. Monti, 39–52. San Francisco: Jossey-Bass, 1982.

Lotchin, Roger W. *San Francisco 1846–1856*. New York: Oxford University Press, 1974.

Marcus, Alan I. "Professional Revolution and Reform in the Progressive Era: Cincinnati Physicians and the City Elections of 1897 and 1900." *Journal of Urban History* 5 (February 1979): 183–208.

Masotti, Louis, Jeffery Hadden, Kenneth Seminatore, and Jerome Corsi. *A Time To Burn?* Chicago: Rand McNally, 1969.

McCarthy, Michael P. "On Bosses, Reformers, and Urban Growth: Some Suggestions for a Political Typology of American Cities." *Journal of Urban History* 4 (November 1977): 29–38.

McCleery, Richard H. *Policy Change in Prison Management*. East Lansing, Mich.: Bureau of Social and Political Research, 1961.

McConahay, John B. "The Effects of School Desegregation upon Students' Racial Attitudes and Behavior: A Critical Review of the Literature and a Prolegomenon to Future Research." *Law and Contemporary Problems* 42 (Summer 1978): 77–107.

McKelvey, Blake. *The Urbanization of America.* New Brunswick: Rutgers University Press, 1963.

Merton, Robert K. "The Latent Functions of the Machine." In *Urban Bosses, Machines, and Progressive Reformers,* edited by Bruce M. Stave, 27–37. Lexington: D. C. Heath and Co., 1972.

Meyer, John W. "The Effects of Education as an Institution." *American Journal of Sociology* 83 (July 1977): 55–77.

Meyer, John W., and Brian Rovan. "Institutionalized Organizations: Formal Structure as Myth and Ceremony." *American Journal of Sociology* 83 (September, 1977): 343–57.

Milgram, S. "The Experience of Living in Cities: A Psychological Analysis." *Science* 167 (March 1970): 1461–68.

Miller, Zane. *Boss Cox's Cincinnati: Urban Politics in the Progressive Era.* New York: Oxford University Press, 1971.

Minutes for the Biracial Advisory Committee of the Ferguson-Florissant Reorganized School District. 2 February 1976. Mimeo.

Minutes for the meeting of the St. Louis County Board of Education. 18 February 1958; 26 September, 10 October 1962; 10 May 1971.

Monti, Daniel J. "Administrative Discrimination in the Implementation of Desegregation Policies." *Educational Evaluation and Policy Analysis* 1 (July–August 1979): 17–25.

———. "Administrative Foxes in Educational Chicken Coops: An Examination of the Critique of Judicial Activism in School Desegregation Cases." *Law and Policy Quarterly,* vol. 2, no. 2 (April 1980): 233–56.

———. "The Relations Between Terrorism and Domestic Civil Disorders." *Terrorism: An International Journal* 4 (1980): 123–41.

Nasaw, David. *Schooled to Order.* New York: Oxford University Press, 1979.

National Academy of Public Administration. *Metropolitan Governance: A Handbook for Local Government Study Commissions.* Washington: Department of Housing and Urban Development, 1980.

Newsweek. 15 September 1980.

New York Times, 12 August 1983.

Note. "The Wyatt Case: Implementation of a Judicial Decree Ordering Institutional Change." *Yale Law Journal* 84 (May 1975): 1338–79.

Nye, R. A. *The Origins of Crowd Psychology.* Beverly Hills: Sage, 1975.

Oberschall, Anthony. *Social Conflict and Social Movements.* Englewood Cliffs: Prentice-Hall, 1973.

Ogbu, John. *The Next Generation.* New York: Academic Press, 1974.

Orfield, Gary. *Must We Bus?* Washington: The Brookings Institution, 1978.

———. "School Segregation and Housing Policy: The Role of Local and Federal Governments in Neighborhood Segregation." *Integrated Education,* vol. 17, nos. 3–4 (May–August 1979): 48–53.

———. "The St. Louis Desegregation Plan: A Report to Judge James H. Meredith, United States District Court." St. Louis Public Schools, 2 May 1980. Mimeo.

Paige, Karen, and Jeffery Paige. *The Politics of Reproduction.* Berkeley: University of California Press, 1981.

Parelius, Ann Parker, and Robert J. Parelius. *The Sociology of Education*. Englewood Cliffs: Prentice-Hall, 1978.

Park, Robert, and Ernest Burgess. *The City*. Chicago: University of Chicago Press, 1974.

Patcher, Martin. *Black–White Contact in Schools: Its Social and Academic Effects*. West Lafayette: Purdue University Press, 1982.

Philpott, Thomas Less. *The Slum and the Ghetto*. New York: Oxford University Press, 1978.

Pivar, David J. *Purity Crusade, Sexual Morality and Social Control, 1868–1900*. Westport, Conn.: Greenwood Press, 1973.

Ravitch, Diane. *The Troubled Crusade*. New York: Basic Books, 1983.

Ravitch, Diane. *The Great School Wars*. New York: Basic Books, 1974.

Reisner, Ralph. "St. Louis." *Law & Society Review* 2 (November, 1967).

Rogers, David. *110 Livingston Street*. New York: Vintage Books, 1969.

Ross, J. M., and W. Berg. *"I Respectfully Disagree With the Judge's Order."* Washington: University Press of America, 1981.

Rossell, Christine H. "School Desegregation and Community Social Change." *Law and Contemporary Problems* 42 (Summer 1978): 133–83.

Rossell, Christine H. "The Atheoretical Nature of Desegregation." *Educational Evaluation and Policy Analysis* 3 (May–June 1981).

Schmandt, Henry, Paul Steinbicker, and George Wendel. *Metropolitan Reform in St. Louis*, 47–61. New York: Holt, Rinehart and Winston, 1961.

Scott, W. Richard. *Organizations*. Englewood Cliffs: Prentice-Hall, 1981.

Sennett, Richard. *The Fall of Public Man*. New York: Vintage Books, 1978.

Silverman, David. *The Theory of Organizations*. London: Heinemann, 1970.

Smelser, Neil. *Theory of Collective Behavior*. New York: Free Press, 1962.

Smith, Al, Anthony Downs, and M. Leanne Lachman. *Achieving Effective Desegregation*. Lexington, Mass.: Lexington Books, 1973.

Smith, Arthur. *Rhetoric of Black Revolution*. Boston: Allyn and Bacon, 1969.

Smith, Michael P. *The City and Social Theory*. New York: St. Martin's Press, 1979.

The State Board of Education and St. Louis County Board of Education's Plan for School Desegregation Pursuant to Court Order of August 27, 1973. State Board of Education, 15 November 1974. Mimeo.

Steinberg, Stephen. *The Ethnic Myth*. New York: Atheneum, 1981.

St. Louis County Department of Planning. *St. Louis County, Missouri Fact Book 1977*. St. Louis County: St. Louis County Planning Commission, 1977.

St. Louis County Star. 30 June 1982.

St. Louis Globe-Democrat. 6 October 1977; 23 May 1979; 4 April 1980; 23 June 1982.

St. Louis Post-Dispatch. 14 January, 6, 8 February, 14 May, 1 September, 29 December 1976; 8 May, 18 July, 2, 16, 18, 20 October, 22 December 1977; 8 January, 5, 9, 10 October 1978; 21 January, 15 March, 19, 25 July 1979; 20, 25 March, 1, 4, 13 April, 4, 24 May, 3, 23 June, 18 July, 12 September, 3, 7 October 1980; 11 March, 5 April, 29 June, 5, 12 July 1981; 13, 22 January, 6, 22 February, 1, 7 March, 29 April, 2, 26 May, 2, 15 June 1982; 29 May, 29 June 1983; 17 January 1985.

St. Louis Public Schools. "Response to Curriculum Study Report." St. Louis City Public Schools, 14 December 1976. Mimeo.

Strauss, Anselm. *Negotiations*. San Francisco: Jossey-Bass, 1978.

Susser, Ida. *Norman Street*. New York: Oxford University Press, 1982.

Sussmann, Leila. *Tales Out of School*. Philadelphia: Temple University Press, 1977.

Sussmann, Leila, and Gayle Speck. "Community Participation In Schools: The Boston Case." *Urban Education*, vol. 7, no. 4 (January 1978).

Suttles, Gerald. *The Social Order of the Slum*. Chicago: University of Chicago Press, 1968.

Tatel, David, and William Taylor. "St. Louis Integration." *New York Times*. 12 August 1983.

Taub, Richard, George Surgeon, Sara Lindholm, Phyllis Otti, and Amy Bridges. "Urban Voluntary Associations, Locality Based and Externally Induced." *American Journal of Sociology* 83 (September 1977): 425–42.

Terreberry, Shirley. "The Evolution of Organizational Environments." *Administrative Science Quarterly* 12 (March 1968): 590–613.

The Evening Sun. 9 November 1981.

Thieblemont, Andre. "Protest Rites at Saint-Cyr: A Contribution to the Study of Military Tradition." *Armed Forces and Society* 7 (Summer 1981): 585–96.

Tilly, Charles. *From Mobilization To Revolution*. Reading: Addison-Wesley, 1978.

Tilly, Charles, Louise Tilly, and Richard Tilly. *The Rebellious Century 1830–1930*. Cambridge: Harvard University Press, 1975.

Turner, R. H., and L. Killian. *Collective Behavior*. Englewood Cliffs: Prentice-Hall, 1972.

Tyack, David B. *The One Best System: A History of American Urban Education*. Cambridge: Harvard University Press, 1974.

Wade, Richard C. "The Periphery Versus the Center." In *Urban Bosses, Machines, and Progressive Reformers*, edited by Bruce M. Stave, 75–80. Lexington: D. C. Heath and Co., 1972.

Warren, Donald. *Black Neighborhoods*. Ann Arbor: University of Michigan Press, 1977.

Warren, Roland. *The Community in America*. Chicago: Rand McNally, 1972.

Wasby, Stephen. "Arrogation of Power or Accountability: 'Judicial Imperialism' Revisited." American Political Science Association, 1981. Mimeo.

Wendel, George. "Previous Attempts at Metro Reform in St. Louis" (table). St. Louis University: Center for Urban Programs, 22 April 1977. Mimeo.

Whyte, William F. *Street Corner Society*. Chicago: University of Chicago Press, 1966.

Wilkinson, J. Harvie. *From Brown to Bakke*. New York: Oxford University Press, 1979.

Willie, Charles, and Susan Greenblatt, eds. *Community Politics and Educational Change*. New York: Longman, 1981.

Wilson, William Julius. *The Declining Significance of Race*. Chicago: University of Chicago Press, 1978.

Wimberley, Ronald C., and James A. Christenson. "Civil Religion and Church and State." *The Sociological Quarterly* 21 (Winter 1980): 35–40.

Wirth, Louis. "Urbanism as a Way of Life." *American Journal of Sociology* 44 (1938): 1–24.

Wittig, Monica. "Client Control and Organizational Dominance: The School, its Students, and Their Parents." *Social Problems* 24 (1976): 193–203.

Wolff, Kurt. *The Sociology of Georg Simmel*. New York: The Free Press, 1964.

Yinger, J. Milton. "Countercultures and Social Change." *American Sociological Review* 42 (December 1977): 833–53.

Yudof, Mark G. "School Desegregation: Legal Realism, Reasoned Elaboration, and Social Science Research in the Supreme Court." *Law and Contemporary Problems* 42 (Autumn 1978).

Zeigler, L. Harmon, M. Kent Jennings, and G. Wayne Peak. *Governing American Schools*. North Scituate, Mass.: Duxbury Press, 1974.

Index